Constitutionalizing Globalization

Constitutionalizing Globalization

The Postmodern Revival of Confederal Arrangements

DANIEL J. ELAZAR

ROWMAN & LITTLEFIELD PUBLISHERS, INC.
Lanham • Boulder • New York • Oxford

ROWMAN & LITTLEFIELD PUBLISHERS, INC.

Published in the United States of America
by Rowman & Littlefield Publishers, Inc.
4720 Boston Way, Lanham, Maryland 20706

12 Hid's Copse Road
Cumnor Hill, Oxford OX2 9JJ, England

British Library Cataloguing in Publication Information Available

Library of Congress Cataloging-in-Publication Data

Elazar, Daniel Judah.
    Constitutionalizing globalization : the postmodern revival of confederal
arrangements / Daniel J. Elazar.
        p.   cm.
    Includes bibliographical references and index.
    ISBN 0-8476-8787-2 (cloth : alk. paper). — ISBN 0-8476-8788-0 (pbk. :
alk. paper)
    1. Confederation of states. 2. International agencies. I. Title.
JC357.E43   1998
321.02—dc21   97-26543

ISBN 0-8476-8787-2 (cloth : alk. paper)
ISBN 0-8476-8788-0 (pbk. : alk. paper)

Printed in the United States of America

♾™ The paper used in this publication meets the minimum requirements of American
National Standard for Information Sciences—Permanence of Paper for Printed Library
Materials, ANSI Z39.48–1984.

This book is dedicated to my closest colleagues,
the Fellows of the Center for the Study of Federalism

Ellis Katz
John Kincaid
Donald Lutz
Stephen Schechter
Alan Tarr

with affection and gratitude

CONTENTS

ACKNOWLEDGMENTS

The beginning of my work on confederation goes back to a 1981 colloquium commemorating the bicentennial of the adoption of the Articles of Confederation by the newly independent states of the United States of America, conducted by the Center for the Study of Federalism and sponsored by Liberty Fund. I owe them a great debt of gratitude for that and so much else. The papers from that conference were published as a special issue of *Publius* (vol. 12, no. 4, Fall 1982) entitled "The Continuing Legacy of the Articles of Confederation."

The study of confederal solutions, of which this is a first product, was funded by grants from the United States Institute for Peace and the Earhart Foundation. I am grateful to the United States Institute for Peace and to Samuel Lewis, then its president, for providing the initial wherewithal to begin this study of confederation and confederal arrangements, and to the Earhart Foundation, its president, David Kennedy, and vice president, Dr. Antony Sullivan, for their continuing confidence in me and my work on questions of federalism.

I would like to thank Deborah Tor and Paul Neal, my research assistants at the Jerusalem Center for Public Affairs and the Center for the Study of Federalism, respectively; Joseph Marbach, Assistant Director of the Center for the Study of Federalism during this stage of the project; Mark Ami-El, Publications Coordinator for the Jerusalem Center; and the secretarial staffs of the Center for the Study of Federalism and the Jerusalem Center for Public Affairs, especially Kim Robinson and Rachel Elrom, for their assistance in the preparation of this volume.

Daniel J. Elazar
Jerusalem and Philadelphia
March 1996

INTRODUCTION

On July 8, 1997, the *New York Times* reported that the Coeur d'Alene tribe of Native Americans (Indians) had launched the first legal gambling site on the Internet based in the United States. With a population under 1,500, this aboriginal people, located in the relatively isolated Rocky Mountains of Idaho, have linked with the most advanced globalized communications network in a clear illustration of the new connection between ethnicity and globalization. The negative responses of the officials of the State of Idaho and many of its sister states claimed this action to be a violation of state laws and the act's murky status in federal law are symptomatic of the new problems of constitutionalization that flow from connections of this type, generated by the new globalization.

In 1982, early in the second chronological generation of the postmodern epoch, Ivo Duchacek, who may have been the first political scientist to combine the study of international relations as a field and the study of federalism, wrote:

> Never before have so many nations and their leaders so frequently and so openly admitted their growing interdependence; never before have they created so many cooperative frameworks and elaborate mechanisms for managing their complex interdependence and its consequences. Simultaneously, however, national leaders and their supporters continue to insist on the sovereign independence of their states with the expectation that the intricate web of regional or global cooperative links will serve their separate interests.[1]

Duchacek continued his discussion by enumerating the hundreds of organizations and associations then already in existence on a globalized basis.

- Over 300 intergovernmental cooperative associations as opposed to only 37 before World War I.
- An increase of 150 percent in the number of what he referred
  to as "intersovereign associations" between 1951 and the time
  he wrote the article.
- Over 2,400 transnational nongovernmental organizations including corporations, trade unions, and religious bodies by
  1978.[2]

Since then, all of those numbers have continued to rise exponentially. The 1995-1996 *Yearbook of International Organizations* lists
12,520 international organizations. While the *Yearbook* categorizes
those organizations in a manner different than Duchacek, the trend is
clearly upward in all of Duchacek's classifications. This includes:

- 266 "conventional international bodies" (federations of international organizations; universal membership organizations;
  intercontinental membership organizations; and regionally
  defined membership organizations);
- 1,497 "other international bodies" (organizations emanating
  from places, persons, or other bodies; organizations having a
  special form, including foundations and funds; and internation-
  ally-oriented national organizations); and
- 3,049 "special types" (inactive or dissolved international organizations; recently reported or proposed international organizations;
  subsidiary and international bodies; religious orders, fraternities,
  and secular institutes; autonomous conference series; and multilateral treaties and agreements).

Globalization and Its Implications

The world today is abuzz with discussions of globalization, especially in the three spheres deemed to count most for human progress:
economics, human rights, and communications. "Progressive" voices
of various shades of opinion are discussing ways in which this
globalization can be advanced so as to increase the opportunities for
human happiness, while "conservative" voices are bewailing
globalization as robbing the world's states of their political sovereignty and the world's peoples of their cultural heritage for what is

perceived as no more than a mess of pottage, and one likely to turn sour at that.

Globalization is indeed upon us. While its extent and effects may be exaggerated from time to time, it is no myth. The benefits of globalization are touted widely and prominently—open markets, free trade, greater prosperity for more people, the development of a common world culture, and greater respect for peoples no longer seen as distant and unfamiliar, greater respect for the human rights of individuals and groups along Western models. Yet at the same time, the "downside" of globalization has also become evident—the weakening, if not destruction, of local cultures and local and national liberties by great international bodies, particularly private corporate commercial bodies, in the name of those benefits. In many respects, globalization has crept up upon us and the mechanisms developed to promote it such as the World Trade Organization or the European Union and their regional counterparts have acquired substantial power with minimal constraints, in practice if not in theory.

Not surprisingly, given the democratic aspirations of our times, closely following on the heels of globalization have come efforts to anchor it in appropriate constitutional frameworks. The need for new constitutional arrangements becomes more apparent to lovers of democracy and liberty as globalization advances. Hence, the effort is acquiring a greater level of consciousness on the part of those engaged in it. However, it is still only at the beginning of being noticed by those not so intimately involved. This constitutionalization is being assisted by the renewed desire for strengthening the local and interpersonal dimensions that have come along with it.[3]

Much if not most of what is happening to bring about this constitutionalization is what classically has been known as federalism; that is to say, the combination of constitutional choice, design, and institution-building to accommodate both existing states and trans-state linkages in a federalist manner by combining self-rule and shared rule in such a way as to ensure that shared rule will be confined only to those functions where it is absolutely necessary or clearly more useful to the polities and peoples involved.

Not only do these efforts rest upon the principles of federalism, whether acknowledged or not, but in their specific applications they represent a certain species of that genus—the confederal species. For many, this may be a surprising development—for much of the modern epoch (mid-seventeenth to mid-twentieth centuries), confederal arrangements were in eclipse as the worldwide thrust toward statism made such "loose" constitutional arrangements look flimsy as compared to federation, a species of federalism considerably more compatible with the then regnant "nation-state." Now in the postmodern epoch with globalization and its companion, regionalization, upon us and moving forward at a fast pace, confederal arrangements have reemerged—indeed, it may be said, are coming into their own. This book is a preliminary exploration of how those arrangements have taken shape in the postmodern epoch, how the decline of statism and the rise of globalization have made federalism in its confederal manifestations the vital constitutional-institutional component that can provide a political framework within which world economic, communications, security, and other trends can and are being accommodated.

The new confederalism rests on three pillars: security, economic integration, and protection of human rights. Each of those pillars serves one of the major sets of actors on the world scene. The security issue serves the states involved in the confederal arrangement. The economic basis serves the commercial and industrial interests of the major economic actors and the human rights pillar serves the individual citizens within the arrangement and also the primordial groups to which they belong. In this way, the new confederalism offers something for everyone in connection with their primary interests. Obviously the three pillars are not as separate as here portrayed and each of the three constituent groups has interests in the pillars other than the pillar of its major interest. That only serves to reinforce the attractiveness of the new arrangements and also offers a mitigating effect against their own side for each set of actors.

One of the major characteristics of the new confederalism is that it is not a matter of the *enlargement* of states as in the old confederalism, whereby small polities felt the need to link with one another to establish larger ones to be better able to survive and/or compete in the world around them, but the *transformation* of states from the effort and ideal of being totally sovereign and self-sufficient to becoming autonomous jurisdictions within a larger system, with sufficient standing in international law and vis-à-vis other states to be able to protect their autonomy except where they, themselves, have conceded it to some collective of which they are also a part, in which they share in the decision-making but cannot act unilaterally. In short, it is a confederalism of state transformation rather than state enlargement. That is what defines the postmodern character of the phenomenon.

In 1980, in "Consociations of Fatherlands," the first piece in which he addressed the issue directly from a federalist perspective, Duchacek suggested that the newly globalizing postmodern world could learn from the American confederal experience of the Revolutionary Era two hundred years earlier.[4] On that he quotes Clinton Rossiter, that confederation seems "to have been just about as viable a form of government as could have been offered to the American people" at that time.[5] He then proceeded to apply the same analogy to what was then still the European Community (now Union) and other contemporary examples of transnational organization limiting state sovereignty.

In his thinking, Duchacek, a federalist, saw confederation as an inferior form of political organization when compared to federation. In this book, we will examine confederation and confederal arrangements not as a way station moving toward federation or as an inferior form of political organization, but as a legitimate form of federal democracy in its own right with its own virtues and vices, strengths and weaknesses, on the premise that what is developing in the postmodern world may indeed restore confederal arrangements to "active duty," as it were, among the forms of regime that offer viable options in today's world.

Duchacek based his view on the fact that the Americans in the 1770s and 1780s were "ready to be Americans," in Rossiter's terms, while the Europeans are not.[6] Our argument here is that the Europeans and others who are considering or embracing federal solutions may want to be Europeans or something else without ceasing to be Frenchmen, Germans, British, or whatever they are, and hence may prefer less fully binding forms of federal organization.

This is not an easy process. Proponents of globalization are unhappy with its slowness and weaknesses, while opponents are fearful of its successes, making them equally unhappy with the phenomenon. But the process goes on, happily or unhappily, and needs to be better understood for what it is so that it can be shaped to better become what we would like it to be.

This writer believes that globalization is upon us "for good." "For good," in this sense, means in a lasting manner, but it is also upon us "for better or for worse" and we have the opportunity to influence it either for the better or for the worse. Federalism and federal arrangements—in this case confederal and limited in character—

offer, in this writer's opinion, the best chance to influence it for the better, to curb its excesses in the concentration of economic power in the hands of those who have only economic interests, and to provide for the introduction of an appropriate political dimension that will support federal democracy and human rights, individual and group, but they must be consciously developed and carefully thought through.

In the words of *The Federalist*, the book of political philosophy that first explicated the United States Constitution and thus laid the foundations for a modern federal theory, regimes are established either by force or accident or by reflection and choice. Regimes using federal principles and arrangements are, more than any others, products of reflection and choice. This is particularly important in the postmodern world. That world was born in part through a series of conflicts on the part of partisans of liberty and democracy struggling to defeat those who would establish other world orders by force, whether Fascist, Nazi, or Communist. As a result of that struggle, we entered into a period of globalization by accident; that is to say, through relatively small and restricted acts to solve immediate problems which led to the development of globalization in the economic and communications spheres. Now, having discovered what has happened, we have a brief window of opportunity to constitutionalize it through reflection and choice. It behooves us to do so or our children will pay the price.

Constitutionalizing Globalization: The Postmodern Revival of Confederal Arrangements is the first product of a larger project on the revival of confederal arrangements in the postmodern epoch, particularly confederal solutions to ethnic conflict.

These confederal solutions, ranging from full-fledged confederations to little more than very limited-purpose associations of states, can be understood as regional and functional cooperatives. These cooperatives vary in importance and scope, in membership, in achievements, and in some cases also in duration. Most important, they vary in the degree to which they constitutionally or empirically bind their members. In fact, they are all of limited purpose and collectively consist of myriad overlapping relationships. Even more critical is that the strongest of them have become what we may call "constitutionally binding"; that is to say, while established voluntarily, they rest upon or have developed elements that formally require a commitment that can only be referred to as constitutional and which from a practical point of view must be maintained if the member is to survive and prosper. Accepting constitutional limits in order to gain their practical possibilities has become unavoidable for their members, but the fact that these are differentially overlapping cooperatives both makes them more universal and mitigates their comprehensiveness.

The nomenclature of these cooperatives is varied. Duchacek cites sixteen different examples:

- International Atomic Energy *Agency* (IAEA)
- General *Agreement* on Tariffs and Trade (GATT)
- *Association* of Southeast Asian Nations (ASEAN)
- International *Bank* for Reconstruction and Development (IBRD or World Bank)
- Economic *Commission* for Europe (ECE)
- *Commonwealth* of Nations (formerly the British Empire)
- European Economic *Community* (EEC)
- *Conference* on Trade and Development (UNCTAD)
- International Finance *Corporation* (IFC)
- *Council* for the Cooperation of the States of the Gulf (CCG or Common Market of the six Arab states on the Persian Gulf)
- United Nations Children *Fund* (UNICEF)
- United Nations *Institute* for Training and Research (UNITAR)
- East African Common *Market* (potential)
- North Atlantic Treaty *Organization* (NATO)
- Warsaw *Pact* (sometimes referred to as the Socialist Commonwealth)
- International Telecommunications *Union* (ITU)

The seeming modesty or comprehensiveness of the name used is, in any case, rarely correlated with the scope and depth of the body in question.[7] Not only that, but the names themselves are different in different states. For example, the United States refers to the universal intergovernmental organization established in 1945 as the United Nations. In other languages, for grammatical or defining purposes, the equivalent term used is "United Nations Organization," an effectively limiting name and actually considerably more realistic as well.

Table 1.1

FORMS OF FEDERAL ARRANGEMENTS

(Political, Economic, and Religious Parallels)

Political	Economic	Religious	Principal Characteristics
1. Union	Multi-Division Corporation	Episcopal Church Polity	Clearly bounded territorial constituent units retain "municipal" powers only while sharing power concentrated in common overarching government.
2. Consociation	Guild Systems	Ethnic Congregation (in centralized or hierarchical church)	Non-territorial constituent units share power concentrated in common overarching government.
3. Federation	1. Economic Community 2. Conglomerate, if the constituent units are represented in the overall management structure	Presbyterian Church Polity	Strong self-government constituent units linked within strong but limited overarching government.
4. Federacy	Customs Union	Autocephalic Church (linked polity of larger hierarchial church)	Asymmetrical permanent linkage between two self-government units with the larger having specific powers within the smaller in exchange for specific privileges.
5. Condominium	Joint Stock Company		Joint rule or control by two units over a third or over some common territory or enterprise.
6. Confederation	Common Market	Congregational Unit or Federation	Strong self-governing constituent units permanently linked by loose, limited-purpose common government.
7. League	Free Trade Area	Congregational Convention	Loose but permanent linkage for limited-purposes without common government but with some joint body or secretariat.
8. Inter-Jurisdictional Functional Authorities	Joint Enterprises	Board of Missions	Joint or common entities organized by the constituting units to undertake special tasks.

The Several Species of Federalism

The several species of federalism include federal and confederal arrangements, symmetrical and asymmetrical. They are shown in Table I.1. The table is necessarily more analytic than a reflection of reality. In many cases, the various forms cannot be separated one from the other in an absolute sense, but, rather, particular polities have combined elements of more than one species in practice, if not in theory. Thus several federations began as confederations and have retained confederal features, and vice versa. This is the most frequent blurring, but since these are the two most widespread species, they also have the most significance.

Alain-G. Gagnon has offered the following definition of federalism:

Federalism may be conceived as a political device for establishing viable institutions and flexible relationships capable of facilitating inter-state relations (e.g., division of powers between orders of government), intrastate linkages (e.g., states or *lander* representation at the central level) and inter-community cooperation. Their emphasis on process, institutions can be seen as arising out of politics, the genesis of institutions resulting essentially from the conflicts and power struggles of economic, societal and political actors. However, the question of territory is also central to any study of federalism and it allows for the expression of both diversity and unity.[8]

While for analytic purposes we can identify a variety of species of federalism, in reality, not only are the lines of separation between them not fixed, but neither is the official terminology used to describe them uniform. Thus, regarding the latter, Switzerland and Canada, both federations, retain their original names, the Helvetic Confederation and the Confederation of Canada. Spain and South Africa are federations in almost every respect, but neither refers to itself as such. Federations themselves range from Nigeria, perennially under centralized military government, to rather centralized India, to the increasingly centralized United States, to moderately diffused Germany, to very noncentralized Canada.

With regard to the differences between federations and confederations, reviewing all the variations, we may conclude that not only are the divisions flexible but that federations serve what are agreed to be single nations in which the federal government has direct contact with the people. Confederations, on the other hand, not only unite several states but different national states or the equivalent thereof, and the federal government must reach the people only or predominantly through those national states. Stated differently, federations are "tighter"—partly national and partly federal, in the words of *The Federalist*, and confederations "looser"—partly federal and partly leagues. Moreover, a successful federation will be based on a common liberal democratic civil society for the whole, while a successful confederation will be based on a union of often distinctive democratic commonwealths.

Another way to think of the distinction is that federations are concerned with nation-building for the comprehensive unit while confederations are most ambiguous on that subject, even if the union is designed to be a perpetual one as in the case of the Articles of Confederation. This is reflected in the lack of all-union citizenship in confederations or making that citizenship entirely derivative from citizenship in constituent units, unlike federations where citizenship in the federation stands at least semi-independently from citizenship in the constituent units. Ultimately, the federal government has the ability to reach out directly to the national citizens even within the constituent units, which offers different possibilities, while such possibilities are distinctly more limited in confederations and confederal arrangements.

There is also more leeway in the forms of regime of the constituent units in confederations than in federations. All the regimes in a federation must be similar in form. Indeed, some would argue, as do Duchacek and Ostrom, that they must be democratic for a true federation to exist.[9] Confederations can have a greater range of regime forms among their constituent units and still survive and thrive.

Here Duchacek goes beyond what this writer would see as possible because he includes bodies that are only slightly more than associations of states linked by treaty as confederal arrangements, beyond what we will consider here, even though we will recognize them as extensions of the same continuum. In this book, the United Nations and similar treaty bodies will be seen as beyond the limits of the confederal definition.

Finally, inter-entity decision-making in confederal arrangements more closely resembles diplomatic negotiation and decision-making among sovereigns than within nation-states. While this should not be regarded as absent from federations, for example, local governments within metropolitan regions conduct much of their business in a manner reminiscent of international relations, the sense of connection between units is much greater.[10]

In some respects, a more precise measure of confederalism is the degree of independent access that constituent states in a particular federal arrangement have to the international arena. Thus, federation and confederation in confederal arrangements, while separable for analytic purposes, in fact exist along a continuum.

We should not regard so many of these arrangements simply as an extension by treaty of accepted international relations among states. Even where the arrangement in question has acquired all the properties of a confederation, it is rarely called that formally. On the other hand, even intentionally far weaker linkages do more than standard treaties. Perhaps the difference is best described in the Treaty of Berne establishing the Universal Postal Union, one of the oldest of the intergovernmental associations. "The countries between which the present Convention has been concluded form, under the designation Universal Postal Union, a single territory for the reciprocal exchange of correspondence."[11] When the whole world or a segment of it is considered governmentally to be a single territory even for a limited functional purpose, that already brings the arrangements for governing that territory, at least for that function, under the rubric of federalism.

This does not obviate the question, Why turn to old terminology to describe new phenomena? It would be possible to invent new terms, but in political language as in so many other things there are great virtues in continuity, even if that continuity embraces certain changes. Certainly the term "democracy" as we use it today is not what the Greeks meant by democracy when they invented the term 2,500 years ago; so, too, with the term "state," whose meaning differs today from its meaning in premodern times.

The important thing is that there are fundamental connections between these differing definitions that justify the use of the same term. That is much more so in the case of the terminology of federalism than in many other cases. In the study of federalism, new terms have been invented where needed. Federation, for example, was invented after 1787 and the invention of the first federation through the United States Constitution. But at the same time it is not only useful but advisable to maintain continuities where they exist, as they do in the realm of confederal arrangements.

Not only that, but by use of a term already loaded with meaning we are helped to avoid implying more meaning than particular phenomena can legitimately bear. There is a virtue to approaching reality from the standpoint that if it looks like a duck, walks like a duck, and quacks like a duck, it is highly likely to be a duck. By the same token, if we see something that does not but which we would like to refer to as a duck, having a prior definition to measure it against helps us to avoid jumping to erroneous conclusions.

In the 1990s this federalizing dimension of globalization began to be recognized on both sides. Students of federalism, less bound by conventional statist thinking, began recognizing the phenomenon a decade earlier, but still only the best students and only in limited ways. In the late 1980s the first students of international relations began to make the discovery from the direction of their discipline. By 1994 the number of articles to appear from both perspectives took a quantum leap forward. So, too, in the other, even more public, forums.

For example, in late 1994 the renowned Salzburg Seminar announced its 1995 core program. Of its eleven workshops, three—"The European Union after 1996," "Transnational Law: Intellectual Property Rights," and "Building and Sustaining Democracies: The Role of Nongovernmental Organizations"—dealt directly with the new confederalization, while four more—"The Globalization of American Popular Culture," "Involuntary Migration, The Impact of the Media on Politics," "Public Policy and World Events," and "Preserving the National Heritage: The Realities, the Politics, the Rewards"—dealt with the environment in which it was taking place.

One of the signs of the times is an upsurge in journal articles submitted on the subjects treated in this book. As co-editor of *Publius: The Journal of Federalism*, I have noticed this increase in the past few years, either through articles actually submitted or authors contacting the editors of *Publius* with regard to possible submissions. This new interest is most welcome and expressed through *Publius* and elsewhere.

From Statism to Multilateralism to Confederalism

What we see before us is the development of a set of international regimes of varying scope and constitutional intensity, almost entirely in the post-World War II period, that are in the process of replacing the pre-World War II international system with a new global order. We can describe that change as the movement from statism to multilateralism to confederalism.

The international system prior to World War II was based upon the Westphalian state system and emphasized the sovereignty of individual states, what we may refer to as statism. Beginning in the middle of World War II, the United States took the lead in an effort to modify statism through multilateralism, which can be defined as the linking of sovereign states to collectively establish multilateral arrangements. In this case, multilateralism began with the states allied against the Axis in World War II. Later it was expanded to include the reconstituted Axis states and the newly constituted Third World states. Multilateralism was fostered to allow the development of new international trade, monetary, and security regimes embodied in the Bretton Woods Agreement and the United Nations Charter and supplemented by the General Agreement on Tariffs and Trade.

None of this would have gotten started or moved forward had the United States not had the economic and military hegemony that it had. The U.S. had assumed the free trade mantle that its former mother country, Great Britain, had worn in the nineteenth century and when its hegemonic position had allowed it to do so, it pressed its point of view on other states, no matter how reluctant.

Even the United States had problems at the beginning. The executive branch of the American federal government wanted to go further than the legislative branch would allow. Hence, the original executive branch proposal for an International Trade Organization was rejected by the U.S. Senate and abandoned, to be replaced by the looser arrangements of Bretton Woods. Similarly, while the U.S. Senate reversed its post-World War I position and ratified American membership in the United Nations, it very carefully restricted American acceptance of United Nations decisions and associated agreements such as the treaty outlawing genocide.

Indeed, for a decade both the economic and political agreements accepted on paper languished in practice, and it was only in the 1950s, as a result of changing circumstances and newly perceived needs, that there were practical steps under both. GATT began to become more effective, despite all the exceptions that it allowed, and the United Nations, paralyzed by U.S.-Soviet rivalry in the Cold War, took on a certain additional strength when the Korean War broke out, as a result of the Soviet boycott of the Security Council at the time. Hence, in the 1950s there began a slow movement to strengthen multilateralism, a movement which took another step forward in the 1970s, especially after 1971. By that time the United States had lost the hegemonic position that it had in 1944 and the agreements were renegotiated, thereby making the voices of the other industrialized member states better able to be heard.

No doubt, the diminution of American hegemony actually allowed the next steps to take place since the former world powers, by that time, no longer were insignificant economically and were able to influence policy more directly. This was particularly true in the case of Western Europe which had the additional strength of the European Economic Community (by then already the European Community). While the EC was not yet capable of truly rivaling the United States, it did make the industrial states of Western Europe a great deal stronger in negotiating with the Americans. At the other end of the world, Japan actually began to rival the U.S. in critical manufacturing fields such as automobiles and electronics. The old hegemonic order moved on to become an oligopolistic one instead, which also allowed smaller and weaker countries more room in which to maneuver.

This had become possible because the EC had moved from multilateralism in Europe and was beginning to become a confederal arrangement. After its crisis of the 1970s, in the 1980s that confederal arrangement became even more real and by the end of the decade the Community was on its way to becoming a confederation, which it did once the Treaty of Maastricht was ratified and went into effect. Meanwhile, the world as a whole was moving beyond multilateralism and into confederal arrangements, marked by the transformation of GATT into the World Trade Organization and the collapse of the Soviet Union and the integration of the ex-Communist Bloc into the worldwide system.

This was not a simple movement but had its ups and downs, fits and starts. For example, the United Nations under its new crypto-federalist Secretary General, Bhutros Ghali, attempted to increase its power through multiplying peacekeeping missions. These did not succeed and Ghali was forced to retreat from that exposed position. Moreover, the civil wars in Yugoslavia, which had been provoked by the problematic moves of members of the European Community, should have offered the EC an opportunity to become the peacekeepers of Europe, but they could not rise to the challenge and merely provided a holding action until the United States was willing to enter the arena and use NATO as its device to allow a joint North American-European peacekeeping effort. Still, by the mid-1990s the world had not only abandoned the old statism but was reaching well beyond multilateralism, which was essentially a matter of international relations among states, well into the development of confederalism as a new norm.[12]

Notes

1. Ivo Duchacek, "Consociations of Fatherlands: The Revival of Confederal Principles and Practices," *Publius: The Journal of Federalism* 12 (Fall 1982):129.

2. *Ibid.*, p. 129.

3. Guy LaForest and Douglas Brown describe this janus-like phenomenon in their book *Integration and Fragmentation* and, along with their colleagues, provide us with a good overview of what is happening in both directions. Douglas Brown and Guy LaForest, eds., *Integration and Fragmentation* (Kingston, Ont.: Institute of Intergovernmental Relations, 1995).

4. Duchacek, "Consociations of Fatherlands."

5. Clinton Rossiter, *1787: The Grand Convention* (New York: Macmillan, 1966), pp. 47-48.

6. *Ibid.,* p. 38.

7. Duchacek, "Consociations of Fatherlands," p. 136.

8. Michael Burgess and Alain-G. Gagnon, eds., *Comparative Federalism and Federation: Competing Traditions and Future Directions* (Toronto: University of Toronto Press, 1993), Ch. 2, Alain-G. Gagnon, "The Political Uses of Federalism," p. 15.

9. Vincent Ostrom, "A Computational-Conceptual Logic for Federal Systems of Governance," in Daniel J. Elazar, ed., *Constitutional Design and Power-Sharing in the Post-Modern Epoch* (Lanham, MD: Jerusalem Center for Public Affairs and University Press of America, 1991), pp. 3-22; and Ivo D. Duchacek, "Comparative Federalism: An Agenda for Additional Research," in Daniel J. Elazar, ed., *Constitutional Design and Power-Sharing in the Post-Modern Epoch*, pp. 23-40.

10. Vincent Ostrom, ed., "The Study of Federalism at Work," *Publius* special issue, vol. 25, no. 4 (Fall 1995).

11. Treaty of Berne, 9 October 1874, Article 3:1.

12. Stephen Krasner, ed., *International Regimes* (Ithaca: Cornell University Press, 1983), pp. 195-232.

Chapter 1

FROM STATISM TO FEDERALISM:
A PARADIGM SHIFT

The world as a whole is in the midst of a paradigm shift from a world of states, modeled after the ideal of the nation-state developed at the beginning of the modern epoch in the seventeenth century, to a world of diminished state sovereignty and increased interstate linkages of a constitutionalized federal character.[1] Over the past several years this has been noted by an increasing number of scholars of both federalism and international relations, as well as statesmen, each group from their own perspective, bringing about a convergence of interests from different perspectives.

This paradigm shift actually began after World War II. Institutionally, it may be identified as having begun in 1944 when the wartime United Nations Allies gathered in Bretton Woods, New Hampshire, to establish a new world monetary system to prevent the world from falling into a disastrous postwar depression of the kind sparked by the Crash of 1929. The United Nations, founded in San Francisco in May 1945 as no more than a league of politically sovereign states with the elevated goal of maintaining world peace, was the next step toward this paradigm shift, although the struggle between the two great powers that led to the Cold War and the Third World's struggle for independence prevented it from having the same political impact as the Bretton Woods system did in the economic sphere.

Despite the developments in Western Europe that have led to the radical diminution of the political sovereignty of the member states of the European Union and similar developments in other parts of the world, particularly Southeast Asia (the Association of Southeast Asian Nations—ASEAN) and the Caribbean, it was not until the collapse of first the Soviet empire and then the Soviet Union itself between 1989 and 1993 that the extensive and decisive character of this paradigm shift became evident to most people, even (or perhaps especially) to those who closely follow public affairs. Most of the latter were, and still may be, wedded to the earlier paradigm that the building blocks of world organization are politically sovereign states, most or all of which strive to be nation-states and maximize their independence of action and decision. While there are a few who have been aware of this paradigm shift as it has taken place and some who have advocated it as a major political goal, for most it seems to have crept up unawares.

The Old Paradigm Shifts

Ambassador Max Kampelman, who has taken account of the shift, referred to it in the following manner:

> The interdependence of the world and the globalization of its economy does not imply or suggest the disappearance of the nation-state, which is showing resilience as an important focus of national pride and ethnic preservation. . . . Abba Eban, in a recent analysis of the prospects for confederation between Israel, the West Bank, and Jordan, commented on the apparent contradiction of a politically fragmented world existing alongside an economically integrated one. He suggests that regional confederations may harmonize the contradiction. . . .
>
> For hundreds of years, international society has been organized on the basis of separate sovereign states whose territorial integrity and political independence were protected and guaranteed by an evolving international law. The United Nations Charter, in embodying and reflecting the values of the state system, reaffirmed the principle of non-use of force across international boundaries and the companion principle of non-intervention in internal affairs. . . .
>
> Into this principle, Woodrow Wilson . . . introduced in the early twentieth century a new principle, that of self-determination of peoples, intended as a blow against colonialism. Its effect, however, introduced mischievous consequences in many parts of the world. Increasingly, violence associated with ethnic conflicts has been justified with assertions of the right of self-determination. What has been misunderstood is the fact that the right of self-determination of peoples certainly does not include the right to secede from established and internationally legitimized nation-state borders. . . .

The world is very much smaller. There is no escaping the fact that the sound of a whisper or a whimper in one part of the world can immediately be heard in all parts of the world—and consequences follow.

But the world body politic has not kept pace with those scientific and technological achievements. Just as the individual human body makes a natural effort to keep the growth of its components in balance, and we consider the body disfigured if the growth of one arm or leg is significantly less than the other, so is the world body politic disfigured if its knowledge component opens up broad new vistas for development while its political and social components remain in the Dark Ages.[2]

Let us understand the nature of this paradigm shift. It is not that states are disappearing, it is that the state system is acquiring a new dimension, one that began as a supplement and is now coming to overlay (and, at least in some respects, to supersede) the system that prevailed throughout the modern epoch. That overlay is a network of agreements that are not only militarily and economically binding for de facto reasons but are becoming constitutionally binding, de jure. This overlay increasingly restricts what was called state sovereignty and forces states into various combinations of self-rule and shared rule to enable them to survive at all. That means federalism, understood in the broadest political sense as a genus involving combinations of self-rule and shared rule rather than as the one species of federalism accepted in modern times—federation.

This has been further exacerbated by the postmodern legitimation of ethnic identity. Every group successful in presenting its claim to separate ethnic identity is able thereby to claim recognition as legitimate and entitled to some measure of self-preservation and political self-expression if it seeks them. Not every potential ethnic group does, nor do all seek the same forms of political self-expression, but more than ever before the possibility of such self-determined groups gaining legitimacy has become great.

The implications of this paradigm shift are enormous. Whereas before, every state strove for self-sufficiency, homogeneity, and, with a few exceptions, the concentration of authority and power in a single center, under the new paradigm all states have to recognize as well their interdependence, heterogeneity, and the fact that their centers, if they ever existed, are no longer single centers but parts of a multi-centered network that is increasingly noncentralized, and that all of this is necessary in order to survive in the new world.

The suggestion that we are witnessing a major paradigm shift is not meant to imply that the outcome will be perfect or even work in every case. Human conflicts remain very real and a new tribalism is the obverse of globalization. In a world that recognizes an increasing number of ethnic groups, some of those groups will come into conflict with the states in which they are located or with each other. Hence, ethnic conflict has become a major world problem and has attracted increasing attention as such, in no little measure because of the horrendous consequences of the more visible ethnic conflicts in our time.

One of the phenomena clearly concomitant with globalization is ethnonationalism. "Ethnic" used in this context can be understood as including racial, linguistic, ethnocultural, tribal, and religious communities, some of which are dispersed within many states, some dispersed as a minority within one, some of which are a majority in one and minorities in others. As the modern state system diminishes in power, ethnic groups reclaim or advance their own claims to national identity. In some cases these claims are old ones and the groups that claim them have been in battle for centuries in their struggle to exercise them.

For every ethnic group that succeeded in gaining control or establishing a state of its own, there are at least ten that remain minorities in other states. Several thousand others are tribes in parts of the world where modern models of statehood did not penetrate until the twentieth century. They never had to surrender their identity, even if they have had to fight to maintain it among the world's peoples. In a postcolonialist era, they have been able to reassert their claims as ethnic ones and in the era of globalization, to seek support for those claims not only within the states in which they are located but around the globe.

Increasingly, these claims overlap and cannot all be satisfied through separation because of the realities of the situation. It is in this context that many have turned to federal solutions.

Federalism probably has received most attention in recent years as a suggested means to solve ethnic conflicts in a world that has rediscovered the harsh realities of ethnicity and has lost its confidence that modernization will bring about their desuetude. But sober students of federalism have long recognized that ethnic demands are among the most exclusivist in the world and that the same ethnic consciousness that makes federalism in some form necessary also makes it all the more difficult and less likely to succeed. Honesty demands that this sad paradox be recognized and its realities be confronted both by the partisans of ethnic self-determination and by the partisans of federal solutions.

Other reasons for the difficulties with ethnic territorial federalism include the diasporic or migratory character of some ethnic groups that are too dispersed to be beneficiaries of what is basically a territorial relationship. Many are very small ethnic communities (two very imprecise and almost undefinable terms) that cannot properly be accommodated within the large polity, at least not to their satisfaction. On the other hand, too small a polity cannot provide for the constitutionalizing of internal ethnic divisions without running great risks.

In essence, a federalism based upon ethnicity requires a high level of coincidence between the ethnic group in question and the territory it occupies. Where more than one ethnic group occupies a territory, that itself becomes problematic. Where one or only one does or where it is overwhelming, it may be tempted to secede rather than maintain a federal relationship with those whom it sees as its enemies. Under such conditions, only the sense of interdependence that goes beyond desires for separate ethnic identity can make federal relationships work. In such cases, confederal arrangements may be preferable or more workable.

During the modern epoch, the "new worlds" of the Western and Southern Hemispheres were settled by emigrants from Europe who founded a number of what Duchacek referred to as ethno-ideological states, of which the United States was the first and preeminent example, and Israel, established in 1948, the last.[3] These states only developed on unsettled or, more accurately, undersettled territories by emigrants who were, at least originally, from the same or similar ethnic stock in the "old world" and who settled in the new in pursuit of the same or similar visions or goals. There they amalgamated into new peoples on the basis of those visions and goals.

This could not be achieved in the old world. For example, the French Revolution attempted to do the same thing in France, an old, indeed, the first of the Western European states, but the historical baggage that France carried with it greatly limited the ideological transformation possible in that country. The twentieth century ideological movements—Communism, Fascism, Nazism, and others—tried to do the same. Not only did all fail, but they did so after bringing great pain and suffering to the countries on which their experiments were tried. Hence we must conclude that ideological transformations are not likely to replace ethnic identities and so offer no way out of these problems.

On the other hand, there are less than two hundred states in the world defined as politically sovereign and thousands of ethnic groups or potential ethnic groups. Thus, many accommodations will have to be made to allow ethnic groups an effective and operative identity within the state system. Even if the five hundred plus federated or constituent states of federal unions are added to the politically sovereign states, we still have something like 3,500 in 700 political entities. In this period of the revival of ethnic identities, and indeed the generation of new ethnic identities in some places, in the case of some groups this is clearly a task for federalism.

Perhaps the solution lies in the extent of the federal bonds as much as in their depth. For most of the modern epoch, at least since the establishment of the American federation through the Constitution of 1787, most of the world has looked upon federalism as federation pure and simple. Other forms of federalism, especially confederation and confederal arrangements that had been considered federal until 1787, not only ceased to be functional but ceased to be regarded as reasonable federal options for governmental organization.

The new globalization has brought with it new kinds of migration. Whereas, in the past, migrations tended to be movements of peoples, individuals, and families from a point of origin to a new destination for conquest or permanent settlement, and either replacement of or absorption into the indigenous population, we now have a continuous migration of peoples, individuals, and families throughout the globe in search of economic opportunity or a better quality of life. Sometimes these migrants are accepted for absorption in their new homes; sometimes they are not and are treated as if they are still attached to their old ones.

In fact, many have become "guest workers" who may never go back to their original homes but are still not absorbed within their new ones. Some are temporary migrants who settle for what they, themselves, consider to be a limited period and seek to maintain their homeland ties. Still others are seasonal migrants. These range from migrant farm workers to the very wealthy who go to live in different climates for different seasons. Still others have resettled in new countries but want to retain serious ties of some kind with their mother country. All of these trends lead in the same direction, to the development of diasporas and various forms of state-diaspora relationships which also affect the old limits of state sovereignty and require new constitutional relationships.

The Rise and Transformation of the Modern State System

The old state system was the product of the modern epoch. Given practical form by the new nation-states of Western Europe, such as France in the late Middle Ages or Prussia in the eighteenth century, these states rested on the idea that by concentrating power in a single head or center, the state itself could be sufficiently controlled and its environment sufficiently managed to achieve self-sufficiency or at least a maximum of self-sufficiency in a world which would inevitably be hostile or at best neutral toward each state's interests and in which alliances would reflect temporary coalitions of interests that should not be expected to last beyond that convergence. The old maxim "No state has friends, only interests" typified that situation.

Centralization and self-sufficiency were the first two defining elements of the modern state. Indeed, the first powerful nation-states were monarchies, advocates of the divine right of kings to protect central authority and power. After a series of modern revolutions, first in thought, led by people like Hobbes, Spinoza, and Locke, and then in practice, kings were stripped of their exclusive powers, even in principle. New power centers were formed, presumably based upon popular citizenship and consent, but in fact with the same centralized powers, only vested in boards and managers, ostensibly representative assemblies, and executive officers speaking in the name of the state. In only a few cases had earlier dispersions of power been constitutionalized and needed to be taken into consideration. This led to the establishment of federations, forms of federalism with clear lines of national supremacy and, at least for purposes of foreign relations and usually defense, extensive national powers. While these may have been mitigated de facto, de jure they were always there to be used.

The third defining element of the nation-state was its striving for homogeneity. Every state was to be convergent with its nation and every nation with its state. Where people did not fit easily into that procrustean bed, efforts were made to force them into it. This was done either through internal pressure (as in France where the French government, in the name of the state, warred against Bretons, Occetanians, Provençals, and Languedocians, among others, even denying them the right to choose names for their children that did not appear on the official Francophone list), or external pressure (as in the Balkans where small national states with minorities outside of their state boundaries regularly warred with one another in an effort to conquer the territories where their fellow nationals lived and either to

exterminate or expel those not defined as being of the same nationality, as in Bosnia today). As a result, modern wars were basically of two
kinds, either imperialistic wars designed to enable more powerful
states to become even more self-sufficient by seizing control of
populations, territories, and resources that could be used in that
direction, or nationalist wars designed to reunite parts of the nation
with the national state.

In the end, none of these three goals could be achieved. In many
cases they were not achieved at all; in others they were achieved
temporarily until those disadvantaged by them succeeded in revolting.
In still others they proved to be unachievable by any sustainable
means. Usually a combination of all three factors prevented their
attainment.

As the late Ivo Duchacek, himself a Czech and thus exposed to the
futility of those efforts in Middle Europe between World Wars I and
II, pointed out in the 1970s, of the then-existing states in the world, 90
percent contained minorities of 15 percent or more of the total population within their boundaries. Of the remaining 10 percent, almost all
had large ethnic minorities of their own living outside of their state
boundaries.[4] Since he documented that fact, matters have gotten more
complex, as we see by the great resurgence of ethnic conflict in one
form or another throughout the world, a factor that has become one
catalyst for the new paradigm in its search for ways to overcome those
conflicts.

Self-sufficiency, in reality, was never achievable. It is well to
recall that modern economic liberalism, which was essentially based
on the principle of free trade, emerged shortly after the emergence of
modern statism to challenge the economic basis of statism, expressed
through mercantilism which sought self-sufficiency. In part, economic liberalism emerged because of the problematics of mercantilism, which were brought to the fore, inter alia, by the American
Revolution against Great Britain. When that policy failed, imperialism replaced it as the means for these modern nation-states to gain
self-sufficiency. Imperialism had failed by the middle of the twentieth
century, not only because the peoples subjugated rejected it, but
because a democratic moral sensibility came to affect the subjugators.

Nor was free trade, in the nineteenth-century liberal sense, the
answer since it was an extension of the nineteenth-century conception
of the "automatic society," that is, the conception that government
could be eliminated or nearly so, to be replaced by "the market" or "the
march of history," or the unshackling of humans' original goodness,
or some other "process" that was believed to work automatically. Free

trade suffered from the same defects as those conceptions when they were applied in the real world.

At the beginning of the modern epoch, those who conceptualized and brought about the revolutions of modernity understood that all society was framed by government and that the institutions of government were necessary to give a society its identity and character. In an effort to establish more space for private social life and for individualism, they developed the idea of "civil society" which preserved that understanding of the role of government in society, which dated back to the beginnings of civilization, but recognized three separate or separable spheres: governmental, public but non-governmental (voluntary associations), and private, each of which they saw as absolutely essential for civil society to realize itself along the lines envisioned. In time, however, their theories were submerged into a kind of mechanical understanding of "society" as superseding civil society and existing in and of itself, with or without government.

The ideologies of the nineteenth century, however widely separated they were in how they conceptualized humanity and what they wanted to do to achieve the ideal society they envisioned, shared this in common. They all believed that their goals could be achieved by releasing automatic mechanisms that would naturally move things in the right direction. This is true whether we speak of laissez-faire which saw the market as the appropriate automatic mechanism, anarchism which saw the goodness of humanity once released from the shackles of civilization as bringing about the desired result, or Marxism which saw historical processes as doing that, or whatever.

By the mid-twentieth century, after attempts to achieve laissez-faire capitalism had led to social and economic disasters such as the Great Depression, and the other attempts had led to one or another form of totalitarianism and the *Götterdämmerung* of World War II, most of the world was disabused of that idea. Free trade, too, ran afoul not only of illegitimate interests of different peoples and polities, but of their legitimate interests. While its value was increasingly recognized, so, too, was the need to harness it within some kind of framework that provided for those regulations and encouragements necessary for free trade to be most advantageous and beneficial to all.

Moreover, the World War II *Götterdämmerung* had itself clarified several points: one, that states potentially powerful militarily had to be somehow harnessed to one another to prevent further and worse catastrophes; and two, that peoples would not submit to rule by others whom they did not see as linked to them in some meaningful way.

The New Paradigm Emerges

All of this was topped off by the introduction of nuclear energy into the equation. The atomic bomb and its successors made it clear to all but the world's crazies that absolute sovereignty was no longer possible, that even the strongest power in the world was limited in what it could do to make its power felt without generating a catastrophic reaction that would be self-destructive. The "balance of terror" of the Cold War years generated by Soviet imperialism but restrained by their nuclear realism, was an effort to harness the old state system to new realities.

Obviously a balance of terror could only be a temporary device. As both great powers and many lesser ones feared, others less interested in maintaining a balance would acquire the same weapons of terror in due course with unforeseen but not very hopeful consequences. So within the balance of terror, especially outside of the very oppressive Communist bloc which tried to use new versions of old imperialist techniques to preserve the power of its leading state and ruling class, efforts began to be made to go beyond the old system to find new ways to gain control of the situation to everyone's mutual satisfaction.

Thus was born the European Community, now the European Union, initially a network of treaties establishing functional linkages between the various states of Western Europe. It dates back to 1949, the very beginning of the postmodern epoch, although the first treaty, the European Coal and Steel Community, was formally signed in 1958. At first the functional links were anchored on the effort to bring the two great continental European rival states, France and Germany, together on a peaceful basis so as to prevent future wars between them. In due course the European Community evolved from consultative agreements to joint functional authorities established by international treaty, to confederal arrangements, to, with the adoption of the European Union Treaty of Maastricht, confederation. Soon, similar efforts were under way in other parts of the world, in part influenced by the EC/EU experience and stimulated by the recognition of similar needs.

Simultaneously, the two great Cold War power blocs, under the leadership of the superpower dominant in each, tried to build ostensibly looser but equally binding links in the realms of economics and defense. Those fostered by the Soviet Union were old-fashioned imperial ties in a new ideological guise. Hence, it was not surprising that they collapsed with the collapse of the Soviet empire in the late 1980s and early 1990s.

Those developed for the free world were developed under the leadership of the United States, which had the generous view that it was in its interest to rebuild Europe and make its components into partners, even though that might bring with it moments of heartburn for the U.S., because in the long run the results would be better for all. So after World War II the United States rebuilt both its allies and its former foes in Europe and the Far East as well, generously providing from its own resources to do so.

In a sense, the postwar world backed into the new paradigm and did not seek it per se. The victors saw as their first task after World War II the resurrection of the old state system with a minimum of modifications. That is to say, they undertook reconstruction of the former Axis powers on a rehabilitative basis so that they could be readmitted to the family of nations, reconstruction of the war-torn Allies so that they would be able to function again as equal members of the world community of states, and various collective security arrangements to try to insure world peace, of which the United Nations was one. As a result of the beginning of the Cold War, the UN became more symbolic than effective, although it was fortuitous that the USSR and its satellites had walked out of the UN before the outbreak of the Korean War, leaving that organization free to take a one-time stand on an issue of that magnitude and to throw its support and cover behind the U.S.-led defense of South Korea.

Even before that, a new world monetary system had been established through the Bretton Woods agreements, formulated at the United Nations Monetary and Financial Conference held at that site in New Hampshire in 1944. The conference resulted in the establishment of the International Monetary Fund and the International Bank for Reconstruction and Development. While little attention was paid to their political implications at the time, their subsequent development and the establishment of an embryonic world economic order in time has had very real political consequences.

In the meantime, the North Atlantic Treaty Organization (NATO) had been set up as a Western collective security pact. In retrospect, we can see that as a major step toward the new paradigm. While it was far from establishing a confederal arrangement, it did establish what Karl Deutsch felicitously referred to as a "security community" under the aegis of the United States, then clearly the only Western superpower.[5]

On the other hand, while efforts to establish federations or decentralized states in West Germany, Japan, and Italy successfully served as part of the rebuilding process and a small number of federations succeeded in surviving decolonization in countries such as India, Pakistan (more on paper than in practice but still surviving), Malaya-

Malaysia, and Nigeria, efforts to federalize aggregations of pre-existing states as federations, such as the abortive United States of Europe, did not succeed at all. In the 1950s, however, the Western European countries did begin to pursue what they called functional rather than federal solutions to their problems of union on a more limited basis. These slowly evolved into confederal arrangements to take the lead in bringing about the paradigm shift.

So, too, were similar efforts initiated in the Caribbean. At first, Britain tried to establish a full-blown West Indies Federation. It failed, but confederal arrangements uniting most of those same islands emerged out of the wreckage. Islands are, by definition, insular; hence federation was too much for them. But although they sought independence, they also perceived that they needed to share certain functions, e.g., currency, higher education, a supreme court.

Similarly, Spain, in an effort to preserve the older statist model but within the context of its economically stronger peripheral regions' drive for autonomy, made some wise decisions to introduce regional decentralization throughout the country. Thus its leaders launched it on the road to federalization, at the same time controlling the secessionist impulse of the Basques, Catalans, and others. In the 1970s, Italy implemented the regional system that the Allies had required it to introduce into its immediate postwar constitution. Belgium, confronted with intensifying ethnic problems between Flemings and Walloons, adopted federation in the 1980s, in an effort to resolve its problem. Thus without in any conscious way abandoning the state system, the federal paradigm in essence sneaked up on an increasingly substantial and significant segment of the world.

In the other direction is the Netherlands, which had become, according to its constitution, a "unitary decentralized state" after the Napoleonic Wars, moving to a form of confederation when it withdrew from its empire. Its Caribbean colonies were transformed into federacies, that is to say, states that were internally independent but were linked to the Netherlands itself in an asymmetrical federal relationship, formally designated the Kingdom of the Netherlands with its own charter, but with its major collective governing institutions those of the Netherlands proper.

All of this was much enhanced by the new economic realities that led to constituent states of existing federations having to insert themselves in the international system as states for purposes of economic development. That drive has only been gaining in momentum since it began.

For example, despite the prohibitions on state involvement in foreign affairs that the U.S. Constitution of 1787 made an exclusively federal power, by the late 1950s several states had opened offices overseas to promote their foreign commerce.[6] This trend has continued and by now is an accepted aspect of American foreign economic policy.[7]

The Canadian provinces have gone even further in this respect. The Canadian government has recognized this involvement and has provided for provincial interest sections in Canadian embassies abroad and Ministry of External Affairs assistance to provinces wanting to conduct their own foreign relations across cultural as well as economic spheres.[8] Quebec has been a leader in this regard for its own nationalistic reasons, but the other provinces have not been far behind.

In the mid-1980s when Duchacek summed up "The International Dimension of Subnational Government," he noted that not only did Quebec have 22 offices abroad, but five other provinces had a total of 21 offices. Alberta had permanent representatives in Los Angeles, New York, Houston, Tokyo, London, and Hong Kong, and had established special relationships with the island province of Hokkaido in Japan, the province Heilongji in the Republic of China, and the province of Gangweon in South Korea.

Thirty-three U.S. states maintained 66 permanent offices in 17 countries, 19 of which were in Tokyo and 11 more in Brussels. Alabama, for example, had a state office in London, a full-time person in Berne, a part-time representative in Frankfurt, and a consulting firm on retainer in Tokyo. In some cases, the major cities in particular states take over a major share of the overseas representative function, in essence promoting the whole state along with their own self-promotion. European countries have followed suit to the point where German federalism scholar Franz Gress has coined the term "intermestic" to suggest the essential combination of international and domestic politics involving the German *länder*.[9]

Transborder relations among cities, cantons, federated states, and provinces in Europe and North America had begun to develop even earlier. Most European constitutions, especially the newer ones, make provision for such relations on the part of their federated states, especially with immediately neighboring polities. Since the European states and their constituent governments are not separated from those of other nations by bodies of water but share common borders with them, they have many more transborder problems that need to be resolved in more appropriate arenas than the national capitals. In addition, the close ties among states established in the European Union affect the constituent governments as well.

In Europe especially, transborder relations among cities are prominent since they involve daily cross-border commuting of workers at all levels as well as normal borderland-area relationships, so much so in some cases that the border is often reduced to a formality. For example, in the tristate region around Basel, Switzerland, involving several Swiss cantons, the German state of Baden-Württemberg, and the French province of Alsace, not only is there heavy transborder commuting, but the Basel airport is actually located in France and connected to Basel by a road in French territory that is accessible only through the Swiss city, while the Basel railroad station serves the neighboring German *land* as well. Similar arrangements can be found in other Western European borderlands.[10]

In North America, elaborate systems of transborder relations have developed along the U.S.-Canadian and U.S.-Mexican borders between the states and provinces of those three countries,[11] covering everything from allocation of water resources to common law enforcement efforts. After World War II the number and extent of these arrangements increased exponentially.[12]

During the Kennedy administration in the United States early in the 1960s, the American states also began to find their way into the international arena. Prior to that, the conventional constitutional wisdom that matters of foreign affairs were the exclusive province of the federal government had prevailed, except where there was a direct domestic state interest, usually having to do with the immigration of one group or another (e.g., the efforts on the part of California to exclude Japanese immigrants at the turn of the century) or matters of political concern to elected office-holders (e.g., the governor of Michigan's vocal support for Ukrainian and Polish independence during the Cold War years). Then, encouraged by the U.S. Department of Commerce, states began to seek markets abroad for their manufacturers to encourage foreign investors to invest within their boundaries and even to implement American technical assistance programs in the developing world.[13]

By the 1970s the line between politically sovereign and federated states was beginning to be blurred. By the 1990s there had almost come to be one "seamless" international system including both the 180-plus "politically sovereign" states and the 350-plus federated (or constituent) states.

Power-sharing arrangements are being tried even in difficult situations. The beginning steps toward a tentative confederal arrangement between Israel, the Palestinians, and Jordan are being taken in the field of transborder connections, particularly with regard to water and power, but also involving nature protection and recreation.

Duchacek wrote before the development of the latest interactive telecommunications and video techniques, which have fostered the ability for people to communicate with each other without passing through any national clearinghouse or system of control by directly entering cyberspace to encounter their counterparts in other countries. The telephone and the photocopier did their share to bring down the Soviet Union. The fax machine and Internet are infinitely more powerful. The possibilities of these new forms of communication are just beginning to be realized.

Thus the new paradigm began to emerge slowly, without conscious planning, and gained momentum as time passed. In the mid-1970s even the European Community looked to many like it would not survive. Then in the 1980s it picked up momentum along with all these other forms of federalism.

The growing weakness of the Soviet empire and the Soviet Union itself contributed to the growing transformation of worldwide international treaty arrangements such as the General Agreement on Tariffs and Trade (GATT) and the then newly established Council on Security and Cooperation in Europe (CSCE) into more constitutionalized leagues that, while remaining dependent upon their member states, also had greater means to bring those member states to reach enforceable multilateral agreements on specifics within the context of their mandates. Each of these cases is a story in itself, a story that needs to be told to better understand the full dimensions of the paradigm shift. Not only did GATT maintain a relatively open trading world for decades, but each round of renegotiations expanded the agreements for open trading and made it harder for any states, including the most powerful, to resist them. After it seemed as if one impasse after another would lead to the collapse of GATT, the 1993 round reached closure as the most extensive of all. This was reflected structurally and symbolically in the part of the agreement that provided that on January 1, 1995, GATT would become the World Trade Organization (WTO), no longer structured as a league but as an international organization.

The CSCE became the vehicle for forcing the Soviet Union under Gorbachev into a program of liberalization that ultimately led to its downfall. It did so by insisting on the application of Western European human rights standards to the Eastern bloc, slowly but inexorably. Today the CSCE has become even further institutionalized as the Office of Security and Cooperation in Europe (OSCE) and has become a more powerful guardian of human rights for all of Europe.

In retrospect, the emergence of globalization and the development of appropriate federal arrangements went hand in hand, but had the basis for globalization not first been established through the Bretton Woods agreements, the United Nations Charter, and the General Agreement on Tarrifs and Trade, there would have been no world frameworks secure enough for federal arrangements to develop the way they did—not as state enlargement but as state transformation.

The Situation in the 1990s

The new globalization is accompanied by a new localization and new forms of localism which in some cases are quite parochial. The two seem to go hand in hand as the world requires a larger scale and arena for some things—in particular, economic development, defense, environmental protection, and human rights—but also seeks smaller scales and arenas to preserve others—in particular, issues of community and identity. In fact, globalization offers greater opportunities to move in both directions. That movement, however, requires political structuring for governance anchored in appropriate constitutional frameworks.

Within this evolving structure, states remain in place, but they become recognizably pluralistic, if not polyethnic. Increasingly, many states have come to recognize their polyethnic character and stop or at least significantly reduce their efforts at homogenization. The full consequences of these changes cannot yet be known, but in conjunction with globalization, they will undoubtedly seriously transform the state system into a network of service states with less emphasis on their exclusivist character.

As the dust settles in the 1990s, we find more federations than ever before covering more people than ever before. These can be seen as the foundation stones of the new paradigm. At present there are twenty-one federations containing some two billion people or 40 percent of the total world population. They are divided into over 350 constituent or federated states (as against the more than 180 politically sovereign states).

Attached to or alongside those federations are numerous federal arrangements of one kind or another, usually asymmetrical (federacies and associated states), whereby the federate power has a constitutional connection with a smaller federated state on a different basis than its normal federal-state relationships, one that preserves more autonomy for the small federated state or is based on some relationship between a Westernized federation and its aboriginal peoples. The United States, for example, has federacy arrangements with Puerto Rico (recently reaffirmed by the people of Puerto Rico in yet another referendum) and the Northern Marianas. It also recognizes several hundred Native American (Indian) tribes within it as "domestic dependent nations" with certain residual rights of sovereignty and certain powers reserved to them. Those now are gaining some real meaning, whether through responsible tribal self-government or through revenues produced for the tribes by the opening of gambling casinos on tribal lands. The Federated States of Micronesia, the Marshall Islands, and Palau, formerly Trust Territories of the United States captured from Japan in World War II, have been given their independence as associated states tied to the United States for purposes of defense and development.

Indeed, one of the manifestations of the new paradigm is the way in which federalism has played a role in restoring democracy in various states. Spain has already been mentioned. Federalism was also reflected in the restoration of democracy in Argentina and Brazil. Indeed, in Brazil the existence of federalism even preserved a modicum of free government during the military dictatorship through the state governors who could remain in power and even have limited elections because of their strength, both political and military. It is an untold story of the Brazilian experience under the generals' rule that Brazil's states kept their state police forces under the governors' control. In the larger states, those forces constituted up to 40,000 trained men who were better organized and trained than the Brazilian army, which was largely composed of conscripts serving limited terms. Thus the governors could fully counter every federal threat to use force.[14] Federalism also has been a means of trying to further extend democracy in Venezuela where the state governors, recently transformed into elected officials, played a crucial role in protecting democracy during the last attempt to oust the president, and seems to be an instrument in slowly transforming Mexico from a one-party into a multiparty polity.

Even more dramatic was the way in which federalism was used to reunify Germany after the collapse of the German Democratic Republic. The territory of the GDR first was redivided into five federated *länder* (federated states), and then those five states joined with the eleven federated *länder* of the German Federal Republic plus Berlin (previously an associated state) to form the expanded federal republic.

Beyond this circle of federations there have emerged the new confederations, such as the European Union, that bind federations (such as Germany), unions (such as Great Britain), and unitary states (such as France) in new-style federal arrangements. Others in this category are the Commonwealth of Independent States (CIS), the successor to the Soviet Union, and the Caribbean Community, constructed around and beyond the Caribbean Common Market

(CARICOM), the heir to the failed West Indies Federation. While both of the latter are not as far along the road to confederation as the EU, both are moving in that direction, each in its own way.

Confederal arrangements are normally easier to achieve and maintain when the states being linked are heterogeneous rather than homogeneous. The more the states approximate the ideal of the nation-state with one nation or ethnic group in one state, the harder it is to combine that state with others. The one possible exception to that rule was when the states of Western Europe formed the European Community, now the European Union. A look beneath the surface of national homogeneity in every major Western European state reveals a diversity of ethnic groups, forcibly submerged by the nation-states, that had already begun to resurface and to develop their own cross-border connections even without the new confederal system.

Many of the states within these new confederations have developed federacy and associated state relations of their own or have decentralized internally, reflecting another dimension of the paradigm shift. Take, for example, Portugal and the Azores or Monaco and France.

The looser league arrangements mentioned above, such as the CSCE in Europe and NATO for the North Atlantic community, which have moved beyond their standing as groups of states linked by treaty to acquire certain limited but nonetheless real constitutional powers, represent the next circle beyond those federations and confederations. In the 1990s these began to be supplemented by regional free-trade areas, the oldest of which, linking Belgium, the Netherlands, and Luxembourg as the Benelux states, has essentially been superseded by the European Community, but the newer of which, such as the North American Free Trade Area (NAFTA) or the Association of Southeast Asian Nations (ASEAN), offer all sorts of promise for the future of their members and for future expansion. For example, the New Zealand-Australian Free Trade Association, which came into existence toward the end of World War II, has begun to integrate those two countries in economic and social fields beyond trade. Increasingly, the relationship is between New Zealand and the states of Australia, rather than simply a bilateral linkage. To make the point even sharper, the recent action of the Gulf Cooperation Council in rescinding the Arab League's secondary and tertiary boycott of Israel was something that those six states, including Saudi Arabia, which is very cautious as an individual state, could only do collectively. As individuals they would not have been able to take such a step in the absence of prior Arab League action.

Last but hardly least are the similar arrangements on a worldwide basis. As we have seen with the latest round of GATT negotiations, these, too, are becoming more than treaties. Despite the fact of the WTO formerly being merely a treaty, the world's leading industrial nations discovered that they could not live without it, so they had to resolve the serious difficulties among them, whether they liked it or not, and move onward.

Finally, there are those international organizations whose standing is such that otherwise politically independent states are virtually compelled to participate in them and to accept those organizations' policies as their own, beginning with the International Postal Union, established in the nineteenth century to regularize world communications. There has been a steady, if uneven, growth in such organizations.

Thus, on the threshold of the third millennium of the Christian era and in the second generation of the postmodern epoch, the paradigm shift seems to be well advanced and moving right along. Indeed, even the most troubled spots of the first generation of the postmodern epoch seemed to be choosing federal paradigms as ways to resolve their presumably "insoluble" conflicts, viz: (1) the Commonwealth of Independent States in the former Soviet Union; (2) the new near-federal constitution in South Africa; (3) the Israel-Palestinian Declaration of Principles, Cairo Agreement, and the Israel-Jordan Peace Treaty, which rest upon the ability of the two sides plus Jordan to establish a network of joint authorities as well as to further develop their separate entities either as states or in the manner of states; and (4) most recently, the British-Irish declaration on Northern Ireland and subsequent local cease-fire declarations, which opened the door to peace negotiations for that troubled area, also along lines that will combine self-rule and shared rule, although still very vague ones.

What is equally interesting is that international law has already undergone considerable change to accommodate the new turn.[15] Since international law in its present form developed out of the Westphalian state system, it had become one of the major barriers to the shift away from statism. Most of those engaged in international relations on a professional basis had studied international law and its concepts and had become wedded to the Westphalian view of state sovereignty, a view that they were influential in helping to continue to dominate conventional thinking about international and interstate arrangements. As political scientists have been saying, while in periods of calm the law may shape reality, in periods of change the law will in the end follow reality and find ways to accommodate and justify it.

Much remains to happen before this new paradigm becomes as rooted as the old one. Included among what has to be done is for scholars and public figures to recognize the new paradigm for what it is, to seek to understand it, and to promote it, each group in its own way. For what can be said about this new paradigm is that while the old state paradigm was a recipe for war more often than not, the new federal one is equally a recipe for peace, if it works.

Notes

1. I use the term "federal" here in its larger historical sense, not simply to describe modern federation but all the various federal arrangements including federations, confederations and other confederal arrangements, federacies, associated states, special joint authorities with constitutional standing, and others.

2. Max Kampelman, "Negotiating Toward a New World: The Art of Conflict Resolution through Diplomacy," Speech to B'nai B'rith, Jerusalem, 13 October 1993.

3. Ivo D. Duchacek, "Antagonistic Cooperation: Territorial and Ethnic Communities," *Publius*, vol. 7, no. 4 (Fall 1977):8-9.

4. Ivo Duchacek, "External and Internal Challenges to the Federal Bargain," *Publius*, vol. 5, no. 2 (Spring 1975).

5. Karl Deutsch and Sidney Burrell, *Political Community and the North Atlantic Area* (Princeton: Princeton University Press, 1957).

6. See Dennis Palumbo in Daniel J. Elazar, ed., *Cooperation and Conflict* (Ithaca, Ill.: F.E. Peacock, 1969).

7. John Kincaid, "American Governors in International Affairs," *Publius*, vol. 14, no. 4 (Fall 1984):95-114; Conrad Weiler, "GATT, NAFTA and State and Local Powers," *Intergovernmental Perspective*, vol. 20, no. 1 (Fall 1993-Winter 1994); Michael Burgess and Franz Gress, "German Unity and European Union: Federalism Restructured and Revitalized," *Federalisme* (1993):121-145; Alice M. Rivlin, *Reviving the American Dream: The Economy, the States, and the Federal Government* (Washington: Brookings Institution, 1992), and Alice Rivlin, "American Federalism: An Economic Perspective," in Knop et al., eds., *Rethinking Federalism* (Vancouver: University of British Columbia Press, 1995), pp. 196-200; John Kincaid "Constituent Diplomacy: U.S. State Roles in Foreign Affairs," in *Constitutional Design and Power-Sharing in the Post-Modern Epoch,* Daniel J. Elazar, ed. (Lanham, MD: Jerusalem Center for Public Affairs and University Press of America, 1991), pp. 107-142.

8. Filippo Sabetti and Harold M. Waller, eds., "Crisis and Continuity in Canadian Federalism," *Publius*, vol. 14, no. 4 (Winter 1984).

9. Franz Gress, "Interstate Cooperation and Territorial Representation in Intermestic Politics," *Publius* (forthcoming).

10. Ivo D. Duchacek, "The International Dimension of Subnational Self-Government," *Publius*, vol. 14, no. 4 (Fall 1984):5-32; Susan J. Koch, "Toward a Europe of Regions: Transnational Political Activities in Alsace," *Publius*, vol. 4, no. 3 (Summer 1974):7-24; James W. Scott, "Transborder Cooperation, Regional Initiatives and Sovereignty Conflicts in Western Europe: The Case of the Upper Rhine Valley," *Publius*, vol. 19, no. 1 (Winter 1989).

11. Ivo D. Duchacek, "Transborder Overlaps between Three Federal Systems: From the Beaufort Sea to Belize," paper presented in San Diego, Western Social Science Association, 28 April 1984.

12. Susan J. Koch, "Toward a Europe of Regions: Transnational Political Activities in Alsace," *Publius*, vol. 4, no. 3 (Summer 1974); James W. Scott, "Transborder Cooperation, Regional Initiatives and Sovereignty Conflicts in Western Europe: The Case of the Upper Rhine Valley," *Publius*, vol. 19, no. 1 (Winter 1989).

13. Dennis Palumbo, *American Politics* (New York: Appleton-Century-Crofts, 1973); John Kincaid, "The American Governors on International Affairs," *American Confederal Experiences, Past and Present,* ed. Daniel J. Elazar (forthcoming).

14. Interviews in Brazil by the author, 21-30 July 1980.

15. Moshe Hirsch et al., *Yerushalayim le'An?* (Jerusalem: Makhon Yerushalayim LeKheker Yisrael, 1994); Ruth Lapidoth, *Yerushalayim-Heibetim Medini'im u'Mishpati'im* (Jerusalem: Makhon Yerushalayim LeKheker Yisrael, 1994); Enrico Molinaro, "Gerusalemme e i Luoghi Santi," *La Comunita Internazionale*, vol. 2 (1994).

Chapter 2

CONFEDERATION AS A SPECIES
OF FEDERALISM

Since the adoption of the United States Constitution of 1787 and the authorship of *The Federalist* by Alexander Hamilton, John Jay, and James Madison, federalism as a term has been identified with modern federation.[1] That is to say, it became the accepted name for the form of government established by the new U.S. Constitution, a form that gave the general government of the United States very real, if limited, powers that it could exercise directly among the citizens of the states who also became citizens of the United States, rather than only through the states as had been the case under the Articles of Confederation. This was the result of a deliberate sleight of hand by the authors of *The Federalist* in pressing their case for ratification. In the essays, Madison used a more generic term, "compound republic," which, in truth, can describe a union as well as a federation, without specifying the differences between them.

Federation in the United States and in most other countries that were to adopt that system of government thereafter, has led to the development or enhancement of a common nationhood, noncentralized, it is true, and with powers divided among the federal government and the states, but all delegated by the people of a common nation. Federation, indeed, is federalism applied to constitutionally defuse power within the political system of a single nation. Federation became synonymous with modern federalism because the modern epoch was the era of the nation-state when, in most of the modern world, the ideal was to establish a single centralized state with indivisible sovereignty to serve single nations or peoples.

39

Before the invention of modern federation, however, federalism
had meant something quite different, what Murray Forsyth referred to
as "unions of states" rather than the constitutionalized diffusion of
power within a single nation-state.[2] Federalism was what we com-
monly know today as confederation. Confederations also are compound polities or species of the genus federalism.

For most of recorded history, federalism meant confederation.
Indeed, until 1788 confederation was considered normative federalism and federation was the newcomer on the block.[3] One of the
achievements of the Federalists at the time of the ratification of the
U.S. Constitution was the sleight of hand that claimed the term
federalism for federation and left confederation out in the cold, with
those who favored the continuation of the American confederation
labeled "Anti-Federalists."[4]

The Federalists' triumph, so in tune with the times, was complete.
While confederation continued to exist in the Netherlands for a few
more years until the Napoleonic conquest, in Switzerland until 1848,
and the German Bund was formed as a successor to the Holy Roman
Empire at the beginning of the nineteenth century, confederation
essentially disappeared as a form of regime in the modern epoch.

Today, however, confederation and confederal arrangements are
being revived as the postmodern form of federalism that seems to be
particularly useful in connecting politically sovereign states that must
accommodate themselves to the realities of new times. These include
the growing interdependence among states deemed politically sovereign, the desire for linkage among states and peoples that will not
require them to merge into new nations but enable them to preserve
their separate national identities and existence, and recognition of the
realities of ethnic distinctiveness and, at times, conflict. This is
tending to develop the major paradigm shift from statism to federalism
principally in the confederal mode.

Confederation and confederal arrangements have been revived in
our time, not as theory at first but in the field, in three ways:

1) in the application of federal solutions to the development of new
interstate linkages;

2) in the replacement of existing polities with confederations as a
result of decentralization; and

3) in the emergence of worldwide links among states that are more
than simple treaties, but less than formal constitutional unions, leading to permanent institutionalization of linkages for purposes of

economic advancement, environmental protection, more efficient service delivery, or greater physical security.

All represent the emergence of a new federal reality of critical importance in the shaping of the postmodern world.[5] Most have their roots in efforts to achieve better positions in world trade or economic affairs. Indeed, they are driven by perceived economic necessity. At the same time, national and ethnic considerations abound in all three cases, making federation too binding a form of union in most cases. Confederation, on the other hand, offers the advantages of partnership and sharing through constitutionalized multicentered forms of polity that bring the advantages of federalism without the threats of tighter union. In all three cases, security and human rights considerations have been secondary and have led to even looser leagues.

Lister has suggested fifteen features that characterize confederation as a class of government:[6]

1. It unites states without depriving them of their statehood;

2. It can unite states whose populations are too heterogeneous to form viable federal-type unions;

3. It requires a written basic law in the form of treaty-constitutions that are legally binding upon the various confederal allies;

4. It presupposes a raison d'être of overriding importance such as a powerful common economic interest or the need of the confederating states for protection against a great power that threatens them all;

5. It provides for a minimalist mandate that leaves most governmental powers to be exercised independently by its member states;

6. It provides for two quite different types of mandate involving collective security and/or economic union. The security mandate always includes the same functions (foreign affairs, war and peace, military integration or coordination). The economic mandate also always includes the same functions (e.g., regulation of external trade and internal commerce, standardization of such things as weights and measures, and the establishment of common or single markets);

7. Confederations require a wide measure of support among the peoples of their member states based on the belief that such ties will enhance their country's security and/or its economic growth and prosperity;

8. As a corollary to this, relations among the member states need to be of a kind that will engender the gradual growth of popular support for, and allegiance to, the confederal union;

9. This popular support and allegiance, however, are subordinate to peoples' primary allegiance to their homelands (otherwise, the union is likely to "graduate" to federal or unitary status);

10. In a confederation, all member states must be ready to settle their quarrels through arbitration or adjudication rather than force;

11. In a confederation, member governments exercise the powers to be confederalized in a joint council that meets regularly and operates under mutually agreed rules of procedure;

12. This council has (i) a voting system in which state representatives vote on behalf of their countries; (ii) a decision-making system whose decisions are legally binding on its member states and are usually based on consensus or broad support rather than simple majorities of those member states; and (iii) a decision-implementing system that delegates the major burden of implementation to its member state governments;

13. Confederal governance presupposes a willingness on the part of the member states to furnish the funds that enable the union to carry out the tasks assigned to it;

14. It also provides for the conduct of the executive and judicial functions of government in ways that are unthreatening to the sovereignty of its member states; and finally

15. It embodies mutually acceptable working solutions to hegemonic and other problems that may emanate from any inequalities of power and resources among its larger and smaller member states.

The Ages of Confederation

It is helpful to understand something of the confederal history of federation to begin our inquiry into this shift. For analytic purposes we may divide the uses of confederation into four quite conventional stages: ancient, medieval (until the mid-seventeenth century), modern (from the mid-seventeenth to the twentieth century), and postmodern (since World War II). A list of the better-known confederations from the ancient, medieval, and modern stages can be found in Table 2.1. The postmodern confederations are to be found in Table 2.2.

All confederations, perhaps all federal arrangements, are for one, another, or a combination of three purposes: for defense, for economic purposes, or for the achievement of some form of virtue. The first two emphasize confederal arrangements through special institutions. The last emphasizes confederal arrangements through special constitutions and laws.

Table 2.1

EXEMPLARY PREMODERN FEDERAL AND PROTOFEDERAL SYSTEMS

Polity	Duration	Location	Form
Adat Bnai Yisrael	13th cent. - 722 BCE	Israel	Union of tribes
Achean League	1st: 6th cent. - 338 BCE 2nd: 281-146 BCE	Greece	Confederation of cities
Boeotian League	4th cent. BCE	Greece	Confederation of cities
Aetolian League	4th cent. - 189 BCE	Greece	Confederation of cities
Decapolis	ca. 106 BCE - CE 117	Roman Palestine	Confederation of cities
Holy Roman Empire	800-1806	Central Europe	Imperial league
Lombard League	1167-1250	Italy	League of cities
Hanseatic League	1158-1669	Germany	League of cities
Swiss Confederation	1291-1848	Switzerland	Confederation of republics
Aragonese-Catalan Empire	1200-1350	Spain	Dual monarchy
Castile, Aragon, and Navarre	1469-1634	Spain	Dual monarchy
United Provinces of the Netherlands	1567-1798	Netherlands	Confederation of provinces
Imperial Spain	1479-1716	Spain and European territories	Multiple monarchy
Iroquois Confederacy	ca. 1600-1760	North America	Confederation of tribes
United Colonies of New England	1643-1691	North America	Confederation of colonies/dominions
Creek Confederacy	formal ties established in 18th century	North America	Confederation of tribes

Premodern Confederations

Premodern confederations for the most part emphasized defense and had minimal economic links. In some cases they tried to cultivate or require certain common virtues among their members in order to be constituents of the confederation.[7] In any case, all relied on comprehensive rather than functional institutions for confederal union.

What distinguished ancient and medieval variants of premodern confederation were that the constituent entities of ancient confederations were themselves integral polities where all citizens were expected to maintain the same religion and cultivate the same virtues. Thus, the confederations often were amphictyonies, formally united by religion, whose union was marked by a central shrine. The Greek leagues are the best examples of such ancient confederations. While only one was actually known as the Amphictyonic League, all were in some measure amphictyonic, while their constituent units saw themselves as local unions of tribes.

The other ancient confederations were tribal. Their constituent units were also organic and often they viewed the confederation itself as having an organic basis in the sense that they saw themselves as being of common descent, in many cases inventing myths of common descent as the basis for their linkage, as among the Bedouin tribal confederations of today.[8] Many tribes maintained confederal connections with one another, but most did not reach the level of political sophistication and differentiation required to speak of them as separable political regimes.

The ancient tribal federal system that apparently did reach that level of sophistication and differentiation was Adat Bnai Yisrael, the polity of the Israelites dating back to the thirteenth century BCE. What we know about it, principally from the Bible, suggests that it did, although it has been variously classified by modern Bible critics as an amphictyonic league, a confederacy, and a federation. To the extent that its political institutions reflected the fact that its tribes were united around the common religion, it may have resembled an amphictyonic league. To the extent that it was seen and saw itself as one nation with a common constitution, the Torah and its law, it was a federation. To the extent that it had relatively few common national political institutions, especially from the time of the Israelite conquest of Canaan until the rise of the Davidic monarchy, it may be considered a confederacy. Like almost all federal arrangements, it does not closely fit any of the models, but combines features of them all. If the Bible is at all accurate, it would have to be considered more a federation than anything else, one with strong amphictyonic and confederal features to be sure, but still one nation with a common constitution and law.[9] However we try to define it in contemporary terms, its people and tribes were united in pursuit of a common virtue: living a God-fearing life under the terms of God's covenant with them.

The various medieval leagues were republican confederations, whereby all constituent regimes were republican, usually oligarchic. While medieval confederations manifested some integral tendencies, they were at best semi-integral in many cases because they had mixes of regimes and, while religiously uniform, were not organized for religious purposes in any way. Rather, they were for defense or trading. Thus, rather than amphictyonies, they were confederal leagues.[10]

The greatest of those confederal leagues was the Holy Roman Empire, which at least nominally united Central Europe under German political and Italian religious hegemony for a millennium. It was monarchic and hierarchic in both its political and religious spheres and was weakened whenever its hierarchies could not hold power commensurate with their authority, which was frequently, especially in the political sphere. The Protestant Reformation ruptured it irreparably, although it was not formally abolished until Napoleon dissolved it in 1806.

Other medieval confederations, for the most part, were leagues of cities, often, but not only, within the Holy Roman Empire. Those leagues were linked for both defensive and economic reasons. The major exception to this pattern was the Helvetic Confederation dating from 1291. It was all republican, although some of its republics were popular and some oligarchic. Its people came from different linguistic communities and, after the Reformation, owed allegiance to different churches. They were united around the pursuit of a common virtue: liberty. The securing and preservation of liberty, particularly the liberty of their communities, was for them the highest virtue and they were willing to make great sacrifices in its pursuit.

From Medieval to Modern Confederations

At the outset of the modern epoch, three important medieval or late medieval confederations were in existence. The oldest was the Holy Roman Empire which had been partially transformed along confederal lines in the sixteenth and seventeenth centuries but never overcame the limitations of its medieval constitution. It was terminally weakened in the late seventeenth and eighteenth centuries, to be finally abolished by Napoleon in 1806, and was succeeded in 1815 by the German Confederation.[11]

The Holy Roman Empire itself also was a truly medieval confederal arrangement based on a medieval corporate society whereby different groups—guilds, religious minorities, or estates—were organized on a nonterritorial basis as permanent bodies, each with a different legal status accordingly. As Europe grew away from those kinds of corporate structures and sought a new kind of egalitarianism, either the reasons or the taste for confederation diminished.

What was characteristic of the Holy Roman Empire was the complete lack of any confederation-wide requirement regarding the regimes of its constituent units. They ranged from what were essentially absolute monarchies (principalities, dukedoms, etc.) to independent cities ruled by oligarchies, and every regime in between. At a certain point, this lack of commonality contributed to the demise of the confederation itself by allowing too severe differences in the governance of the confederal states that affected the decision-making processes of the confederation as a whole. This gave advantage to some members over others in an age when that was becoming less acceptable.

Equally, if not more important, were the great differences in size of the constituent entities which, given the different regimes, generated a very serious big-state/small-state problem. In its later years, this was resolvable only with the emergence of Prussia, a very big state, as the dominant one, which was fatal to the empire, as it was later to the German Confederation, the empires's successor.

Prussia was also an absolute (if relatively benevolent) monarchy. As Prussia's power grew, so did the power of its rulers or ruling family. The combination initially led it to assume a dominant role in the Holy Roman Empire constellation by virtue of its very great military power and the concentration of decision-making in one king plus his courtiers. Since federal arrangements presuppose a very substantial degree of equality, especially on essentials, this broke the framework and the viability of the system and brought it to an end, encouraged by Prussia itself.

The second oldest was the Swiss Confederation which came into existence at the end of the thirteenth century (1291). It survived a number of external and internal threats, including the Reformation, while strengthening its confederal character, although it was reconstituted after the Treaty of Westphalia in 1648. After nearly passing out of existence as a result of the Napoleonic conquest of Switzerland, it reemerged as a modern confederation in 1815 within expanded boundaries as a result of the Napoleonic occupation. It came into being for defensive purposes, pursued its common economic interests, and cultivated its common virtue. In modern times, those purposes were preserved, but because Switzerland had been designated neutral in the aftermath of the Napoleonic Wars, the confederation had to internalize the need for both defense and virtue, and increase its economic role at a time when the rest of Europe lost interest in Switzerland from a political perspective.[12]

Switzerland had maintained republican standards for its constituent entities from the first. (Liechtenstein, for example, as a principality, could not become a constituent entity in the Swiss confederation because it was not republican. To this day its relations with Switzerland are those of an associated state in certain limited economic ways.) While there were differences among the republics as to whether they were ruled democratically or oligarchically, these were manageable even as the differences in the size of the constituent entities grew; so the Swiss confederation could even survive the Napoleonic conquest of Switzerland and reorganize itself, first as a modern confederation and ultimately as a federation. The modern history of Switzerland in this respect is very illuminating. The Swiss were not happy with the Napoleonic efforts to establish a unitary Helvetic Republic. They also had tired of the oligarchic rule in most of the constituent republics of the old Swiss Confederation, so in 1815, when they restored the confederation, they did so in such a way as to weaken those oligarchic characteristics. The confederation remained fully functional until it adopted a federal constitution similar to that of the United States in 1848, in an effort to become more like a nation-state.[13]

Within a generation, however, they found that the whole idea of confederation did not serve them well in the modern world of that time. They concluded that they needed more unity through stronger framing institutions. Matters were brought to a head by the brief Sonderbund conflict of the mid-1840s. The result was the establishment of the Swiss federation in 1848 to provide those new framing institutions.

The third was the United Provinces of the Netherlands, established in the latter part of the sixteenth century as a result of the Low Countries' revolt against Spain. In the Netherlands, the provinces began as more or less equal in size and power (although Holland did have some advantage in both respects) and with similar mixed regimes. As time went on, the monarchic principle grew more powerful in certain provinces, strengthened by the growth of the oligarchic principle in all. Ultimately this proved fatal, since the emerging liberal forces within the Dutch republic rightly or wrongly identified the confederation with anti-liberalism and threw in their lot with the Jacobins and the Bonapartists. This was a false assessment, but it was sufficiently powerful to prove fatal to the confederation when the liberal forces were supported by the power of Napoleon's armies.

The confederation died as a result of the Napoleonic conquest. The unitary, constitutionally decentralized monarchy that emerged after Napoleon's defeat had federation-like characteristics, but in the face of the conservative reaction of the European powers of the time, it could not move further in that direction.[14] Actually it was quite centralized for many years, then became a model consociational polity, and now is part of two confederations—the Kingdom of the Netherlands and the larger European Union.

Modern Confederations

Modern confederations were confederations of constituent polities or governmental confederations. What was characteristic of them all was that they were designed from the first to be perpetual unions, even if the covenants that established them in some cases had to be reaffirmed at regular intervals. Not only that, but they were comprehensive confederations, that is to say, they were held together on a comprehensive rather than a functional basis. All of these confederations had general governments that served comprehensive purposes. All the regimes, general and constituent, were republican.

Four modern confederations are considered to have been successful, that is to say, to have lasted long enough to have been effective while they lasted. One, the Helvetic Confederation, dates back to premodern times.

Although the Holy Roman Empire was pushed over the edge by Napoleon, his conquests, and their consequent disruption of the old European political order, the Germans were not yet ready for unification. Rather, they experimented with other confederal arrangements in the post-Napoleonic era that were more attuned to the modern age. They too, however, were plagued by the same two weaknesses that afflicted their predecessor and within half a century collapsed under the weight of an even more aggressive and powerful Prussian state. What emerged was a united Germany, nominally federal but in fact ruled by the organs of government of Prussia.

The United Provinces of the Netherlands and the United Colonies of New England, formed in 1643 on the very eve of the modern epoch, were both products of the Reformation (Switzerland, re-formed at the very end of the Reformation, can be considered in this category for certain purposes as well).[15] Both were formed for a combination of defensive purposes and in pursuit of liberty as a virtue, especially federal liberty, that is to say, the liberty to observe the covenants of Reformed Protestantism. Although they came to an end for different reasons, both did so after Reformed Protestantism had spent its energy and could no longer sustain the demands for a federalism of virtue. Only the nineteenth-century German Bund was formed primarily for defensive and economic purposes through the Zollverein. It may be that the desire for German unity was a form of virtue, but it played a much more circumscribed role as such.[16]

In all four confederations, the constituent units were the principal exercisers of the sovereign powers of government. Together they delegated limited powers to a general government, which had to work through them in order to reach their publics. In a statist age, this proved unsatisfactory since it did not allow those polities to function in any respect as states. Hence, they sought a compromise between centralized unitary statism and confederation, and found it in federation. In continental Europe it was presented by political theorists in just those terms. For those theorists, federation could recognize the organic nationhood of each polity while at the same time preserving the virtues of community and noncentralization simultaneously.

There were other experiments with confederation in the modern epoch, either within the territory of the former Holy Roman Empire or in Latin America, as well as in the United States of America under the Articles of Confederation. All were short-lived. Most were way stations on the road to national unity, either federal or unitary.

In that respect, the United States of America is the ideal type, beginning as a confederation at a time when the Americans already saw themselves as a people, although not a single national community: they saw their states as their primary communities.[17] Similar governmental considerations expressed themselves in Central America, in Colombia, and in other parts of Latin America. In a few cases—Central America, for example—nationalism remained localized within the constituent units of the confederation and led to its dissolution. In most others, as in the United States, a wider nationalism led to the establishment of national unification on a new federal basis.

With the end of those confederal experiments, confederation, as such, disappeared for the rest of the modern epoch, replaced by nationalism in its various forms. Federal ideas and arrangements were retained only through federations that could appear to the outside world as fitting the conventional definitions of statehood, while internally remaining noncentralized. Not only confederations, but also confederal arrangements disappeared except on an imperialistic, that is to say, hierarchical, basis where imperial powers established unions of crowns or protectorates over semicolonial (e.g., Austria and Hungary, Sweden and Norway) or colonial territories (e.g., Uganda, Nigeria, the Indian princely states) that formally remained independent but actually were closely ruled by the imperial power.

Postmodern Confederations: The Revival of the Species

With the end of the modern epoch, the nation-state also began to lose its monopoly in the international system. The nation-state itself did not begin to disappear. Quite to the contrary, in the first postwar generation, not only the idea of the nation-state but statism in its most virulent form spread to the former colonial territories. Newly independent colonies in what was soon to become known as the Third World, insisted on all the prerogatives of political sovereignty that they could.

But it was already too late. The nuclear age, coupled with the East-West confrontation, pushed almost all the world's states into one bloc or another, or perhaps into the nonaligned bloc which was almost as much of a limitation on independent state activity in the international arena. No states could do what modern politically sovereign states were presumed to be able to do. Sovereignty just could not keep its promises in a world of growing interdependence.

While all this was happening, new confederal experiments began to emerge. After an abortive beginning, the idea of confederating for defense took a very definite backseat to confederation for economic purposes.

The shift from security to economic development as the primary interest of confederations simply reflected new needs that led to new interests. Nevertheless, this brought confederal arrangements into convergence with a modern politics which emphasized interests over virtue, and a postmodern politics which identified economic interest as the primary reason for linkage. It is not that security did not remain a great interest, but while in the modern epoch, security had become an interest deemed to be best protected by the nation-state through the balance of power, in the postmodern epoch it only could be protected by nation-states in alliance with one another under the aegis of a great power. Moreover, economic interests came to be deemed the principal ones that warranted federal arrangements that went beyond treaties of alliance.

We might summarize by pointing out that in premodern times the emphasis was on polities concerned with virtue, security, and prosperity, in some combination. The development of modern federation permitted a distinction to be made whereby the constituent polities in federations were to be more concerned with virtue, while general governments were to be concerned with interests, in this case, primarily security and prosperity. The postmodern epoch seems to be in the process of adding a third arena, with primary responsibility for matters of virtue, such as they remain or have become in the postmodern epoch, left to the constituent or federated states; with large federations and the "sovereign" states sharing responsibility for matters of security and economic affairs with transnational and transconfederal leagues; and with confederal arrangements that are gaining primary responsibility for matters of economic prosperity. This does not mean exclusivity since all three arenas or at least two of the three have responsibilities with regard to each task, but a system seems to be forming whereby primary responsibility is lodged in one or another.

Postmodern confederations increasingly are characterized by unions of states claiming political sovereignty but, unlike in the modern epoch, not necessarily independence. This distinction between sovereignty and independence reached the headlines in connection with the breakup of the Soviet Union. While most of the union republics of the USSR that initially claimed sovereignty but not independence, ultimately claimed independence as well, within Russia itself there are autonomous republics, part of the Russian Federation, that claim sovereignty but have deliberately avoided claiming independence.

Worldwide, some of these sovereign states have limited their independence by uniting into semiformal confederations, usually regional, whose governing institutions are woven out of a number of joint authorities, each with specific functions assigned to it and governed directly or at one step removed by collegial bodies embracing all of the member states. All of them claim to have democratic republican regimes and require their constituents to have the same. Those that do not, do not survive. The network of authorities confederated through collegial institutions is also supported by a common confederal law within the specific areas of agreement, usually interpreted and overseen by a common constitutional court.

Lister has suggested four main applications of confederal institutions:[18]

1. Some groups of small states and ministates may wish to form confederal-type unions in order to enhance their economic clout. By placing themselves in a position to come forward with mutually agreed positions on specific issues, they would maximize their bargaining power with larger and more powerful entities.

2. Some multiethnic states threatened with break-up may wish to experiment with confederal institutions in the hope that they might provide a viable alternative to dissolving all political ties.

3. Groups of contiguous states, large and small, may contemplate the formation of confederal ties with a view to optimizing the benefits to be derived from an increasingly interdependent world economy. Such groups might also utilize such ties to enhance their collective security in an increasingly dangerous world.

4. Finally, the world community as a whole, in light of the great dangers that appear to lie ahead, will surely be focusing on how it can deal effectively with those dangers. In this wider context, the confederal model also warrants careful consideration.

These postmodern confederal systems offer several improvements over modern confederation. The idea that all regimes were to be republican was already present in most modern confederations. Modern confederalism also contributed the idea that unions, even if they were only confederal, were to be perpetual, that is to say, secession had to be by mutual consent of either all or a majority of the parties involved. Modern confederations also sought to establish comprehensive general governments supported by equally comprehensive constitutions. Even if limited in the powers delegated to them, all of those powers and the institutions to carry out those powers were embodied in a single comprehensive constitution providing for a single comprehensive, if limited, government.

The elimination of this last requirement is a major key to the success, so far, of postmodern confederations that have been able to build themselves up as fast as their constituents desire, but only that fast. The invention of this last technique of building linkages has opened wide new horizons for postmodern confederation.

The end result has been a slow growth of confederal arrangements and, in some cases, confederations. Table 2.2 supplies a list of current examples.

Table 2.2

CONFEDERATIONS AND CONFEDERAL ARRANGEMENTS

Confederations
　　1. European Union (EU)
　　2. Caribbean Community (CARICOM)
　　3. Commonwealth of Independent States (CIS)

Leagues
　　4. Association of South East Asian Nations (ASEAN)
　　5. Benelux Economic Union
　　6. Central American Common Market
　　7. Council of Europe
　　8. Council on Security and Cooperation in Europe (CSCE)
　　9. The Nordic Council
　10. North Atlantic Treaty Organization (NATO)
　11. Western European Union (WEU)

Associated States (Asymmetrical Confederal Arrangements)
　12. Andorra (condominium of Spain and France)
　13. Aruba (Netherlands)
　14. Bhutan (India)
　15. Cook Islands (New Zealand)
　16. Federated States of Micronesia (United States)
　17. Liechtenstein (Switzerland)

18. Marshall Islands (United States)
19. Monaco (France)
20. Netherlands Antilles (Netherlands)
21. Nieu Islands (New Zealand)
22. Palau (United States)

It should be noted that confederal arrangements come in two forms: symmetrical and asymmetrical. Symmetrical relations involve equality among all the partners to the arrangement so that each adheres to the relationship under the same terms as the other adherents. There are often situations, usually referred to as associated state relationships, in which smaller territories connect with larger ones on a basis that gives them a special linkage and a special status. The existing arrangements are listed above. Associated statehood relationships are roughly parallel to federacy relationships which represent asymmetrical federations. Under those, the relationship is not only established on mutual agreement, but can only be dissolved or altered by mutual agreement. With regard to associated state relationships, they, too, are established by mutual agreement, but they provide in their constitutional documents for ways and means to alter or dissolve them by one party or the other.[19]

Assymetrical relationships make possible the survival of the small republic within situations in which a certain amount of interconnection is needed, not only on a globalized or regional basis but with a particular larger state, to enable that survival to occur. Associated state relationships have also been used to bring about the revival of small republics, particularly with regard to the United States and its relationship with the former Pacific trust territories, the Federated States of Micronesia, the Marshall Islands, and Palau. Thus, associated state arrangements much strengthen the possibility of using confederal arrangements to make possible the survival of small polities in a globalized world.

Understanding the Federalist Paradigm

While this book is about confederation and confederal arrangements, it is well to recall that confederation is only a term for a certain kind of federal solution located on a federalist continuum based on its own characteristics of constitutionalized and noncentralized power-sharing, emphasizing the combination of self-rule and shared rule through different arenas of governance, and cannot be definitively and uniquely demarcated in every case. Many students of federalism have foundered in seeking overly clearcut definitions. In the real world, some federal polities are more like federations and others more like confederations, but frequently mix elements of both.

Federalism in a political sense fundamentally involves the combination of self-rule and shared rule, the efforts of people and polities to maintain a maximum degree of independence while participating with others on a constitutionalized but noncentralized basis to accomplish those tasks that they either seek, or out of necessity find it necessary to undertake together. There are various forms of self-rule and shared rule, all of which can be considered expressions of the federal principle or federal arrangements. All federalism is based on noncentralization, that is to say, multiple power centers, at least some of them constitutionally authoritative, that not only prevent the development of a single power center but prevent control over decision-making by a single power center. Decentralization, on the other hand, implies that there is a center that can decide what is to be centralized and what is not. In noncentralized systems no such center exists, while the relations among the several centers must be conducted on a constitutionalized basis through negotiated cooperation, i.e., bargaining based on the premise that what must be done together must be done in a manner that emphasizes sharing.

Federalism involves compound polities. In federations these tend to have single national identities. In confederations each constituent unit can preserve its own national identity within the framework of the constitutional links establishing the larger entity in which they all share. It is particularly in the case of confederations that the emphasis is on the constituent units, but wherever there are federal arrangements the model is essentially cybernetic, that is to say, based on multiple arenas, many channels for communication among them, and a variety of different mechanisms for mobilizing them to undertake particular courses of action in place of a single channel. This is very different from the idea that efficiency is gained through concentrating everything within single channels or power pyramids. Federal systems play to diversity and rely upon diversity to achieve more by providing more room for interplay of various forces to accomplish those tasks allocated to them or which they have assumed.

To use a biological analogy, there are several species of the genus federalism. Nevertheless, the two main species are federation and confederation; all of the others can be related to either one or the other.

Following *The Federalist,* if a federation seems to be some combination of a unitary state and a confederal one, a confederation can be seen as being some combination of a federation and a league. What is characteristic of the federalist continuum as distinct from a unitary one is that the federalist continuum is based upon a cybernetic model, a matrix of different-sized arenas of governance in which powers are distributed to both larger and smaller arenas that, while larger or smaller, are not ranked hierarchically. Thus, for some purposes smaller arenas may be more useful and powerful, and for others, larger ones. As in a cybernetic model, the model for federalism is the matrix for which the common constitution and the general government serve as framing institutions, embracing and linking the smaller arenas (Figure 2.1). A good (and dynamic) analogy would be a power grid in which different loadings are directed to different cells within the matrix. The character of the institutions and the distribution of powers indicate whether the matrix is more of a federation or more of a confederation.

The matrix model represents the concretization of the paradigm shift, replacing "higher" and "lower" with smaller and larger arenas whose size does not suggest the degree of their importance but rather their appropriateness for different tasks. Governments transformed into framing institutions cannot be reified and can be changed through popular action. Moreover, since all are authorities-as-agents of the people, none can claim that they are sovereign over others, whether people or other governments.

This stands in sharp contrast to the hierarchical model of a power pyramid with its apex at the top and various levels broadening downward, either with a clear chain of command or always with a tendency to move in that direction (Figure 2.2). In that model, there is a strong tendency for all important political questions to rise to the apex where they become court politics, where the courtiers' primary interest is to influence the ruler or circle of rulers at the top.

There is yet a third, organic model, based on the relationship between the center and periphery, which is particularly popular among students of democratic societies today (Figure 2.3). It occurs when a polity and society develop organically, with those most powerful gravitating to the center where they form an elite or congeries of elites, and the remainder of the population remains on the periphery, perhaps influencing the elites in certain ways but, under normal circum-

Figure 2.1

THE MATRIX MODEL

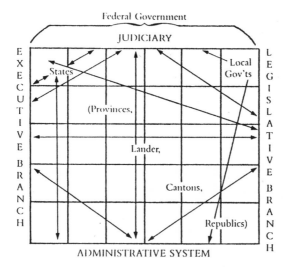

Figure 2.2

THE POWER PYRAMID

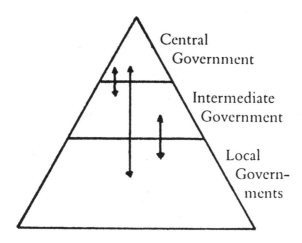

Figure 2.3

THE CENTER-PERIPHERY MODEL

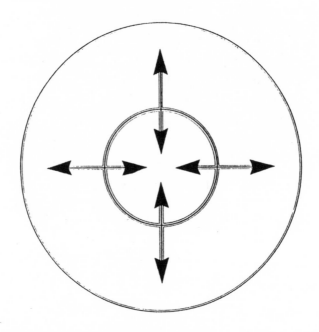

stances, responding to their lead. In fact, it is not significantly different from the hierarchical model in its practical effects since, without
constitutional barriers, the iron law of oligarchy soon moves the latter
in the direction of the former.

A comparison of these three models reveals the differences (Table
2.3). The hierarchical model is founded by conquest (force), either by
external powers or through internal actions such as a coup d'état or the
conquest of a market by an entrepreneur. The organic model emerges
through the accretion that comes from organic development (accident). The covenant model is established by a pact among equals
(reflection and choice). The words in parentheses indicate how the
authors of *The Federalist* refer to the three models which are identified
in *Federalist,* Number 1. The model that best expresses hierarchy is
the pyramid; the one that best expresses the organic model is two
circles, one within the other; while the covenantal model is best
expressed through a matrix. Those visual expressions in turn express

Table 2.3

MODELS OF FOUNDINGS/REGIMES

Hierarchical	Organic	Covenantal
Conquest (force)	Accretion (accident)	Pact (reflection and choice)
Pyramid	Circle within circle	Matrix
Hierarchy	Center-Periphery	Frame and Cells
Administration - top down bureaucracy	Politics - club - oligarchy	Constitution - written
Politics - court	Administration - center - outward	Politics - open with factions
Constitution - charter	Constitution - traditional	Administration - divided
Apotheosis - army	Apotheosis - Westminster system	Apotheosis - federal system
Excess - totalitarian dictatorship	Excess - Jacobin state	Excess - anarchy

hierarchy, the center-periphery relationship, and a frame with cells within it.

In the hierarchical model, the public institutions, arranged in the order of their importance, are: (1) administration from the top down; (2) politics, mainly involving the politics of the "court" surrounding the ruler; and (3) a constitution, if one exists, in last place, expressed as a charter handed down by the ruler to those below him. In the organic model, (1) precedence belongs to the politics of a club or clubs; (2) it is followed by administration from the center outward; (3) the constitution is usually embodied in documents that express traditional practices as they have developed after those traditional practices have become entrenched. In the covenantal model, (1) the constitution takes precedence because it establishes a relationship between the various parts and the whole. It is a written constitution because it must be available to all who are governed by it for them to see and understand. (2) Politics is next in rank after the constitution; it is an open politics designed to allow all citizens to participate in political affairs. (3) Administration is last, used essentially to enable the polity to provide the services it is called upon to provide through the constitution and politics. It is divided administration, shared by the framing institutions and the various cells.

The apotheosis of hierarchy is an army and its excess is totalitarian dictatorship. The apotheosis of the organic model is the Westminster parliamentary system and its excess is the Jacobian state. The apotheosis of the covenantal model is the federal system and its excess is anarchy.[20]

Confederations, like federations, fall within the matrix model. Their differences are best expressed by the differential weighing of the cells within the model. In a federation, the largest arena carries the heavier weight, while the basic constituent arenas carry a weight of their own and a permanent status within the matrix like that of the largest arena. Within those arenas, there are others, many of which can be redesigned according to need, at least in theory. In a confederation the largest weight is with the basic constituent arenas that constitutionally and practically are the fulcrum of the whole model.

It is possible to look at the foregoing three models of polity as shaping different political cultures as well as different forms of political organization, with the matrix model the critical one for federal political cultures. Beyond that, Duchacek argues that there is or can be a distinctive confederal political culture which he identifies as being expressed between four major, interconnected themes:

1. Awareness of some common interest, either external threat or opportunity, bringing cross-boundary cooperation on a territorial or functional basis.

2. Explicit retention of territorial sovereignty and self-rule with the primary loyalty oriented toward the territorial community.

3. Cautiously specific delegation of some power to a collective decision-making body.

4. Self-definition and self-determination of territorial interest groups.[21]

In his examination of confederacies going back to ancient times, Duchacek sees these themes repeated in different political arrangements, in combination with other cultural characteristics in each political arrangement, with great consistency. Whether those elements represent a confederal political culture or what Duchacek referred to as "political constants" is a matter for consideration, but that they are very real is clear.

Duchacek saw that the shared perception of an external challenge or, better, threat was particularly operative in all premodern and modern confederal arrangements. As suggested above, in postmodern ones this threat, which was essentially a matter of military threats, has given way to economic challenges whereby prosperity demands entering into such arrangements in order to develop economically.

With regard to the preservation and promotion of intraconfederal peace and harmony in premodern and modern confederations, these were often connected with the sharing or joint development of particular territories as in the case of the western lands of the United States which, in what was perhaps the most far-reaching act of the U.S. Congress under the Articles of Confederation, were transferred to the United States government and provision was made for settling them and organizing them into states which should be admitted as equal partners of the original thirteen in the confederation.

In a more contemporary case, Antarctica, outer space, and the seas have become the common property of the nations of the world for development on a joint or shared basis. Antarctica involves physical lands and has involved the harmonization and limitation of national territorial claims. The sea and space, which cannot be so divided, involve issues of territorial waters and airspace that encompass only the smallest fraction of the whole, while the rest is organized by treaty or convention through other forms of sharing or joint operations that do not involve permanent claims over particular pieces of water or space, but only rights to use or exploit them. We have yet to develop appropriate means to handle the humans who occupy such common spaces either temporarily or permanently, relying upon older ideas of nationality and residence to accommodate them.

Encompassing the third element calling for a confederal response, Duchacek listed five groups of problems:

1. *Economic and financial* matters (international trade, tariffs, currency flow and stability, credits, unequal distribution of resources and development, depletion of energy, peaceful uses of atomic energy, etc.).

2. *Social and health* problems (population explosion, famines, illiteracy, infant mortality, epidemics disregarding sovereign boundaries, drug traffic, etc.).

3. *Ecological* issues (pollution and depletion of planetary resources, protection of some animals, conservation of the ozone layer,
tampering with world climate, etc.).

4. *Free movement* of persons, news, views, and art; cooperation in
the use of communication satellites; distribution of radio wavelengths;
extradition of criminals and prosecution of terrorists across national
boundaries.

5. *Standardization* of statistical data and procedures, measures,
safety rules in air transportation, shipping registration rules, and many
other highly technical issues that result from the present rapid and
multiple contacts among men and nations.[22]

In dealing with any or all of them, there needs to be some
delegation of state powers to supranational organizations or to some
collective decision-making body and, as Duchacek puts it, cautious
delegation at that, complete with various controls designed to keep
control over that delegation in the hands of the delegating states. All
the ways and means to devise intergovernmental relations within
federations or other polities have been utilized in this connection, as
have others, depending more upon functional or territorial agreements
among states that are far more limited. These range from delegating
powers on specific matters to specific external bodies and ensuring
that the delegating states are represented in the composition of those
bodies, to the development of uniform legislation that has to be
enacted by each state involved, so that while it never becomes more
than state legislation for the individual states, it is uniform and
adopted uniformly by all the associated states. This latter is the
procedure chosen by the Nordic Council to bring harmonization of
legislation in various fields to Scandinavia.

This system of delegating powers for specific functions has come
to be known as functionalism. Some of those who have espoused it
have been partisans of the nation-state who seek to limit its loss of
powers by providing for a very limited delegation of functions only
where necessary. Others have been federalists who recognize the
impossibility of achieving a more ambitious federal project in one or
two comprehensive acts and therefore seek to introduce federalism
through the spread of such functional arrangements. Both positions
converge in the development of confederal arrangements.[23]

With regard to explicit retention of territorial sovereignty, at the
beginning of the modern epoch federalism as a theory provided the
means to displace the modern statist notion of sovereignty by vesting
sovereignty in the people rather than in any human political artifact,

even the state. But this begs the question as to who or what constitutes the people. As a rule, in federations, a people is constituted in two ways: as the whole nation but through its constituent entities. In confederations, peoples are constituted in the constituent entities and sovereignty does not adhere to the confederation as a whole except derivatively.

At the same time, as we have noted in the recent experiences revolving around the breakup of the Soviet empire, there is a difference de facto as well as de jure between sovereignty and its full exercise as independence. Peoples and states can justify claiming sovereignty without seeking its unilateral exercise. Thus almost every confederation formally provides for sovereignty to be vested in the people of the constituent units.

Earlier students of federalism emphasized the difference in where sovereignty is vested as making more of a difference in influencing the form of the regime than it does in fact and concluded, as a result, that federation and confederation were totally different forms of government instead of being two species of the same genus. The events entailed in the breakup of the former Soviet Union and its empire at the end of the 1980s brought home a point that had been raised before but not with such specificity, namely, the difference between sovereignty and its full exercise as independence.

Peoples and polities can and indeed do claim to be sovereign without claiming the right to fully exercise that sovereignty—to be totally independent. They only reserve to themselves the right to decide how and in conjunction with whom they will exercise those of their powers that they are willing to delegate and emphasize that they have the sovereign authority to do so. That is a distinction with an important difference. For those who accept the idea of state sovereignty, this distinction allows for the possibility of federal linkage of sovereign entities without surrendering sovereignty or insisting that sovereignty is precisely equal to independence in all spheres. The sovereignty that is retained in every case is territorial sovereignty, and what is relinquished in a confederation is functional sovereignty in some areas. In a federation, territorial sovereignty is shared or transferred to the overarching power, to the general polity.

As indicated above, in confederal arrangements, powers delegated by the politically sovereign member states are limited to specific functions and do not include granting the general government the power to levy taxes directly on the people. General government taxes functionally become levies on the constituent states with the constituent states in fact reserving the power to meet those levies or not, even if by the constitution they are required to do so.

On the federalist continuum we can trace out movement between the more federal and more confederal poles. Canada, for example, was founded between 1862 when its constitutional convention was convened and 1867 when the results were enacted into law by the British Parliament as a relatively centralized federation in response to the American Civil War which frightened the Canadians. (While it was given the name "confederation," to distinguish it from the American system, in fact it was just the reverse.) After initially promoting a strong federal government, it shifted between the late 1880s and the 1930s to a more noncentralized federation. It then entered into a period of reconsolidation which ended in the 1960s, at which point it began to move increasingly in the direction of confederation in the real sense, transferring more powers to its provinces and undertaking more decision-making in the kind of collegial frameworks, e.g., conferences of first ministers including both the federal prime minister and the provincial premiers, that are characteristic of confederal arrangements.

Yugoslavia, which was founded as a unitary state after World War I, became a federation under Communist leadership after World War II and then began to devolve powers to its six constituent republics and two autonomous provinces within Serbia. After the death of Tito, it moved to collective leadership based upon those eight entities and became a confederation in all but name. When Croatia and Slovenia wanted to change the polity constitutionally into a confederation and were opposed by Serbia, matters broke down and Yugoslavia was plunged into secession and civil war whose final outcome is not at all clear at this writing, but which is likely to lead to a group of separate confederations among the six republics or their parts.

The dissolution of the USSR broke up a fictive federation into a set of new, politically sovereign states loosely linked as a "commonwealth." That commonwealth is now moving more toward confederation as the independent states find that they need each other for economic and security purposes. Meanwhile, Russia itself is moving in the direction of becoming a conventional federation and perhaps Georgia and Ukraine will move in the same direction.

A Final Word

We are at the beginning of an exciting era of political innovation and transformation of the kind we have not seen since the seventeenth and eighteenth centuries. Following Thomas Kuhn, what we seem to be witnessing is a paradigm change, in this case, from statism to federalism, of which confederal arrangements are one aspect. Not that modern states are likely to disappear soon, if ever, but that those states are acquiring an overlay of confederal arrangements, in some respects supplementing and in some respects replacing their present patterns of authority and functions. This paradigm shift is already of significance and is likely to be of enormous significance in a very short time.

When Arthur MacMahon and K.C. Wheare published their pioneering works on federalism shortly after World War II, it was easy to distinguish between federations and unitary states. The biggest questions were addressed to the federations themselves. Were they really federations or quasifederations? What constituted a "pure" federation? Both MacMahon and Wheare addressed those issues but did not have to go any further.

By the time that this writer published his first comparative analysis of federalism in 1968, matters were already more complex and one could, without much stretching, distinguish between federations and federal arrangements, but confederal arrangements still seemed to be of historic interest only. This remained true for the literature that appeared over the next twenty years. Most scholars still studied federalism in one country. The few who took a comparative approach such as Rufus Davis, Ivo Duchacek, and Carl Friedrich focused exclusively on federations and had enough difficulty with them.

By the time that *Exploring Federalism* was published in 1987, this author already could take note of emerging confederal arrangements of a serious character. Still, only twenty existing federations containing a third of the world's population could be identified. Although various kinds of federal arrangements embracing another 40 percent were also identified, the distinction between those polities that were federal or utilized federal arrangements and those that did not was still relatively clear. Less than a decade later, it no longer is.

The great expansion of confederal arrangements has come to reach more of the world's states than not, so that today all of the major powers, most of the intermediate ones, and quite a few of the smaller ones are involved in one kind of confederal arrangement or another. The efforts to revive confederation may only prove to be steps to domination of the world by profit-oriented economic interests, bloody local wars between aggressive nationalities, or they may turn out to be the first steps toward building a truly new democratic world order based on the widest possible extension of the federal principle and shared rule.

Notes

1. Alexander Hamilton, John Jay, and James Madison, *The Federalist* (Cambridge, MA: Belknap Press, 1961). See also Martin Diamond, "The End of Federalism," *Publius* (special issue on "The Federal Polity"), vol. 3, no. 2 (Fall 1973):129-152.

2. Murray Forsyth, *Unions of States* (Leicester: University of Leicester Press, 1981).

3. *The Federalist*.

4. One need only consider the intellectual argument within the United States between John C. Calhoun and his followers and Daniel Webster and his followers. Cf. Ross Lentz, *The Writings of John C. Calhoun* (Indianapolis: Liberty Press, 1991).

5. Daniel J. Elazar, *Federal Systems of the World: A Handbook of Federal, Confederal and Autonomy Arrangements,* 2nd ed. (Harlow, Essex, UK: Longman Current Affairs, 1994).

6. Frederick K. Lister, *The European Union, the United Nations and the Revival of Confederal Governance* (Westport, CT: Greenwood Press, 1966), pp. 33-34.

7. Edward A. Freeman, *A History of Federal Government in Greece and Italy,* 2nd ed. (London: Macmillan, 1893).

8. Ludwig Ferdinand Clauss, *Als Beduine unter Beduinen* (Freiburg im Breisgau: Herder, 1933).

9. Harry Orlinsky, *Ancient Israel* (Ithaca, NY: Cornell University Press, 1964); John Bright, *A History of Israel* (London: SCM Press, 1972); Daniel J. Elazar, "Polity in Biblical Israel," in Daniel J. Elazar, ed., *Authority, Power and Leadership in the Jewish Polity: Cases and Issues* (Lanham, MD: Jerusalem Center for Public Affairs and University Press of America, 1990).

10. Henri Pirenne, *Early Democracies in the Low Countries: Urban Society and Political Conflict in the Middle Ages and the Renaissance* (New York: Harper and Row, 1963); Numa Fustel de Coulange, *The Ancient City* (Garden City, NY: Rand McNally, 1962).

11. James Bryce, *The Holy Roman Empire* (New York: Schocken Books, 1961); George F. Nafziger, *The Armies of Germany and the Confederaton of the Rhine, 1792-1815* (West Chester, OH: G. Nafziger, 1993); Peter Burg,

"State and Nation in the German Confederation (1815-1866)," *History of European Ideas*, vol. 15, no. 1-3 (1992):31-38.

12. Daniel J. Elazar, ed., "Communal and Individual Liberty in Swiss Federalism," *Publius*, vol. 23, no. 2 (Spring 1993); Wilhelm Oechsli, *History of Switzerland 1499-1914*, trans. Eden and Cedar Paul (Cambridge: Cambridge University Press, 1922).

13. Oechsli, *ibid.*

14. Ernst Heinrich Kassman, *The Low Countries, 1780-1940* (Oxford: Clarendon Press, 1978).

15. Murray Forsyth, *Unions of States, op. cit.;* Piter Geyl, *The Netherlands in the Seventeenth Century* (London: E. Benn, 1961-1964) 2 vols.; Harry M. Ward, *The United Colonies of New England, 1643-90* (New York: Vantage Press, 1961).

16. William Otto Henderson, *The Zollverein* (London: F. Cass, 1959).

17. Jack P. Greene, "The Background of the Articles of Confederation," *Publius*, vol. 12, no. 4 (Fall 1982):15-44; Aaron Wildavsky, "What If the United States were Still Governed under the Articles of Confederation?," in Daniel J. Elazar, ed., *American Confederal Experiences, Past and Present* (forthcoming).

18. Lister, *The European Union, the United Nations and the Revival of Confederal Governance*, p. 49.

19. R. Michael Stevens, "Asymmetrical Federalism: The Federal Principle and the Survival of the Small Republic," *Publius*, vol. 7, no. 4 (Fall 1977):177-203; Daniel J. Elazar, *Exploring Federalism* (Tuscaloosa: Alabama University Press, 1987), pp. 50-61.

20. Elazar, *Exploring Federalism*, pp. 33-38.

21. Ivo D. Duchacek, "Consociations of Fatherlands: The Revival of Confederal Principles and Practices," *Publius*, vol. 12, no. 4 (Fall 1982):153.

22. *Ibid.*, p. 157.

23. See David Mitrany, *A Working Peace System* (Chicago: Quadrangle Books, 1966), for a presentation of functionalism at its height in an advocacy manner. See also Louis A. McCall, *Regional Integration: A Comparison of European and Central American Dynamics*, Sage Professional Papers in International Studies, 4-02-041 (Beverly Hills: Sage, 1976).

Chapter 3

CONFEDERATION AND FEDERAL LIBERTY

One Genus: Two Species

Conventional accounts of American history treat confederation and federation as two very different ways of dealing with the problem of political organization. Indeed, within the limited context of American history, this approach can be understood as reflecting the sense of profound transformation brought about by the U.S. Constitution of 1787. In a larger sense, however, the American experience shows federation and confederation to be two species of the same genus—federalism, each seeking in its own way to combine liberty with appropriately effective government.

As we enter a new era of globalization that will require new political forms, it behooves students of politics everywhere to reexamine the American experience under confederation as well as federation, and most especially the principles underlining the confederal experiment, to try to understand exactly how both species of the same genus were given their modern form in the new United States. Such a reexamination is especially appropriate at this time because the serious revival of confederal options around the world since World War II inevitably leads us back to the original American experience.[1]

In the century following adoption of the Articles of Confederation, there were other confederal experiments in Europe and Latin America, all of which foundered in the face of the nationalistic tendencies of the modern epoch which emphasized the linkage of nation-building and state-building on a centralized basis or, at a minimum, along the lines of federation. In the postmodern epoch, on the other hand, consti-

69

tutionalized transnational political organization based on shared economic and cultural foundations has become more acceptable, leading to a renewed interest in the possibilities of confederation.

The modern character of the American confederation and its connection with federalism are important to note at the outset. One of the reasons for ignoring the close relationship between the confederal and federal experiences of the American confederation is that students have treated it as if it were simply a late example of a premodern league rather than a perpetual union of states. Indeed, this view was developed directly and explicitly by the authors of *The Federalist* as part of their polemic against the Articles of Confederation and on behalf of the new federal constitution. One can understand their reasons for trying to identify the existing confederation with the ancient and medieval European leagues which were premodern expressions of the federal principle. However, it behooves us to question the accuracy of what they did. Their descriptions of the weaknesses of those leagues are generally accurate, and their attribution of some of those same weaknesses to the American confederation was also justified; but in the heat of the political battle, they went beyond that. Whether they properly classified the American confederation with those leagues needs to be examined more closely.

The polity established by the Articles was a "Confederation and perpetual Union" as described in its preamble, while the Constitution of 1787 was designed to "form a more perfect Union." Therein lies the similarity and the difference. The confederation established by the Articles was perpetual and had virtually unlimited power within its sphere. It was far more than an alliance since, when a state acceded to it, it could no more withdraw than can a state from the federal union. Moreover, in international law, the United States of America was an independent entity constituted by its states and not simply a committee of them. It was a confederacy (Article I) that came into existence only after ratification by all of the member states. Were it merely a treaty or alliance, it could have come into existence for those states ratifying it immediately upon their ratification. In fact, it hardly can be said to have "come into existence" because, in reality, the Articles represented a formal constitutionalization of what had been established in 1775 by "the United States in Congress assembled," an entity that continued to function from 1775 to 1781 even while the Articles were pending ratification.

Here we will suggest that confederation and federation as developed in the United States after 1775 were both modern devices. As such, American-style confederation, no less than federation, was a different form of political organization from the earlier leagues. That is one reason why the study of the American confederal experience does not lead us away from federalism, but improves our understanding of federalism as a genus and the application of federal principles and arrangements in the real world.

What Constitutes Liberty?

The central interest of both federation and confederation and, indeed, for true federalism in all its species, is the issue of liberty. All forms of federalism begin with the assumption that government in some form is necessary and that the development of appropriately effective government is a major human task. In this respect, federalist theories are realistic. The other "given" of federalism is that humans are born free and that good government must be grounded in a framework of maximum human liberty. The task of constitution-makers is to develop a regime for each people that secures liberty even while recognizing and allowing for government in its coercive aspects where absolutely necessary.

To say that liberty stands at the center of federalist striving is to open the door to the question of what constitutes liberty in the federal context and how federalists deal with the problematics of liberty. On one level, these questions lead to what may be the decisive difference between confederation and federation. Federations are communities of both polities and individuals, and emphasize the liberties of both. The American federation has placed even greater emphasis on the liberty of individuals than on the liberties of its constituent polities, an emphasis that has grown more pronounced over the generations. Confederations, on the other hand, are primarily communities of polities that place greater emphasis on the liberties of the constituent polities. It is the task of the constituent polities to protect individual liberty, more or less as each defines it, although the constituent polities of confederations of republics must conform to at least minimum standards of individual liberty in order to preserve the republican character of the whole. The minimum guarantee of individual liberty in the Articles can be found in Article IV, which gave the "free inhabitants in each of these states . . . all the privileges and immunities of free citizens in the several states," "free ingress and regress to and from any other state," and "all the privileges of trade and commerce" —in other words, basic civil and commercial rights.

Thus, to understand a confederation, it is necessary to understand, first and foremost, what constitutes the liberties of its constituents and how those constituents see confederation as protecting those liberties. American pluralism has strayed far from the concept of group liberties to become almost exclusively individualistic in character. This is not surprising, given the character of American society. No doubt, one of the reasons why it was possible to convince a majority of Americans, voting by states, to abandon confederation for federation was because, even in the Revolutionary era, the states were not able to command a level of identification stronger than that of individual self-interest and the growing common perception that Americans were Americans, first and foremost.

Had the states been perceived by a majority of their citizens to be primary organic communities as John C. Calhoun later argued, there is little doubt that the Constitution of 1787 would have been rejected on behalf of state liberties. As it was, the real challenge to that document revolved around the protection of individual liberty (e.g., the need for a bill of rights in the federal constitution). Not that the principle of state liberties was totally rejected—the political liberties of the states were deemed to be very important as evidenced by the Tenth Amendment—but they were not primary in the American scheme of things.

Because of this special character of American pluralism, Americans have a very difficult time understanding issues of group rights. That made federation easy for them. But for much of the world, group rights—variously defined as national, local, or ethnic liberties—are of the essence. For them, confederation may be the most viable way to attain the combination of liberty, good government, and peace that federalism promises.

On another level, both species of federalism must deal with the perennial problematics of liberty. Whether articulated or not (and in the United States, it usually is not), the foundation of their effort rests on the distinction between natural liberty and federal liberty. Natural liberty is unrestricted, the freedom of the state of nature, whether understood in Hobbesian or Lockean terms. In the end, it is the liberty that leads to anarchy, or the war of all against all. According to federal principles, proper liberty is federal liberty, that is, the liberty to act according to the terms of the covenant (*foedus*) which calls the body politic into existence. Every proper polity is established by a pact among its constituents that is covenantal insofar as it rests upon a shared moral sensibility and understanding and is legitimate insofar as it embodies the fundamental principles of human liberty and equality. Behavior that does not fit within those terms is, in effect, a violation of the covenant and a manifestation of anarchy. Hence, it can be stopped and its perpetrators punished by the appropriate institutions of government.

In sum, federal liberty is liberty established by agreement. The content of any particular agreement may and will vary. Thus, John Winthrop could understand true liberty as that flowing from the covenant between God and man in which God dictated the terms of the agreement and which man pledged to accept. On the other hand, James Wilson of Pennsylvania, one of the authors of the Constitution of 1787, could understand federal liberty as a strictly secular expression of the compact establishing civil society. Today, when the Supreme Court of the United States holds the state and federal governments to standards of behavior based upon the U.S. Constitution, even when the implementation of those standards places heavy restrictions on individual behavior, in effect, it does so on the grounds that the constitution is a compact entered into by the people of the United States that, *inter alia,* delineates what constitutes federal liberty within the American system.

This discussion would not be complete if we did not recall that one of the basic tensions that informs American civilization is the tension between natural and federal liberty. Admiration for the former has been expressed in various ways in American history from the eighteenth-century ideal of the "noble savage" to the "natural man" of the nineteenth century, to "doin' what comes naturally" in the first half of the twentieth, to the "let it all hang out" of our times. Indeed, natural liberty was clearly dominant in the land from the mid-1960s through the 1970s.

Federal liberty found its first expression in the theopolitical stance of the Puritans, and has retained favor among those applying religious standards and moral expectations to the American people and their polity—including the eighteenth-century revolutionaries, the antislavery forces of the antebellum years, the Populists and Progressives of the late nineteenth century, and those who fought the civil rights battles of the 1950s and 1960s. All of the foregoing believed that people were not naturally free to commit certain wrongs, but, as citizens or residents of the United States, living under its constitution, could be required to act or refrain from acting in ways that violated the terms of that constitution.

The Articles of Confederation had as the focus of their concern the federal liberty of the constituent states. Hence, they had what was at once a more limited and far broader definition of federal liberty with which to work, restricting the freedom of the constituent states in those few fields where it was deemed necessary for a uniform confederal standard while allowing each in its own way to determine what constituted federal liberty for its own citizens.

Federation and Confederation

Returning to the differences between federation and confederation, we may begin with the classic distinction, namely, that in federations, the federal government can reach out directly to its citizenry as well as through the constituent polities, while in a confederation, the confederal government must reach individual citizens only through the constituent polities. This definition is accurate as far as it goes, but it is not complete. We must add the point made above that a federation is more concerned with the preservation of individual liberty, while a confederation places greater emphasis on the preservation of the local liberties of its constituent polities.

A third characteristic distinguishing federations from confederations is that the former have a common law of some scope that is enforceable throughout the federation, while the latter tend to leave matters of law to the constituent polities except as explicitly provided in limited areas determined to be of such general concern that they must be governed by a common law. This is a matter of the greatest importance; some might even say the heart of the matter. Federation is possible only where a sufficiently comprehensive common law binding all citizens of the constituent unit is possible. By the same token, confederation is a viable means of establishing federal ties in situations where the parties to the bargain can only tolerate specific and limited common laws.

The Articles provide for a common law of war and peace and a common foreign relations. Implicit in the Articles is a common republicanism which is so taken for granted that it finds expression only in the prohibition against granting titles of nobility in Article VI.

The Confederacy also had full powers over coinage, weights and measures, and postal services.

The most ambiguous elements in the Articles are those relating to interstate commerce and the general welfare. On the one hand, it is clear from Article IV that the United States is to be a single entity for commercial purposes, but without eliminating the powers of the states to protect their own respective economies, as suggested obliquely in Article VI. Similarly, there are two references to the general welfare, one in Article III with regard to the revenue-raising powers of the new Congress. Both references are general and open-ended.

A fourth dimension must be added having to do with the ends of the polity. Every polity is devoted to the attainment of certain ends, to the achievement of justice as it is conceived by those who constitute it. In this respect, the extent to which the general government possesses power, while crudely related to the defined ends of the polity, is not determinative of those ends. One of the perceived problems of the American confederation is that the confederal government was not adequate for the achievement of the ends for which it was instituted. We have already mentioned two elements involved in determining the ends of federal polities, namely, liberty, however defined, and good government, however defined. In both cases, federal polities, because they are constituted in a formal way by a pact or articles of agreement, are likely to be more explicit about their understanding of these and other ends to which they are devoted. These ends are generally stated in the preambles to their constitutions, but may also be stated or explicated in the body of the constitutional document(s).

As a general rule, confederations have more limited ends than federations. With respect to the United States, the principal difference between the Constitution of 1787 and the Articles of Confederation was one of means rather than ends. In this respect, the Preamble to the 1787 Constitution specified that what was proposed was the establishment of "a more perfect union," not a new one. What was changed were the means of effectuating the union, which required the expansion of the powers granted to the federal government even in order to obtain already agreed-upon ends.

The major shift with regard to ends was from an emphasis on the liberties of the individual states to the establishment of liberty, justice, and domestic tranquility for the people of the United States. Article III of the Articles sets forth the ends of the Confederation:

The said states hereby severally enter into a firm league of friend-
ship with each other, for their common defence, the security of their
Liberties, and their mutual and general welfare, binding themselves
to assist each other, against all force offered to, or attacks made
upon them, or any of them, on account of religion, sovereignty,
trade, or any other pretence whatever.

Contrast it with the Preamble to the Constitution of 1787:

We, the People of the United States, in Order to form a more perfect
Union, establish Justice, insure domestic Tranquility, provide for
the common defence, promote the general Welfare, and secure the
blessings of Liberty to ourselves and our Posterity, do ordain and
establish this Constitution for the United States of America.

We would not want to minimize this shift. In a certain sense, it is
of the essence; but it is not, as some would have it, the exchange of a
loose league for a consolidated union. There is more of a shift in
emphasis than in underlying form. We do not wish to enter here into
the question of how effective or ineffective the Confederation was;
that dispute is well-known. One thing is clear, however. While we
cannot and never will know whether the potentialities within the
Articles of Confederation could have been developed to deal with the
problems of a growing United States, the confederal government was
not simply a failure. It had a number of accomplishments, not the least
of which involved the extension of its powers into new spheres,
whether with regard to the organization of western lands (after all, the
Confederation Congress established the basis for the admission of new
states into the United States), in banking (the Confederation Congress
established the first bank in the United States as its instrumentality),
or in the initiation of support for educational and eleemosynary
development.

Following Madison, the distinction between the two regimes can
be summarized as follows: the Constitution of 1787 provided a government that was partly national and partly federal to replace the
Articles of Confederation which established a regime that was partially federal and partially a league. The first combination came to be
known as federation; the second came to be known as confederation.
The tension built into the former is between the national and the
federal elements, while the tension built into the latter is between the
federal and the league elements. Since federal arrangements always
involve one or another set of built-in tensions, the character of the

tension of each particular arrangement is the major clue as to the species of federalism involved.

The difficulties—often fatal—of confederation flow from this basic tension. In our consideration of whether confederation can be a viable federal option, we must raise the question as to whether (or under what conditions) the confederal tension can be sustained in a polity on a long-term basis. This is a real issue in the European Union today.

The American Rationale for Confederation

The American Confederacy and the Articles of Confederation which established and guided it must be understood as a Whig mechanism, an extension of the commonwealth principles that informed constitution-making in most, if not all, of the individual states. It has the classic dimension of an Old Whig or Commonwealthman polity, American style. It is covenantal rather than contractual since it relies principally on the states' moral commitment to making the Articles effective for the enforcement of its provisions. It not only required consent but emphasized it in the Whig manner by requiring the constant renewal or reaffirmation of consent at almost every step in the governmental process. In this respect, it relied on another Whig principle, republican virtue, as the mainstay of the polity since it was implicit that only if republican virtue flourished would the states live up to their moral commitment.[2]

The Whig reliance on republican virtue was tied in with the emphasis on homogeneous polities in which community would exist to foster republican virtue and a shared public interest. That is one of the major reasons why the United States as a whole could be no more than a confederation in the Whig scheme of things. It was too diverse to properly foster or maintain either. (That is why in the debate over the ratification of the Constitution of 1787 the Federalists concentrated their attack on the notion that the states could be sufficiently homogeneous, arguing that they also were too large.) For the Whigs, the states had that capacity, which was another reason why each state was to vote with one voice in the Congress and was to be responsible for implementing (i.e., appropriately adapting) the acts of Congress.

In Whig tradition, the Confederacy's principal institution was the legislature, formally titled "the United States in Congress assembled."

It, in turn, was tied as closely as possible to the people or, more accurately, to the polities it represented, following the Whig pattern of exercising control first over governmental power and then over the governors who exercise it. The members of the Congress were delegates chosen and supported by those who sent them, and sat for limited terms only, again a classic Whig control device, also found in most of the early state constitutions. There was heavy reliance upon consensual action by several bodies in order to implement programs, particularly the United States in Congress assembled and the individual states, but also Congress and its Executive Committee with minimum sanctions to bring about cooperation among them and a heavy emphasis upon each accepting its moral responsibility (or consenting) to do its share.

The practical deficiencies of the Whig approach to governance soon became apparent in the states as well as the Confederacy. A great part of the triumph of the Federalists over the Whigs lay in their genius in creating better mechanisms of governance, through which Whig principles could be embodied in Federalist institutions. Ultimately, it was this synthesis of Whig principles and Federalist institutions that created the golden age of American federalism. We should have learned from the Confederation years and the period since 1865 that, to the extent that one or the other is abandoned, the country suffers, but more on that below.

The existence of the Confederacy was taken for granted from the first. There was never any debate as to whether the states should be united. The debate centered around the character of the union, not its existence. For all intents and purposes, the union came into existence no later than 1775; indeed, the very process of declaring independence reflected the degree to which the United States of America already existed. In this sense, the union began with the people of the several states seeing themselves as Americans in certain respects from the first, and as linked to one another as Americans across state lines.

This is another way in which the American Confederacy was a Whig confederacy, a confederacy of commonwealths that was to embody commonwealth ideals, not like the European leagues, or even the United Netherlands which was a union of provincial oligarchies. There is no question as to the republican and popular character of either the American regime or its constitution. The U.S. was born free under its first constitution as much as under its second. Indeed, the argument in later years was that it was even born freer under its first than under its second. This is an argument that many do not accept, but it is testimony to the ideals embodied in that first American confederation. In other words, the fundamental principles of American government were established under the Articles, namely, that the United States was to be a commonwealth of commonwealths resting on popular and republican bases, able to function only through the cooperative interaction of its components in a non-hierarchical way and committed to partnership to advance common goals for the general welfare.

The great acts of the Confederal Congress reflected this overall thrust. Those acts included the acquisition of the western lands as the common property of the United States, provision for their settlement and organization as future states of the Confederacy, the initiation of a national banking system, the provision of a common defense force, and the negotiation of treaties of peace and alliance with the European powers having interests in North America. These and other acts of the Confederacy all involved the application of the aforementioned principles in concrete ways. Their success is attested to by the fact that they were continued or reenacted under the new federal constitution and continued to provide a basis for American development long after the Confederacy gave way to the new regime.

Whig Principles and Federalist Mechanisms

The history of the adoption of the Constitution of 1787 can be examined from the perspective of how the Federalists constructed a stable and lasting extended republic by taking the essence of the Whig rationale and standing it on its head so as to overcome its weaknesses. Cutting through the polemics surrounding the struggle over ratification of the Constitution of 1787, we can begin to understand the degree to which the second U.S. Constitution represented a supplement to the first, a synthesis of old principles and new practices as well as a departure from the first constitution. While the constitutional convention produced a well-articulated Federalist theory in contradistinction to the Whig theory, it is important to note that the former was not the exclusive theory of all members of the convention or even of those who were most active in drafting the new constitution. We are suggesting that the radical Federalists, in building the theory behind the U.S. Constitution, incorporated Whig principles to some degree (we need further research to determine to what degree) while transcending them in the invention of the mechanisms of government for which the constitution is justly famous.

The two most original elements of Federalist theory are the idea of the extended republic as a means of controlling the evils of class and faction, and the idea of the separation of powers as a means of providing energetic yet controlled government. Both were simultaneously extensions and transformations of Whig theory. The Federalist theory of the extended republic followed the confederal precedent of the Whigs but, rather than relying on expectations that shared understanding of the commonwealth in politically homogeneous polities would promote good government, the Federalists realistically recognized the problems of class conflict and factional struggles and sought to control them through the device of a large federal republic that would dilute their intensity.

So, too, the principle of dispersing power among various units that must function cooperatively or concurrently was not foreign to the Whigs. The crucial addition of the Federalists was the invention of the tripartite separation of powers based on the presidency as the separate executive branch, a judiciary headed by a supreme court, and a bicameral legislature with one house representing the people and the other the states. Those who held Whig principles had little difficulty adjusting to this invention which, as a mechanism, offered clear advantages over the kinds of power-sharing that lay at the root of the Whig system, especially since that earlier division between Congress and the states was incorporated into the new constitution, albeit on somewhat different terms. Indeed, the Whigs had already come to the tripartite division in their own state constitutions.

The matter of the extended republic was somewhat more difficult for the Whigs to assimilate. It represented a greater theoretical departure. The Whig premise was that only where those who held the power of government were subject to direct oversight of the citizenry were they likely to be properly controlled. Each extension of government beyond local control presented its own complications for the Whigs. Governments serving larger arenas had to be fenced in with more restraints, albeit moral restraints more than mechanical ones, other than the limited bag of Whig tricks such as selecting representatives for the shortest possible terms of office with maximum possible rotation and bound as closely as possible to those who selected them.

Now here was James Madison turning that theory on its ear and arguing just the reverse: that the extended republic offered greater republican stability, not so much because of better formal divisions, but because it prevented the division of society into two classes, the few creditors and the many debtors, which was the case in small republics since time immemorial. This was an argument to be conjured with precisely because it addressed the great question of liberty that preoccupied the Whigs. To the extent that the Constitution of 1787 was based upon this argument, it did represent a radical change.

For our purposes, the great change wrought by the Constitution of 1787 was to constitutionalize power and its limits, to set forth clearly the expanded powers of the federal government, but also to clearly limit them through mechanisms and institutions designed to keep a potentially powerful government under control. The federal system had become more national in its thrust but was counterbalanced by becoming more explicitly federal in its organization, in contradistinction to the Articles which were more federal in their thrust but more like a league in the organization they established.

In accomplishing this, the new constitution moved the American people from a reliance upon covenantal principles—that is, moral obligation as a means of ensuring compliance with agreed-upon arrangements—to compactual ones, in which the means of compliance and the penalties for noncompliance were specified and enforceable. To say this is to oversimplify to some extent. But, allowing for that oversimplification, in the main it is the best way to describe the fundamental transformation of principle from the first to the second constitution.

The claim that the United States is indeed a polity founded by covenant can be sustained only in light of the document itself. The Declaration of Independence was the covenant that established the American people and set forth the basic principles to guide them as a people.[3] The Articles of Confederation must be read in light of the Declaration of Independence since many of its silences or ambiguities relate to the widely understood and widely accepted principles of the Declaration. In that respect, it is an operational gloss on the covenant itself and, like it, relies on moral commitment for the enforcement of obligations. Thus, both the Declaration and the Articles make references to the Deity: The first "appealing to the Supreme Judge of the World," and the second recognizing that "the Great Governor of the World" inclined "the hearts of the legislatures" of the respective states "to ratify the said articles of confederation and perpetual union." Both references should be understood as more than piety. As in every covenantal document, they are designed to invoke moral obligation. God is made a witness to the proceedings and to the consent freely given to the result. The Constitution of 1787, on the other hand, is long on sanctions or, more accurately, grants of power to Congress to enforce its terms, but contains no reference to Heaven. It is thoroughly secular in its means and ends, a compact rather than a covenant.

On one level, the failures of the Articles of Confederation attest to the limits of covenants without operative sanctions in human society. Nevertheless, a strong measure of Whiggism survived to help inform the new federal constitution and direct it toward larger ends than those that the radical Federalists proposed as appropriate for the more perfect union. The Whig influence was felt in somewhat contradictory ways, and not necessarily in ways that met the expectations of the old Whigs of the revolutionary generation; but that is all too often the way of human affairs, and we need not be surprised at that result.

The resurgence of Whig influence came simultaneously with the struggle over ratification which, in one sense of course, the Whigs lost. Fearful of the extensive powers granted the federal government under the new constitution and unwilling to fully trust procedural devices and intricate mechanisms to restrain federal power, the Whigs insisted on the addition of a Bill of Rights to the new constitution, which was done as soon as the new government was organized. The idea of a Bill of Rights was classic Whig doctrine, though in the case of the federal constitution, Whigs seemed to have imbibed Federalist principles by demanding a Bill of Rights that was enforceable and not simply a declaration of principles designed to generate moral obligation on the part of the governors toward the governed, as was the case with the declarations of rights in the state constitutions. Thus, in the adoption of the Bill of Rights itself the new synthesis began to be manifest.

Even more far-reaching was the decision on the part of the Anti-Federalists, most of whom were Whigs, to accept the new constitution and actively participate in the organization and administration of the new government. By accepting the results of the struggle over ratification, those who shared Whig principles in one way or the other almost immediately gained substantial power within the new federal government and were able to use that power to interpret the new constitution in a manner consistent with their Whig ideas.

Perhaps one of the best examples of this was Albert Gallatin's introduction of cooperative federalism as the accepted form of intergovernmental relations in the years of Thomas Jefferson's presidency. Rather than exploit powers granted the federal government to enable it to operate directly within the states in pursuit of federal

goals, Gallatin developed ways and means of federal-state cooperation whereby the federal government and the states undertook to
implement joint programs. In doing this, Gallatin restored the important Whig control device of cooperative action, albeit within the
framework of the federal constitution, which relied less upon good
will than heretofore and more upon latent federal powers. Gallatin's
efforts were to influence the course of American government and
administration from that time forward.[4]

In short, the adoption of the Constitution of 1787 did not simply
substitute Federalist for Whig principles, but created a new tension
between the two sets of principles that has played itself out through
Federalist institutions and a federal, as distinct from a confederal,
regime. That tension remains with us.

For the first two generations under the constitution, the United
States resembled a confederation almost as much as it did a federation,
as those who espoused a confederal approach shaped a federal constitution to their ends. In the third generation, those who tried to push the
confederal approach too far precipitated a civil war, with the inevi-
table backlash toward federal union. After the corresponding excesses
of Reconstruction, however, the federal balance was restored for two
more generations, only to be upset in the direction of centralization
once again. It was during those generations that Americans lost sight
of the principles of the founding generation, both Federalist and Whig.
Both covenantal and compactual theories of the polity were rejected
in favor of the then more fashionable organic and evolutionary (Dar-
winian) theories. Concomitantly, hierarchical views of the state came
to replace the idea of the federal commonwealth. Progressives and
reactionaries, socialists and capitalists, reformers and stand-patters
were swept up by the new styles. Only among the midwestern and
western Progressives did the Whig outlook continue to prevail while
the Federalist outlook came to be confined to politicians with a stake
in the system as it existed.

It was only in the post-World War II generation that we began to
rediscover the teachings of the Federalist founders, principally through
the work of Martin Diamond, and only toward the end of that generation did we begin to pay attention to the Whig founders. We are still
engaged in the latter exploration. Only insofar as we understand the
ideas and actions of both sets of founders will we be able to understand
the origins of the American federal commonwealth and to steer the
ship of state in the right direction.[5]

Conclusions

Confederation, as conceived and practiced by the American people between 1775 and 1789, was not merely an imitation of earlier European leagues. Rather, it was an attempt to develop a species of popular government within the federal genus that would reflect the extension of Whig principles to a polity expanded to a size beyond that of any in history other than the autocratic Russian empire. As such, it merits serious consideration for what it can teach us about the problem of federal arrangements in extended republics.

While the result, the United States of America as a confederation, was rejected after less than half a generation (incidentally, the minimum time needed for a regime to consolidate itself) and replaced by a presumably radically different approach to the organization of government, in fact, what emerged was a synthesis of the Whig and Federalist approaches, based upon a perennial tension between the two. That tension has accompanied the American people in its experiment with self-government ever since, at times more self-consciously, and at times less. The roots of that tension lie in the effort to combine federal liberty with good government. The tension itself has been a creative one that deserves to be fostered. The best way to do so is to begin by understanding the premises of Whig as well as Federalist thought underlying the American political system, as well as the federal mechanisms used in the governance of that system.

Students of federalism have been discussing the degree to which federalism and democracy are interrelated. All generally agree that there is a relationship of some closeness. Among the scholars there are those who see federalism and democracy inextricably intertwined.

This is especially true of those who see federalism strictly as federation. They are prepared to argue, as do Ostrom and Duchacek, that federal systems in nondemocratic polities are no more than shams. Duchacek further argues that there must be a federal political culture to accompany federal structures and processes for federalism to be real.

Without disagreeing with either, this writer argues that the existence of the federal form will have an influence toward certain dimensions of democratization even if the full conditions of democracy are not present. In other words, federalism has a certain independent influence that moves matters towards liberty of some kind by the very fact of its being. This does not obviate the close relationship between federalism and democracy and indeed the desirability of that connection, only that it is not an all or nothing at all matter.

This is particularly relevant in the discussion of confederal arrangements. Whereas federations require more close identification of federalism and democracy to be truly federal, there is more room for variation in confederal arrangements, although the direction remains clear and, whatever it may be, it must be pursued by all of the members of the arrangement, if not always at an equal pace. The extent of the confederal arrangement to some extent determines how equal the pace must be. Full confederations are similar to federations in that respect, whereas less intense confederal arrangements offer more leeway.

Consequently, only in a democratic age could confederal arrangements be revived on the scale that they are being revived today, where even states that clearly are not democratic move to pretend that they are and appear to conform with certain basic practices associated with democracy, particularly in the field of liberties and rights, in order to be accepted into the community of nations and certainly to be accepted into even the looser confederal arrangements that have developed since World War II such as the CSCE and the WTO. Indeed, those arrangements themselves become tools to promote democratic republicanism.

Notes

1. For the literature on the confederation, see "The Continuing Legacy of the Articles of Confederation," a special issue of *Publius*, vol. 12, no. 4 (Fall 1982).

2. It is important to note that the term "republican" did not come into general use in a positive sense until the winter of 1775-76, as the colonies moved toward independence through their new union, "the United States in Congress assembled." See Donald S. Lutz, *Popular Consent and Popular Control* (Baton Rouge: University of Louisiana Press, 1980), pp. 1-22.

3. For an analysis of the Declaration, see Daniel J. Elazar and John Kincaid, *The Declaration of Independence, The Founding Covenant of the American People,* a working paper of the Workshop on Covenant and Politics of the Center for the Study of Federalism.

4. Rosanne Rothman, "Political Method in the Federal System: Albert Gallatin's Contribution," *Publius,* vol. 1, no. 2 (Winter 1971):123-141.

5. Martin Diamond, "The Ends of Federalism," in "The Federal Polity," a special of *Publius*, vol. 3, no. 2 (Fall 1973).

Chapter 4

FEDERALISM IN THE NEW EUROPE

In 1992, Europeans, particularly the Spanish, celebrated the quincentennial anniversary of Columbus's discovery of the new world of America. In the way that history works, Columbus himself did not know that he had discovered America and he did not know that his discovery was going to set off further explorations leading to the discovery of all the remaining new worlds on earth, including Australasia. But in his case of mistaken identity he really did open the path that led to the establishment of new societies in North and South America, Australia, New Zealand, southern Africa, and the Caribbean.

Columbus's discovery came in the same year as the last Muslim rule in Western Europe was ended. Indeed, the two events were related. The Spanish conquest of the Muslim Kingdom of Granada in southern Spain also led to the expulsion of the Jews from Spain, inaugurating a period of two centuries during which the Jews were essentially expelled from the major countries of western Europe and the remaining Muslims left powerless. About a century or so thereafter, those who remained as individuals were physically expelled and have only returned as immigrants since World War II.

Thus in 1492, Europe turned outward to direct its energies to the tasks of discovery, exploration and settlement of new worlds. Europeans also made a last effort to maintain a unified Christendom in Europe itself based on efforts to give Catholic Christianity a religious monopoly in Western Europe. It was an effort that failed before it started. By 1492 Martin Luther and the other great Protestant reformers were already alive. In 1517 the Reformation began, which ended that unity for Christian Europe.

The 1492 consolidation of Spain that followed on the three events mentioned above meant that Spain soon joined France in pioneering the development of the European state system which was to become dominant after the mid-seventeenth century, first in Europe and then over much of the world, ending the possibility of political unity in Europe as well.

The principle of the European state system was that every state was sovereign, that is to say, dependent upon no one else, able to make its own decisions on every matter, including matters of life and death, peace and war. As a state, it was to strive to be self-sufficient, namely, not to be dependent on any outside factors so that it would have no external constraints, economic or any other, to inhibit those decisions, which led to European colonialism and the idea that if a European state did not have the resources to produce what it needed at home, it should conquer some territory (with its people) that did, or settle in some place that had and thereby increase its self-sufficiency. A third expectation was that the populations of these new states should be homogenous, if necessary by expulsion or repression of those who were different. However achieved, they should be homogenous.

The Spanish expelled those who were different; the French repressed them, forced them to adopt French as their language, and even prohibited them from taking names that reflected their old local identities. To this day in France there is a list of officially approved names. When a couple goes to register the birth of their child they have to register his or her name and that name must be a name on the official list. This was done to make sure that Bretons and Occitanians, people from Languedoc and Provence would not choose names in their local languages, but that they would choose proper French names. This law, a part of the nation-state-building days of France, remains on the books and enforced to this day. It has been modified only to allow a limited appeal process.

The state system the Europeans introduced was both a beneficiary and a simultaneous development along with the discovery and colonization of these new worlds. That state system, which became the norm and the standard in international relations, also provided the framework and the vehicle for modern European wars. The human race is certainly no stranger to wars. It seems that humans will find something to fight about no matter what. Nevertheless, the wars of the modern epoch were exceptionally ferocious, combining as they did the involvement of whole populations (total war) and modern technologies of destruction. We postmoderns live in the aftermath of a secular age of total wars. The Peace of Westphalia in 1648 put an end to the religious wars in Europe and opened the modern epoch. For the next 300 years secularization in the world was often advanced by the argument that religion led to wars and, therefore, if people seriously maintained their religious attachments and religious beliefs there would be more wars.

By now, we know that human beings will fight over anything if they have a mind to fight—dominoes or a cup of coffee—and once religion ceased to be the cause of wars in Europe, imperialism and nationalism took its place. We would be just as foolish to say today *ex cathedra* that nationalism causes war, as it was earlier to blame religion, but in any case, the nation-state system did become the vehicle for bloody wars, both external and civil.

The New Europe and Federalism

Now, 500 years later, matters have taken a new turn. Europe, after a generation or so of decolonization, has turned inward. It trades with the world; it does not seek to conquer territories so much as to conquer markets. The idea that states can be self-sufficient is demonstrably impossible in our times. Certainly in the nuclear age, there is no state that is sovereign, not the United States, not (when it existed) the Soviet Union, nor any of its successors . All states are interdependent and the world today is striving to find some way to accommodate the realities of national aspirations along with the realities and the necessities for interdependence.

Not only that, but Europe has become a place of attraction for millions of Muslims. Islam is now the largest non-Christian minority in Western Europe. It is probably the most active and strongest religious force in Western Europe because the Muslims who come are still, for the most part, religiously committed, even if they are not orthodox, whereas the Europeans, except perhaps for the Swiss, have the lowest rates of religious concern and affiliation in the world today.[1]

After bringing the world to the brink of destruction twice in this century because of its wars, Europe lost its place as the center of Western civilization. The United States not only became a world power, but inherited Europe's role. The shift was further stimulated by the decolonization that was taking place, first in the former European colonies settled by Europeans and then in our time in Asia and Africa where the Europeans had colonized without settling major populations of their own. Europe seemed to have ceased being a guide or a model for the world.

The Search for Federal Arrangements

Fifty years later, Europe is again at the cutting edge, now in developing new postmodern political arrangements. It is almost as if Europe is reasserting itself as the main street of the world, as the center of the action, and what Europe is doing is a matter of great interest for all the world. Europe is undertaking three massive experiments in federalism. In Western Europe it is undertaking an experiment in building a "Community" that is going to go beyond the Common Market to bring federal links—perhaps union—to the mother states of the state system, the first states to develop the European state system in the late Middle Ages or early modern times.

In Eastern Europe, in the territory west of the ex-Soviet Union and east of the Common Market, the experiment is taking a very different form. Virulent nationalism, which in the short term seems to be the worst expression of the old European belligerency, has erupted within the republics that were once Yugoslavia, but which also can be seen in a much more mild ("velvet") form in the struggle between Czechs and Slovaks in what used to be Czechoslovakia.

These nationalist explosions are all based on a hidden premise that none of these small nation-states that have emerged will have to go it alone. Slovenia and Croatia would not have seceded from Yugoslavia had they not had expectations that someday they will get into the European Community. So, too, with Slovakia. The Baltic states are in the same category. So even in the ethno-national struggles we are seeing a hidden federalist agenda that is stimulating some of the most virulent nationalism that we have witnessed since World War II.

Further to the east in the Commonwealth of Independent States, an effort is being made to combine nationalism and federalism into some kind of workable and viable system that will allow people to find their own self-expression, yet at the same time develop institutionalized, constitutionalized ways to maintain or foster their necessary interdependence.

Many years ago, the late American political scientist Martin Diamond defined federalism by taking a line from the movie *The Man Who Came to Dinner*. In it, Jimmy Durante, the American comedian who played a madcap Broadway musical composer, came in, sat down at the piano and started banging out the song "Did you ever have the feeling that you wanted to go but the feeling that you wanted to stay." In Europe today that is probably the best definition of federalism that one can find. Let us look at how these three efforts to both stay and go, or go and stay, are working themselves out in the three major divisions of Europe.

First of all, look at the European Community/Union. Fifteen years ago, most European academics were bemoaning the fact that the European Community was about to dissolve, that it had failed, that it had no chance of staying alive. They were very wrong. Not only was this situation reversed in the 1980s, but in 1991, through the Maastricht Treaty, the European Community took what may turn out to be a gigantic step toward a federal Europe. That is, not merely a common market with open borders that already had turned into a de facto confederation whereby still politically independent states cooperated together in a constitutionalized way to achieve common ends, but actually into a new confederation *de jure*. The term "The United States of Europe" is not used because it was discredited in a premature effort to achieve this result after World War I, but that is basically where Maastricht may lead if it is carried out according to the momentum that it has generated.

In the fifteen years prior to Maastricht, there was a dramatic turnaround toward moving in the direction of federation. Many people in the EC states believe it is now going too far and too fast, if it ever should happen, but which many of the leaders of the European Union support. The Maastricht Treaty essentially provides that the European Union will acquire comprehensive, if limited, sovereign powers, not simply by treaty but through a constitution that will enable the EU to intervene not only in the substantial but still limited aspects of economic life and those matters related to economic life, such as working conditions and economic and political rights that affect the joint economy and working conditions, but that it will extend into every sphere including the social sphere.

The opponents of Maastricht claimed that this was going much too far, that the European Union does not need this degree of consolidation in order to achieve the objectives for which the Common Market was established even as it has been expanded to promote the sense of common community which many in western Europe have been seeking and which anybody who watches television will see in such acts and symbols as the Eurovision contest every year, the regular display of the European flag with its twelve stars on a field of blue, and the effective adoption of the last movement of Beethoven's Ninth Symphony as the anthem of the Community. These symbolic acts have already reached into the hearts and minds of many Europeans, especially the younger generation. Ratification of the Maastricht Treaty had to be unanimous by all twelve member states to take effect. It did not have such easy sailing because Denmark, the first to take action on ratification, put it to referendum and it was voted down. The Irish, who voted next, voted it up. Opposition to the treaty was so strong that the French government felt the need to put it to a referendum in which it barely passed. In essence, it was sent back for changes in the direction of a looser union. The British did not put it to a popular vote. That is not the British way. Prime Minister Major provided a pro vote in Parliament to prevent his government from falling but only after a bitter debate that also called for some serious changes in the instruments.[2]

In any case, the problematic reaction was on the table and promised changes were necessary before ratification could succeed. Denmark did vote again under pressure and approved the referendum but just barely. In any case, the treaty was ratified in the end.

In fact, there are three groupings in the struggle over whether the European Community will become a federation, will remain a strong confederation, or become a little stronger confederation but not a closer union. Jacques Delors's group seeks the maximum amount of federalization, a stronger, more unified federal system. The second is the group that follows the views of Margaret Thatcher, who remains an important force, even though she is no longer prime minister of Great Britain. They will resist federation in any way, manner, or form, hoping to keep the Common Market but to keep it modest. A major spokesman for the third position is Prime Minister Maartens of Belgium, who has called for undertaking a slow strengthening of the confederation so that the end result will be more union but not more consolidation. Unfortunately, his position, which more closely reflects the reality, has not attracted the public attention that either of the first two have gained.

Subsidiarity: The Other Side of Hierarchy?

These are positions that are actively being fought about today. Without going into the details of that struggle, what is significant is that the European Community is the product of Catholic Europe. The states that originally formed the Community, and that even today form the majority of the member states, are states whose predominant religion and whose predominant spirit of organization came out of Catholicism, reflecting the same spirit that sought to unify European Christendom from the late Roman Empire or the early Middle Ages onward.

The European Community reflected a certain school in this Catholic or post-Catholic world, that of Montesquieu and de Tocqueville rather than that of the Bourbons or the Jacobins, but it came out of a civilization that had long strived for unity on a hierarchical basis. When one listens to Jacques Delors talking about Europe, one hears the voice of that spirit. The predominantly Protestant nations of Europe, for the most part, did not join in the European Community. Denmark is an exception. Britain is an exception. The Netherlands, with a large Catholic-background population that may now be a majority, is something of an exception. Britain joined very reluctantly, the Netherlands much more positively, Denmark somewhere in between. Only later did the other Nordic countries reluctantly move toward membership.

Those Protestant-inspired countries, even in their post-Protestant phase, share a different vision. Their vision was of a Europe of countries that were not quite reified nation-states in the manner of the Catholic states of Europe, countries that were citizen-states, where the citizenry were given a much larger role in determining the composition and powers of government. The conflict to which the European Union addresses itself, however, is not first and foremost that conflict between states in the Catholic spirit and states in the Protestant spirit. There is instead an intra-Catholic conflict. It is a conflict born of the French Revolution, between the Jacobins who invented what we have to call (forgive the oxymoron) totalitarian democracy and those who sought a liberal democratic heritage, of whom the Baron Montesquieu was one exponent and Alexis de Tocqueville another. This struggle reached its first peak at the time of the French Revolution when the Jacobins sought to change first France and then the world from the center by centralizing everything and then remaking it—from the calendar to land ownership, everything. On the other hand, the line of thought represented by Montesquieu advocated separation of powers and power sharing between the nation, its local communities, and regions.

The European Community, to the extent that it was founded by Frenchmen—it was founded essentially by Jean Monnet of France and Konrad Adenauer of Germany—who came out of the de Toquevillian tradition, was an answer to the Jacobins. But the leaders were themselves raised as Jacobins. In the end, it seems that they have been overwhelmed by their own culture to expect that a federal Europe means a strong central government in Brussels, a strong bureaucracy to effectuate the activities of that central government, and a hierarchical structure of power acquired from the Catholic Church modified by a Catholic concept, namely, subsidiarity. In the Church, subsidiarity means that decisions should be made and actions executed at the lowest possible level.

There is still too much statist hierarchy embedded in European political culture and, consequently, political thought. On one hand, the relationship between the member states and the EU is portrayed as a matter of subsidiarity, which is not the way at least a goodly number of the member states perceive it. (They do not see themselves as having built the EU as the apex of a new pyramid in which they are merely an intermediate level.) On the other, there also is the tendency to subordinate the federated states within the member states by transforming them into mere "regions," that is to say, into administrative organizations of the central government for certain purposes, when in fact, in those member states that are federal or nearly so, the federated states have considerably greater powers in a nonhierarchical framework.

They were in theory, but in a hierarchical system the top decides which is the lowest possible level. This is not the way of federal decision-making which views federal political systems in other than hierarchical terms to begin with, as noncentralized matrices of constitutionally distributed powers, but it is an effort to federalize a hierarchical system. It is an effort to create a community of nation-states in which the bureaucracy at the center will have the final say. That is the crux of the problem. It is now more or less agreed in Western Europe that there will be some kind of federal solution for the European Union. Whether it will be confederal or federal is the issue that is being confronted now. It is of enormous significance that in the very heartland of the European state system, the very originators of it have essentially abandoned the notion of the reified, totally independent, totally sovereign state seeking self-sufficiency, and are now struggling over what kind of constitutionalized interdependence they will have. They have even come to the conclusion that treaties of interdependence are not enough, that real powers have to be transferred from the states to the European Union. The only question is to what extent and how much. This marks a change in European thought after 500 years. The struggle is a very vital and important struggle, but the struggle itself suggests the change that has taken place.

Intrastate Devolution

Simultaneously within the states of Western Europe there has been another phenomenon of the same order taking place and that is devolution. In other words, if there is any other sign that is needed to show that Europe is in the process of essentially abandoning the statist road, it is what is happening within those same states that came together to form the European Community, while internally they began the substantial process of decentralization.

The four that are probably farthest ahead in this are Germany, Belgium, Spain, and Italy, all of which have adopted noncentralized systems of government since World War II. In the first two cases, they have adopted federalism. West Germany after World War II adopted a model federal system. Forty years later, when it absorbed East Germany, it first required East Germany to break up into its original five federal states—five *länder*. In essence, East Germany did not join West Germany, the five *länder* of East Germany joined the eleven *länder* of West Germany to become the new German Federal Republic.

Belgium, which was faced with an ethnic conflict between Flemings and Walloons after World War II, devolved step by step until it moved to the point where in January 1991 it officially became a federation in an effort to accommodate that conflict. Spain, which still avoids the term, had been struggling for true national unity since 1492—since even a little before 1492 when Ferdinand of Aragon and Isabella of Castile married and formed the dual monarchy that ultimately led to what they had sought, namely, the consolidation of the countries of Spain into one Spain. Nevertheless, the unity of Spain remained an imposed one, never accepted by the smaller peoples of the Iberian peninsula. After Franco died, in 1978, Spain adopted a new democratic constitution that provided for constitutionalized devolution of substantial powers to autonomous regional communities in every part of the country. Nearly two decades later, we can see that Spain thereby established a federal system for itself, and a successful one at that.

Italy's postwar constitution provided for a system of fifteen regular and five special regions. The five special regions were activated immediately; the others were not made operational until the 1970s in a reform designed to overcome the near paralysis of the national government, thereby establishing a constitutionally decentralized polity which has had considerable success in governing. Now the growing force in Italy is the Lombard League which consists of a very high proportion of northern Italians who want to divide Italy into at least three federal units, mostly so they can stop having to support the south, which they consider simply throwing money at the Mafia for nothing.

Portugal and, in a certain way, even the Netherlands and France have moved toward a greater regional decentralization. Portugal adopted its own version of regionalization including home rule for its island provinces. The Netherlands, which had been one of the early modern European confederations until the French Revolution, has been devolving powers once again to its provinces and municipalities. France has established a system of regions and empowered them within its hierarchical system. The United Kingdom and Denmark have also taken modest steps along this road. Only Greece, Ireland, and Luxembourg have not. Greece is the odd man out in the EU in any case. Luxembourg with its 999 square miles can hardly be expected to decentralize and Ireland with its own particular situation does not need to.[3]

Scandinavian Confederal Linkage[4]

There is a very different confederal arrangement in Scandinavia. The five states of Scandinavia (Finland, Sweden, Norway, Denmark, and Iceland), plus three of their autonomous territories (Aaland Islands attached to Finland and the Faeroe Islands and Greenland attached to Denmark) have over the years built themselves a very special confederal arrangement to accommodate their very special interests in wanting to be united for certain common Scandinavian purposes but remain fully separate as states.

The history of Scandinavia once was one of periodically recurring wars between its five countries and the colonization of one or another, in whole or in part, by one of its neighbors. Thus, Finland for years was governed by Sweden which also governed Norway and Denmark at different times, with their outlying possessions at least nominally under Swedish suzereignty as well. Norway stayed part of Sweden until 1905, although it had its own constitution during the nineteenth century. Denmark at one time controlled all of Scandinavia, to the displeasure of the Swedes and Norwegians.

By the mid-twentieth century, all of these states and islands were independent or sufficiently autonomous to satisfy their respective demands. But separation was not fully satisfying either since they all shared a common Scandinavian culture (Finland and Greenland least of all) and common aspirations in both foreign and domestic social policy. To meet those needs, the Scandinavian states formed the Nordic Council and its ancillary institutions.

The Nordic Council is one of the earliest transnational arrangements that has hovered on the edge of becoming constitutionalized. Indeed, it belongs to the first period of such arrangements, the latter half of the nineteenth century, beginning in the 1840s with discussions of a postal union and ending in 1914 when the effort to establish a customs union failed as a result of the outbreak of World War I. The pronounced ethnic, cultural, and at least to some extent historical similarities of the five Nordic states and their location in the extreme north of Europe contributed to the interest in coordinating or uniting activities in nonpolitical spheres even while the five were engaged in various disputes in the political arena, especially the struggle of Norway to become independent of Sweden, Iceland to become independent of Denmark, and Finland to become independent of Russia. At the same time, the historical experience that they all had at one time or another of being politically subordinate to one of the others has also kept them apart, not only making them reluctant to extend constitutionalized ties into anything smacking of the political realm, but also fearful of too binding a connection in other realms.[5]

The Nordic efforts at closer integration have gone through four phases to date. The first was before 1872 when discussions were widespread about technical linkages in fields such as posts. The second was from 1872 to World War I, when the advocates of greater integration tried to promote a Nordic customs union and even a Nordic common market, while others sought to achieve a common legal basis for modern Scandinavian life. The former efforts were not successful, while the last was and set the pattern for what was to be characteristic of Nordic integration.

World War I put an end to all of these efforts, which only partially resumed during the interwar period and only reemerged after World War II. It can be said that, in this respect at least, World War I set back efforts at Nordic integration as it no doubt did other efforts in the European heartland. There were, however, some initiatives, another failure at customs union and the establishment of the Nordic Council itself as a consultative body.

It was not until after World War II, when the fourth phase opened in 1947, that serious efforts again began in the development of common institutions as well as common goals to be carried out. It has achieved a measure of success, but was essentially aborted or distorted by the rise of Western European integration.

As a result of these contradictory pulls, the five states have confined themselves to a loose common council and have achieved the desired level of integration principally through harmonization of laws. Thus, from 1872 onward, there has been a strong and rather successful effort to develop a uniform commercial code, common family law, and common criminal law through the regular meetings (officially once every three years) of the appropriate government officials from each state to prepare common contents which each state could then enact as part of its own state law. Here, what were contrary pressures in other fields served the common interest in that the laws of all five came from a common tradition of Scandinavian law reinforced by the periodic unification of the states, often by conquest, in earlier times.

Customs union was harder to attain, but finally was. Instead of proposed common markets, a common Scandinavian bank was established but only after much pulling and hauling. On the other hand, a postal union came early and similar links with other forms of communication followed by treating them as technical rather than political matters. Citizens from each of the five countries can pass into any of the others without border controls and various efforts in cultural cooperation have succeeded, again resting on their common Scandinavian culture. At one time it seemed that there might be an outer European bloc comparable to the European Community, consisting of the Scandinavian countries plus the United Kingdom through the European Free Trade Agreement, but the reluctance of all of its members to relinquish sovereignty or any of its attributes and the ultimate decision, first on the part of the United Kingdom and Denmark, that if sovereignty was to be compromised, it was better compromised within the more powerful collection of states known as the European Community, stamped *finis* to that possibility.[6]

On the other hand, the existence of the Nordic Council has also enabled nongovernmental organizations in the region, some working for greater integration of the five states and some merely interested in particular tasks of doing business, improving cultural expression, and promoting economic development, to thrive.

In the end the most characteristic element of the Nordic effort is the informal development of common draft legislation which is then enacted into law in the respective states to be a kind of integration through law, but not through overarching law. If there is to be any future for the Nordic confederal arrangement as a confederal arrangement, it will probably be through that pattern, and much of it will be within the expanded European Union that now includes Sweden and Finland as well as Denmark. In that sense, the Nordic Council and its ancillaries are characteristic of other confederal or other proto-confederal agreements in Europe that include parts of the European Union plus states outside of it.

In the course of these developments, the Nordic Council, while scrupulously adhering to the fiction that it is a mere treaty between politically sovereign states, has introduced many of the elements that we have identified as belonging to new-style confederations. While all of the member states were in place by 1955, in 1970 the Faeroe Islands and Aaland were given their own representation on the Council through Denmark and Finland respectively, and in 1984 Greenland was given its, also through Denmark. It is important to note that the Faeroes, Iceland, and Greenland have stayed out of the European Community even though in the case of the first and last their mother country has been a member for a long time. They claim that their cultures as well as their economies are at stake.

The Council itself has six committees dealing with economics, legal matters, cultural affairs, social policy, the environment, and budgets, with the budget committee coordinating the executive committee's processing of the Council of Ministers budgetary proposals and supervising the activities financed by the Council of Ministers. The Council has a presidium to govern it between Council sessions consisting of no more than two members of parliament from any one country and with a total of no more than eleven. The presidium is served by a secretariat with a staff of approximately 100. The Council of Ministers is defined as a "cooperation organ." On it are representatives from all five states and the three autonomous territories. Its composition varies depending on the issue before it. Its chairmanship is rotated annually among each member state. The person responsible for the work of the Council is a member of the government of each state who serves as Minister for Cooperation. State prime ministers are directly responsible for drawing up the political guidelines for cooperation. The Council cannot make any decision until the issue is prepared by its secretariat, processed by the relevant executive committee, and decided unanimously. A unanimous decision is binding on the member states. Occasionally, decisions must be ratified by the parliaments of the member states. The secretariat is permanently located in Copenhagen. The Nordic Council defines Nordic cooperation as part of larger European cooperation, not an alternative to it, based upon the shared values of the Nordic countries. Those shared values used to include neutrality, which they now see as becoming less significant in the new Europe, whereas social democracy and environmental protection are now central.

The Nordic Council sees its special regional interest in European cooperation as focusing on the Polar and Baltic regions. The Baltic Sea is badly polluted and the Nordic states are working to curb the pollution. They have also organized NEFCO, the Nordic Environment Finance Corporation, to improve environmental technology, for use in the Eastern and Central European states that contribute so much to the pollution on the south side of the Baltic. Research methods and expertise to improve the environment are concentrated in the Nordic Institute of Marine Biology located in Norway and staffed by experts from all the Nordic countries.

Nordic Information Offices have been opened by the Council of Ministers in the Baltic capitals. They make funds available to promote cooperation between the Nordic and Baltic countries.

In addition, within the Nordic part of the Baltic, the sea's three main islands and archepelagos—Bornholm, Gotland, and Aaland—are developing a permanent cooperation scheme backed by the Council of Ministers. This cooperation arrangement crosses the old definitions of territorial status. Aaland is an autonomous territory, part of Finland, whereas Bornholm and Gotland are Swedish counties. Because of the location of these three island groupings, they dominate the strategic crossroads of the Baltic, thus giving them a special importance for trade, if no longer for defense. They are being encouraged to work together to present a united front to the European Union as well as the Nordic Council and the Baltic states.

On another front, the five Nordic countries established the Nordic Industrial Fund in 1973. Today it is one of the largest Nordic financial institutions with an aggregate portfolio that amounts to some ECU67.5 million and annual grants exceeding ECU13.5 million. The Fund's objective is to "promote the technical and industrial cooperation in the Nordic region by initiating and financing joint projects involving enterprises and research institutions from at least two of the Nordic countries." Non-Nordic firms can participate in projects as long as those terms are met. Its work has been mostly in what is considered "frontier industries"—information technology, biotechnology, materials technology, and environment technology. The Fund chooses target areas upon which to concentrate at different periods of time. The Fund is designed not only to advance Nordic industrial skills in these areas but to make Nordic firms more competitive.

It should be clear that the Nordic Council has increased its role precisely in those activities associated with the most advanced forms of economic and educational progress and has tried to become what is sometimes called a "change agent" in connection with progress in those fields. Of course, it does so within the common social policy framework for which its member states are noted, namely, the provision of equal opportunity for all, which in these days means in particular the elimination of gender bias. The Council of Ministers has supported a joint Nordic action program in this area.

The Nordic Council is also active in promoting a common Nordic culture in fine and practical arts, music, and literature. In 1962 it established the Nordic Council's literature prize, today the region's most prestigious literary prize, devoted to encouraging modern Nordic literature. The Nordic Council's music prize was established in 1965 for similar purposes. In 1978 the Nordic Arts Centre was established at Sveaborg outside of Helsinki to give joint Nordic recognition to the visual arts.

The Nordic Investment Bank (NIB), headquartered in Helsinki, was established in 1976 to channel international capital to the Nordic countries. It is now a major regional bank with a higher credit rating than any other Nordic bank. It, too, provides major credit for environmental projects. NEFCO is an NIB subsidiary. It also handles Nordic investment aid abroad.

The Nordic Council also provides funds to advance the industrial development of various segments of its membership, for example, funding research in improving fishing for the three westernmost islands in the community.

The Nordic region also has had a free labor market since shortly after World War II. Citizens can not only move from one country to another without cumbersome restrictions, but are covered by the social security system of the country of domicile without respect to their citizenship. Since it was introduced in 1954, more than a million people have moved across state borders within the Nordic region, mainly between Finland and Sweden and Denmark and Sweden, aside from those who live along the frontiers and cross the border for work purposes daily. This is made easier by establishing common occupational qualifications adopted by the parliament of each state and thus shared by all.

All this is supported by the region's strong trade unions. There, too, the Nordic Council of Ministers has established the Nordic Institute for Advanced Training and Occupational Health (NIVA), located in Helsinki, to work with the various national institutes of occupational safety and health to diffuse research and technological developments among the council members. Significantly, the courses are conducted in English.

In 1988 the Nordic Council of Ministers launched NORDPLUS to encourage Nordic university students to transfer between the universities in Nordic countries for at least part of their studies. Thousands of students and a thousand teachers have done so on NORDPLUS grants. One of the other aims of NORDPLUS is to build networks between universities and university departments. In addition, the Council of Ministers has established NorFA, the Nordisk Forskereaddan Nelsesakademi, an institute for advanced studies intended to improve the quality of research and increase its quantity in Nordic countries.

Mixed Hopes in Eastern Europe

What about east-central Europe? In the twentieth century, east-central Europe has moved from being part of a traditional empire to national independence, to totalitarian rule, to national independence again. Almost all of the states of today were part of the Austrian-Hungarian empire, which did not fall until after World War I. There are still people actively engaged in world affairs today who were born and raised as citizens of the Austrian-Hungarian empire. Poland, which was not, was part of the Russian empire, so it had an imperial experience also.

After perhaps 30 years of national independence, sometimes under homegrown dictatorial regimes, these countries came under totalitarian dictatorship in the form of Nazism or Communism or both for another 40 or 50 years. Now they are engaged in experiments with freedom, all this in the space of hardly more than 70 years. Not surprisingly, the experiments in freedom first have taken the form of a revival of nineteenth-century nationalisms.

Each of the nations that were striving against the Austrian-Hungarian empire and were repressed, first by the Nazis and then by the Communists, are now seeking some form of self-expression but with an interesting difference. The interesting difference is that they are all doing so, even the most virulent cases, as in Yugoslavia, expecting to be part of some European confederation, either the European Union, which is the dominant expectation, or, some suggest, a revival of the old Austrian-Hungarian empire with one or two other countries on a democratic basis to form a loose confederation of Middle European states. If these states were to go into the EU, they would probably pull Europe more towards confederation than federation because the original twelve would not want to take them in as federation partners. They might be willing to take them in as confederates, though this idea may have been a casualty of what has happened in Yugoslavia.

Indeed, after 1989 and the liberation from Communist domination, such a confederation was a major topic of discussion. It has suffered eclipse because virulent nationalism is now running its course throughout the area. Originally, Croatia and Slovenia even proposed a looser confederation for Yugoslavia; they just wanted to constitutionalize the powers that they had gained over the years since Tito's death. They were frustrated by Serbia for its own reasons.

The Czechs and Slovaks separated in 1992, but what the Slovaks meant by separation was, again, a loose confederation. They did not get it because the Czechs saw no gain in that. East-central Europe is a mixture of virulent nationalism with some hope for handling the problems of markets and externalities through confederation. Eastern European thinking is based on three paradigms—the paradigm of Yugoslavia, which is the whole thing gone crazy; the paradigm of Czechoslovakia, where the Czechs have been too civilized to fight about anything; and the paradigm of Hungary, which is self-sufficient, does not see itself as having any minorities of consequence within its boundaries, but which is looking for outside linkages, particularly economic, perhaps with Austria, perhaps with the European Union. All three are seeking national separation based upon the possibility of confederation. In the long run, the only way they can separate is if they can find partners for confederation.[7]

Finally, there is the ex-Soviet Union. These states, too, have had a history very similar to eastern Europe in the twentieth century, from empire to totalitarian dictatorship to experiments with freedom. The difference is, of course, that these republics represent much greater diversity because they extend into Muslim central Asia and into pagan eastern Siberia, and include peoples with all kinds of backgrounds, cultural histories, and diversities. The USSR was, perhaps, the most polyglot of imperial domains in its time and now its successors are not quite sure how to handle that polyglot character.

The CIS states are confronted with the necessity of transforming an ersatz federation, a federation that existed only because their Communist rulers thought that they still had to preach Communism to everybody in their own language, not because they really wanted any kind of diffusion of power. They must decide how they can accommodate national independence, either through some kind of links between republics or without them and whether real federation is possible, whether they have even the human resources in the sense of people with the requisite cultural resources to maintain the kinds of trust and cooperation that are necessary to maintain any federal system. In a sense, this is their most difficult problem because they have a very difficult problem of trust, and without trust, polities cannot have any kind of real power-sharing, no matter how well constitutionalized power-sharing might be on paper. So they are going through an immense struggle. Nevertheless, it is a struggle that at every turn is turning towards some kind of federal or confederal solution.[8]

Take, for example, one of the hardest problems between the ex-Soviet republics. Understandably, Ukraine has very little trust when it comes to Russia respecting its independence. After all, it was subdued by one Russian empire after another. So when Ukraine has all those former Soviet naval vessels in its ports, it is not so easily persuaded to share them with the Russians. In turn, the Russians claim that, since they built that fleet and supported it, it is basically theirs. For now they have reached an interim agreement for joint control. We have yet to see whether that will work or not. The fact that with all their antagonism, both republics felt the necessity to do so may mean that they have come to realize that confederal links are their only peaceful way out.

The Baltic republics, which have left the CIS entirely, have done so because they have established, first of all, the Baltic common market, but also because they are all placing their hopes on achieving membership in the European Union. They are confronted with internal national and boundary conflicts, especially since the Communist government of the USSR, even while preserving the forms of federalism, shifted territories and populations from republic to republic more or less at will. Crimea, for example, which was in part shifted to the Russian Federation from the Ukraine, was divided in unnatural ways. Now the Crimeans have their own agenda. Part of the republic called Moldova was shifted from Bessarabia, Moldova's original name, to the Russian Republic so that the Russians could see to it that the Moldovans would not have direct access to the Black Sea and, in return, Moldova was given a piece of Russian territory, mixing the two populations. This has led to a civil war within that republic.

On one hand, these boundary problems have been exacerbated, but on the other, they may actually promote staying together because if the republics fully broke apart, then they would lose access to their historic territories more quickly than they might otherwise. There, too, reason (a precarious device, to be sure) suggests that the future will require some kind of combination of internal federalism, in Russia for sure, perhaps even in the Ukraine, with some kind of external or larger confederation.

The Revival of Confederation?

What does all this suggest? All this suggests that Europe, sitting on the cutting edge, is leading in the revival of confederation, a form of federalism that moderns thought was gone and unworkable. It may still be unworkable, but the experiment is one that really bears watching.

The American inventors of federalism held that all sovereignty is in the people as a whole or in their parts and all governments have delegated powers only. Therefore it is possible to achieve democratic republicanism by separating and sharing the powers delegated. That became the modern federalist answer to the European state system. Whether this process was recognized fully or not, in fact this is what happened. The new societies—the United States, Canada, Australia—became the bulwarks of modern federation in their striving for independence or relief from mother country control without adopting the state system as the Europeans developed it. Their main argument was that a nation had to have national unity—agreeing in this with the

European state theory—but it had to be democratic unity, which could be done in a federal way.

Today, at the outset of the postmodern epoch, the Europeans have concluded that they must go beyond the state system. To do so, they have revived the very confederal option that they rejected at the outset of the modern age, in new postmodern terms. This may or may not turn out to be a workable option, but it is a very important attempt. It is being tried in three variants:

1) in the European Union in the west;

2) in some kind of looser, shadowy affair in the middle; and

3) in a very active way in the east, in what used to be the USSR.

These three sets of regional arrangements within Europe will develop within a larger confederal framework for Europe as a whole. As stated above, federalism breeds federalism, just as statism breeds statism. The transformation of the European Union into a confederation was accompanied by Europe becoming an anchor in a series of looser confederal arrangements that will be described in Chapter 5, ranging from the Western European Union to NATO to the Council of Europe to the CSCE. Each of these has become constitutionalized in its own way, albeit in a manner much looser than any confederation would be. Moreover, each has as its principal anchor the European Union. Only in NATO is the EU one anchor of two, with the United States being the other. This interlocked network of confederal arrangements provides further support for maintaining the peace of Europe and keeping wars confined to local or regional venues.

This leads to another point of history. Five hundred years and more before Columbus, Charlemagne's empire was divided into three smaller empires, one for each of his sons. The westernmost, in the land of the Franks, would develop into the Kingdom of France, a centralized, unitary monarchy until the French Revolution, and which later became a centralized, unitary republic. The easternmost kingdom consisted of the principal territory of what is today Germany, anchored in what became Prussia. Politically, it remained segmented throughout the Middle Ages, a collection of kingdoms, duchies, counties, electorates, or what have you, loosely linked through the Holy Roman Empire. Only in modern times did its main state, Prussia, emerge as the dominant kingdom in the region and take the lead in forging a united and quasifederal, and then federal, Germany.

In the middle, from the North Sea down the Rhine Valley, through Switzerland and into northern Italy, was the middle kingdom, the territories Charlemagne bequeathed to his son Lothar (hence,

Lothringen in German; in French, Lorraine). In this middle kingdom, itself historically a borderlands area that included the eastern and northernmost parts of the old Roman empire and the western and southernmost parts of the Germanic-speaking regions, medieval federalism was born and survived, providing a federalist basis for the Holy Roman Empire, for the Helvetic Confederation, now Switzerland, and the United Provinces of the Netherlands, now the Kingdom of the Netherlands. Belgium also functioned as a federation of counties, although it only became formally federal in recent years.

It was in the regions that were once part of that middle kingdom that Reformed Protestantism became the dominant form of Christianity during the Protestant Reformation. The Reformed Protestants invented the federal theology that almost immediately became the foundation for Calvinism and the political confederations that constituted the region's first step toward modernity. In our times, virtually every one of the founders of the European Union was born within the territory that had once been part of that middle kingdom. While most were Catholics by birth, they were oriented from early on toward a federalist tradition. The unity of the European Union has been referred to as the revival of Charlemagne's dream. Its federal character is also Lothar's monument.[9]

This is an experiment that the whole world should watch because, in a world that is growing more interdependent, where the old model of state sovereignty has been seriously weakened by events, if not in the hearts and minds of people, but where, nevertheless, there are cultures and boundaries and nationalities that are real, maybe, just maybe, the Europeans will lead us all in a direction that will enable us to live and live well in the next century.

Notes

1. For religious affiliations of Europeans, see *Europa Year Book* (London: Europa Publications, 1994).
2. Richard Corbett, *The Treaty of Maastricht* (Essex: Longman Current Affairs, 1993); Laura Cram, *Policy-Making in the European Union* (London: Routledge, 1997).
3. Daniel J. Elazar, *Federal Systems of the World*, 2nd ed. (Essex: Longman Current Affairs, 1994).
4. *Ibid.*, pp. 334-335; and *Europa Year Book* (London: Europa Publications, 1994).

108 Chapter Four

5. *Ibid.*
6. Richard McAllister, *From EC to EU* (London: Routledge, 1997); Jeremy J. Richardson, *European Union: Power and Policy-Making* (London: Routledge, 1996); Richard Corbett, *The Treaty of Maastricht*; Laura Cram, *Policy-Making in the European Union.*
7. Carol Skalnik Leff, "Could this Marriage have been Saved? The Czechoslovak Divorce," *Current History* (March 1996):130-134; Oldrich Dedek, et al., *The Breakup of Czechoslovakia: An In-Depth Economic Analysis* (Aldershot, England; Brookfield VT: Avebury, 1996); Robert Henry Cox and Erich G. Frankland, "The Federal State and the Breakup of Czechoslovakia: An Institutional Analysis" (unpublished manuscript, 1995).
8. Barbara Jancar-Webster, "The CIS—Confederal Solution to Ethnic Conflict?" (unpublished manuscript, November 1994); Daniel J. Elazar, *Federal Systems of the World.*
9. Paul Belien, "...That Limited Government Works Best," *Wall Street Journal Europe*, 9 June 1994, p. 6.

Chapter 5

THE REVIVAL OF CONFEDERATION IN EUROPE

Confederations and Federations

From the time of the adoption of the United States Constitution in 1787-89 until the founding of the European Community in 1958, the historical trend in the world for those seeking federal solutions to their regime problems was federation, that is to say, the establishment of a strong general government to serve as a framework uniting constituent polities and their governments, usually intended to contain a single nation, all subject to a common constitution as supreme law of the land. Federations gave important functions, including foreign affairs, defense, management of the economy and taxation, among others, to a federal government that exercised the powers granted it directly upon the citizenry of the federation.

As a rule, modern federations were designed to establish new national entities and to diminish previous loyalties. The United States, for example, is a country built upon the migration of individuals and families from many different ethnic, religious and racial groups from around the world. "America" was, for them, new territory and they spread across it from sea to sea to sea. Hence, the United States has never had a convergence of its political boundaries with different ethnic or racial identities. Consequently, in the United States, federalism helps diffuse the pressures of ethnicity and race, and vice versa.[1]

In Germany, on the other hand, confederation proved inadequate because of the basic sense of ethnic unity of the German people, despite their one-time division into many identifiable subgroups (Saxons, Prussians, Bavarians, etc.) and independent polities. Federation, as in the U.S., has served the cause of democratic republicanism.[2]

In Canada the existence of two territorially grounded "founding nations" or ethnic communities, British and French, has led to periodic constitutional crises in our time. The British also were divided into English, Scottish, Welsh, Irish, and Cornish but, forced to confront the French, for most purposes united into one group. This also has led to the maintenance of the ethnic identity of later arrivals (e.g., Jews, Italians, Ukrainians) in a multicultural context as a crosscutting pressure, for better or worse.[3]

In Switzerland, linguistic and religious differences rest on what once were ethnic differences between Allemanians, Burgundians, Italians, and Rhaetians. Over time, political, geographic, and religious changes have made those differences crosscutting rather than reinforcing, maintained only within a sense of common Swiss nationhood.[4]

Before 1777 the modern idea of the centralized, homogeneous nation-state led to the definition of federalism as the loose linkage of such states in confederations. In the end it contributed greatly to the disappearance of confederations or confederal arrangements during the second half of the modern epoch, between the late eighteenth and the mid-twentieth centuries, as exclusive national statehood became the norm.

Throughout the nineteenth century, democratic republics, large and small, found federation a useful way to achieve democratic unity, a trend that continued through the immediate aftermath of World War II. New federations were established in Latin America, Canada, and Australia. After World War II, formal federations were established in Central and Eastern Europe as well, often to give the illusion of democratic unity.

A major reason for the triumph of federation was the need to reconcile constitutionalized power sharing with the overpowering thrust of statist nationalism for external purposes. A federation could appear to be a single state in the international arena and could satisfy the aspirations of a common nationalism, while "inside" it maintained its diversity.

The fact that federalism was preserved at all as a device for political organization in the modern years of statism and nationalism, to better allow the democratic organization of political power through the combination of self-rule and shared rule, was due to the great invention of the American Founding Fathers. Their task was made easier by the fact that the people of the United States saw themselves as sharing a common American nationality that increasingly superseded local ties, but even the United States had to fight a civil war before the issue was deemed settled and a common American citizenship given preeminence.

"Community": An Interim Stage

Today, confederations are often used where the separate ethnic or national loyalties of the constituent states are very strong and their people wish to preserve them, but at the same time see the advantage of long-term or permanent links with other states and peoples. In that sense, the elements of ethnicity seem to be among the critical factors in distinguishing between success or failure in connection with federal solutions.

The excesses of statism and nationalism revealed by the Fascist and Nazi movements in the twentieth century weakened the Western world's commitment to nationalism as an ideal per se and raised questions about the kind of exclusivist statism that had been a dominant feature of the modern epoch. As the world moved into a postmodern epoch, the states of Western Europe, exhausted by two world wars, sought new forms of unity in diversity, beginning tentatively with a set of treaties establishing economic linkages so that they could better compete in the world market. Over the next 40 years there evolved a European Union which became a new-style confederation, as much a new political invention as the U.S. invention of federation in 1787.[5]

The European Community essentially became a confederation in a formal way on January 1, 1994, as the European Union. It is by far the most advanced and comprehensive example of the new phenomenon. Indeed, just as the United States of America under its Constitution of 1787 became the model for modern federation, we may expect the European Union under its various treaties to become the model for postmodern confederation. Not only that, but many studies of the European Union, especially under its previous name, the European Community, explore and document the evolution of the EU from functionalism for economic purposes to confederation.[6]

From the first, the vision for European unification was a federal one, and the conventional expectation of those who sought it was federation, a United States of Europe. When Western European efforts at federation failed in the immediate aftermath of World War II, the federalists were replaced by the so-called "functionalists" who developed a system of linkage of functions, piece-by-piece, through the establishment by treaty of unifying "authorities" for specific but limited fields. It is they who laid the foundation, wittingly or unwittingly, for the new-style confederal arrangements that emerged and the reinvention of confederation, while strenuously denying that they had any federalistic intentions, for strategic reasons. Thus, the development of a new-style confederation has been overlooked by many. Until very recently, the EC continued to be understood by functionalists and federalists alike as a way to *avoid* federal solutions.

It hardly need be said that the failure of the "United States of Europe" movement and its replacement by a functionalist approach was the result of the still intense nationhood of the states of Western Europe. Every Western European state was seen as serving a particular nation. This was particularly true of those continental European states that formed the core of the EEC at its beginning. The inventors of the Westphalian system, they were still its strong adherents. At the same time they had come to recognize that old enemies, particularly France and Germany, had to be linked somehow in a golden net that would keep them from warring with one another. They also realized the economic need for extending that net to include at least certain basic functions. Thus, without giving up their nationalist ideals, they were ready for limited but very real functional linkages.

Three principal features stood out and marked the EC as a new-style polity: One was a general admission requirement to full membership that admitted member states into the governing councils and gave each an appropriate share of the bureaucracy of the EC on a more or less equal basis. The second was the transfer of powers to the EC on a functional basis, whereby specific and limited functions came within the purview of the Community institutions on a far more substantial basis than in any of the old confederations. Where the EC was explicitly granted authority and powers, its institutions could, at least in part, work directly with the citizens of the member states, although in all cases it had to work through the individual states themselves. Third was a constitutional court that was empowered to make far-reaching decisions within the limited sphere of EC authority.

It was this mixture of reliance upon the member states by the EC in order to act and the authority to reach out directly to the people on a limited basis, with each particular combination determined by separate agreement among the member states, that gave the new confederation form. Moreover, the new confederation quietly insisted upon democratic republicanism as the required regime for member states, a step that became particularly visible in the cases of Greece, Portugal and Spain, which passed from dictatorship to democracy as a condition of their entrance into the European Community.

After a period in the 1970s when it seemed that the Community itself would fail, it took on new vigor in the 1980s and there began to be talk about further union. That led to the Single Europe Act which took effect on January 1, 1993 and to the Treaty of Maastricht which took effect January 1, 1994 which, despite abjuring that goal, was designed to move the EC toward federal union. Both have subsequently run into problems. The Single Europe Act is now in effect on paper but has not been immediately effective in practice. While the Maastricht Treaty was ratified in the end by all twelve member states as it had to be, the ratification came with such reservations and revisions that it is more likely to strengthen the confederal aspects of the new European Union than to move it in the direction of federation. By now it is clear that the nations of Western Europe, realizing the necessity to do so, are committed to the EU, but they are not willing to give up their national identities expressed through states that retain substantial independence even while seeking limited union.

While some, including this writer, have been arguing that the European Union had been in the process of reviving confederation as a form of government at least since the 1970s and that by the time of the Single Europe Act, adopted in 1987, the EC had moved from being a confederal arrangement to a confederation, the Maastricht Treaty affirmed and constitutionalized the confederation beyond any doubt. The formalization of the change was reflected in the change in name from the European Community, a functionalist choice, to suggest the low profile of the original treaties, to the European Union, a name that seemed to promise more than confederal linkage and that could satisfy federalists as well as confederalists.

The Maastricht Treaty

Both the writing and the ratification of the Maastricht Treaty essentially involved a struggle between federalists and confederalists: the former proud to claim the name and the latter, led by Britain, reluctant to identify themselves with federalism in any way, following the vaunted model of British pragmatism. The federalists succeeded in giving the EU a new overall structure while the confederalists succeeded in limiting its application, thereby keeping the confederal mode of operation.

The treaty finally negotiated was constructed on the basis of three pillars: that embracing the original economic community, an intergovernmental pillar dealing with foreign and security policy, and a second intergovernmental pillar dealing with the Union's internal affairs. The first is embodied in Titles II, III, and IV of the treaty which amend the EEC, ECSE, and Euratom treaties and formally name them the "European Community." The second is embodied in Title V. The third is embraced in Title VI which covers justice and home affairs. All three are bound together through Titles I and VII, the Preamble and final provisions which bring them together to establish the European Union.

This complicated arrangement was designed to satisfy the anti-federalists' fears. Originally those fears seemed to be an expression of the UK government only, but as the difficulties that emerged in the ratification process indicated, the peoples, if not the governments of most of the other Community member states, shared many of the same feelings and were reluctant to go even as far as the treaty as finally concluded went, causing a major reassessment in the minds of the EU leadership. The treaty did not even use the term "federal," but "ever closer union." Even though British Prime Minister John Major accepted many federalist elements of the treaty, including subsidiarity, he attempted to define the new way without using the term "confederation." As he put it, "At Maastricht we developed a new way, and one much more amenable to the institutions of this country—cooperation by agreement between governments, but not under the Treaty of Rome."[7]

The final product was, when consolidated with the existing EC treaties upon which it rests, hundreds of pages in length. The result has been described as not so much a constitution as a collection of basic laws. Lister lists seventeen functions that fall within the confederal dimensions of the EU:[8]

1. Elimination of customs duties between member states (Articles 12-17);
2. Setting of the common customs tariff (Articles 18-29);
3. Elimination of quantitative restrictions in the trade between member states (Articles 30-37);

4. Common agricultural policy (Articles 38-47);
5. Free movement of workers (Articles 48-51);
6. Right of business establishment (Articles 52-58);
7. Right to provide services (Articles 59-66);
8. Free movement of capital (Articles (67-73h);
9. Common transport policy (Articles 74-84);
10. Rules to ensure free competition (Articles 85-94);
11. Harmonization of national taxation laws (Articles 95-99);
12. "Approximation" of national laws (Articles 100, 100a and b, 101 and 102);
13. Common visa requirements (Articles 100c and d);
14. Convergence of economic policies (Articles 102a-104c);
15. Common monetary policy (Articles 105-109m);
16. Common commercial policy (Articles 110, 112, 113, 115);
17. Consumer protection (Article 129a).

Lister lists another ten in which the EU functions more as a governmental organization:

1. Social provisions (Articles 117-125);
2. Education, vocational training, and youth (Articles 126-127);
3. Culture (Article 128);
4. Public health (Article 129);
5. Trans-European networks in transport, communications, and energy (Articles 129b-d);
6. Industrial cooperation (Article 130);
7. Economic and social cohesion (Articles 130a-c);
8. Research and technological development (Articles 130f-130p);
9. Environment (Articles 130r-t);
10. Development cooperation (Articles 130u-y).

To these ten areas must be added the two areas of "foreign affairs and security" and "justice and home affairs." In most of these 27 activity sectors, the member states are also entitled to carry out many functions on their own.[9]

Most observers see the treaty's main achievement as the establishment of the objective of economic and monetary union along with a timetable for its achievement. The EMU is designed, according to Article II of the treaty, to

promote throughout the Community harmonious and balanced development of economic activities, sustainable and uninflationary growth respecting the environment, a high degree of convergence of economic performance, a high level of employment and social protection, the raising of the standard of living and quality of life, and economic and social cohesion and solidarity among Member States.

Most of this was already embodied in earlier Community treaties. The goal of currency union, however, was established precisely in treaty form. Indeed, the treaty gives the Community exclusive authority over money, superseding any independent activity by the member states in that field.

The European Central Bank is to be established by 1999. Its precursor, the European Monetary Institute, began operation on January 1, 1994, prepared by the Committee of Central Bank Governors of the member states which had existed since 1964. In all of this, coordination of exchange and inflation rates and deficits of the member states needs still to be developed appropriately and properly. There yet have to be developed ways in which the member states collectively govern the Community's central bank, yet share their powers with the institutions of the EC.

The second pillar, designing a common policy in the fields of internal and external security and foreign affairs, is built on the experience of the European Political Cooperation Procedure (EPC) and the new Common Foreign and Security Policy (CFSP) provisions of the treaty. The CFSP remains intergovernmental in character and is not within the jurisdiction of the European Court of Justice. It must pursue its objectives through "common positions" and "joint actions." This can be translated into the current practice of EPC or into new initiatives worked out through an elaborate procedure involving qualified majorities if there is no proposal before them from the Commission, which means that they must gain a majority of at least 54 out of a possible 76 votes cast by at least eight countries. Ultimately, this should lead to a common defense policy, a task whose elaboration and implementation is entrusted to the Western European Union, at least until 1996.

The third pillar, relating to justice and home affairs, is an effort to go beyond the ad hoc machinery handling technical cooperation in fields such as law enforcement policy, customs, asylum, extradition, deportation, visa policy, and immigration. These introduce EC institutions into the process directly. Administrative costs for increasing coordination are to fall within the EC budget. The Council of Ministers is responsible for the overall program and a new body, the "K4

Committee," has been established to undertake coordination between the different intergovernmental activities. Both the European Parliament and the Court of Justice continue to be largely excluded. Most decisions are to be by equal vote of the member states.

The treaty provides that the EU is to be served by "a single institutional framework" presided over by the European Council made up of the heads of state or government and the president of the EC Commission. The powers of the European Parliament, still the weakest of the EU institutions, are also expanded. Draft laws now need to be brought before it for two readings, not merely for consultation. Five specific innovations have been introduced by the treaty, which otherwise simply codifies precedents and practices already developed by the European Community:

1. The incorporation of the principle of subsidiarity; namely, what can be done at a lower level should be, and not raised to a higher level.

2. The establishment of a limited European citizenship.

3. The introduction of a co-decision procedure between Parliament and Council.

4. The involvement of Parliament with the Council in the appointment of the Commission.

5. The setting up of the Committee of Regions to better deal with the substate governments of the members.[10]

Subsidiarity has been taken to heart as a concept by the EU leaders, although it is, in fact, a very anti-federalist idea. It was originally a Catholic doctrine designed to modify the hierarchical structure of the Catholic Church, originally for enhancing the role of the lower or smaller orders in the Church. The Founding Fathers of the European Community, so many of them coming from the Catholic tradition, lit upon this device, and applied it as a civil one to the Community. It first surfaced in the Tindemans Report on European Union of 1975 and was first formally used in European constitutional legislation in the European Parliament's 1984 draft treaty drawn up by Altiero Spinelli, one of the foremost ideologists of the Community. It was written into the Treaty of Maastricht with the encouragement of the Commission and the insistance of the Germans as a basic guideline for future activity, to control the flood of single market legislation since 1985, which member states and various interests were opposing on the grounds of too much interference in the minutiae of daily life. The German government was particularly interested in protecting the constitutional position of the *länder* within the Community and the German federal system. The British also insisted on subsidiarity to retain greater independence and freedom of action. As Duff says, "unsurprisingly, it is defined ambivalently."[11]

The great advantage of including the principle of subsidiarity in the treaty will be to establish the principle of "states rights" within the EU. How that will play out remains to be seen.

The introduction of EU citizenship is a major step forward. As introduced in the treaty, it is limited to citizens of the member states and confined to electoral rights, i.e., voting and standing for office in local and European elections, confirming the right of citizens to petition the European Parliament, the establishment of an EU ombudsman, and the possibility of sharing consular services outside the EU. It does not provide greater protection for other civil or human rights and only nationals of member states are included.

What the citizenship provision does do is strengthen the European Parliament as the voice of European citizenship, require the adoption of a uniform electoral procedure, and recognize trans-European political parties for the first time.

Introduction of the "co-decision" procedure which grants the right of legislative partnership with the Council to the European Parliament is potentially a major step. It does not make the Parliament a co-equal partner of the Council, but does give it a larger say in reviewing draft acts, as in the case of the annual budget of the EU. The treaty prescribes co-decision procedures for matters relating to the internal market, free movement of workers, trans-European networks, environmental policy, R&D, and cultural policy. Co-decision is a step beyond cooperation, the previous definition of the Parliament's power. Procedures in all of these areas will have to be developed through usage.

The Parliament has also been given a role in the selection of the Commission President and is required to approve the Commission as a whole. It has always had the power to dismiss the Commission as a whole, which it has never dared to use. Now, by simple majority it may block the nominations to the Commission by the member states' governments.

The establishment of a new Commission of the Regions by the treaty potentially confronts a major problem in the evolving EU, namely, how do constituent states of member federations express themselves within the Union. To date, regionalism in the Community has treated all regions equally, whether German *länder* and Spanish autonomous communities on one plane, Scotland and Wales on another, and Greek municipally-based regions or English planning regions on yet another. The Commission's powers are mostly the powers of consultation. A solution has not yet been found for distinguishing between federated states and other kinds of regions in relations with the EU, but new arrangements will be developed with the German *länder* and the Spanish regional governments, which are expected to assert themselves in the new body, while pressure for further decentralization within non-federal member states should grow.

Perhaps the social protocol is the weakest aspect of the new treaty since the UK is not included in it, by its choice. What is surprising is that the other eleven states went ahead even without the UK. The social protocol is a new initiative. The fact that it is asymmetrical will also make a difference in its application. Asymmetricalism is becoming more widespread in the Union's governance. Denmark has followed Britain by opting out of stage three of the EMU and the single currency, and it has gone further to opt out of the defense activities of the Western European Union (WEU). The WEU comprised only ten of the twelve member states in 1994 (it may now include thirteen out of the fifteen). On the other hand, Belgium, the Netherlands, and Luxembourg are united as Benelux, and those three plus France and Germany are united in the Schengen Agreement.

In the end, the Maastricht Treaty has enlarged the powers of the Community and transformed it into a union, but it is a confederation of commonwealths, not a federation. The treaty was written in that spirit and was further interpreted in that way even before it went into effect. In addition, on January 1, 1995, three new states—Finland, Sweden, and Austria—joined the EU after their peoples voted to do so in separate referendums. Norway, however, again rejected membership. How this will play out under Maastricht also remains to be determined.

Beyond the European Union

The EC/EU was designed strictly with its own needs in mind, as was the United States in 1787. In fact, it has become a pacesetter for a world in transformation where the simultaneous desire to maintain separate polities, either for nationalistic or democratic reasons, and the need to be united in larger political communities for security and economic reasons has to be reconciled. The result has been the emergence of efforts—at least tentative—at confederation outside of the EU as well.

Moreover, in the same way that one set of federal arrangements has begotten others in the United States and in other federations, the same thing seems to be happening in Europe. While the EU remains at the core of those arrangements, all of Western Europe and, in some cases, Europe as a whole, has developed quasi-confederal arrangements that link the European states not members of the European Union with those in the Union for limited purposes of commerce, defense, regional development, and human rights protection. Some of those non-EU states are already in the process of being accepted for membership in the EU and others may be accepted in the future, but in any case it seems that there will be a two-tier confederal approach that will ultimately embrace all of Europe west of Russia.

In addition to the European Union, the other major European confederal-type organizations are the Western European Union, the Council of Europe, the Conference on Security and Cooperation in Europe (CSCE), the European Bank for Reconstruction and Development (EBRD), and the North Atlantic Treaty Organization. The Western European Union was established in March 1948 as a treaty for collaboration in economic, social, and cultural matters and for collective self-defense between the UK, France, the Netherlands, Belgium, and Luxembourg. Its defense functions were transferred to NATO in December 1950 and in 1954 the Federal Republic of Germany and Italy acceded to the treaty. Nevertheless, it was in abeyance until October 1984 when it was reactivated as a means of strengthening the European contribution to the North Atlantic alliance. In June 1992 its mission was further broadened to include peace-keeping and humanitarian operations to be undertaken at the request of other international organizations. Spain and Portugal joined in 1988 and Greece in 1992. Denmark and Ireland are linked to the WEU as observers and Norway and Turkey as associated members.

The Council of Europe emerged from the Congress of Europe held in 1948 at the Hague, which brought together 1,000 influential Europeans from 26 countries. The Council includes 31 member states and is the organization bringing together all European democracies. Its statute was signed in London in May 1949 with ten founder members.

The North Atlantic Treaty was originally signed in April 1949. Greece and Turkey entered NATO in 1952, the Federal Republic of Germany in 1955, and Spain in 1982. It acquired political as well as military goals from the first, but it remained essentially a military alliance and provided the security umbrella under which European unity could develop in other spheres. After the demise of the Warsaw Pact in 1991 marking the end of the Cold War, it began a transformation to enter other, more political spheres of activity including coordination and cooperation with other international institutions, and involvement in international peace-keeping operations. It has also reached out to the former Communist bloc states with forms of associate membership, establishing the North Atlantic Cooperation Council to include 22 additional states from the former Eastern bloc.

The Conference on Security and Cooperation in Europe was founded on August 1, 1975 with the signing in Helsinki of the Final Act of the CSCE. Signatories included 25 participating states, all the European countries that existed at the time except Albania, plus the United States and Canada. Achievement of the Final Act came only after several years of negotiation. It declared a set of political commitments that established the basis for relations and cooperation among European states along the East-West divide in the political, economic, cultural, human, information, and military confidence-building spheres.

At first the results of the new CSCE were minimal. A second meeting only took place in late 1977 and early 1978 which simply reaffirmed the earlier commitment and called for further meetings. While experts meetings took place in the following years, it was not until 1980 that the second follow-up meeting was convened in Madrid.

It took three years of negotiations in Madrid, until September 1983, for agreement to be reached on next steps, which meant that it took until then for the Soviet Union to modify its intransigent position and accept the changes that were taking place within and around it. The highlight of the second follow-up meeting was its emphasis on human rights as an essential factor in developing international cooperation and the provision of first steps toward making that aspect real. There followed another series of experts meetings.

Then on the 10th anniversary of the signing, a commemoration meeting took place in Helsinki to reaffirm the agreement for yet another time. It was not until the following year, however, that some concrete steps began to be taken. The conference on confidence- and security-building measures in disarmament, which had opened in Stockholm at the beginning of 1984, concluded on September 19, 1986 with agreement on what came to be known as the Stockholm Document designed to reduce military tensions and the risks of confrontation, including an arms control agreement with on-site verification provisions.

Figure 5.1

OVERLAPPING MEMBERSHIPS IN EUROPE

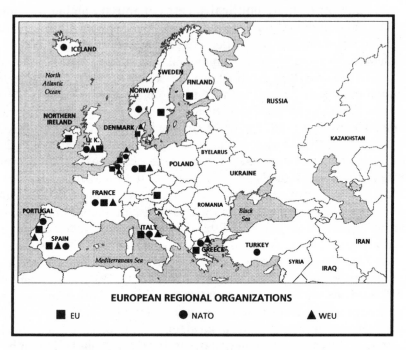

EUROPEAN REGIONAL ORGANIZATIONS

■ EU   ● NATO   ▲ WEU

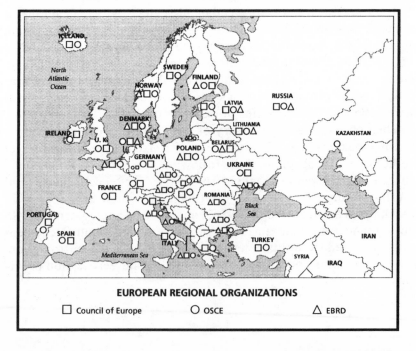

EUROPEAN REGIONAL ORGANIZATIONS

□ Council of Europe   ○ OSCE   △ EBRD

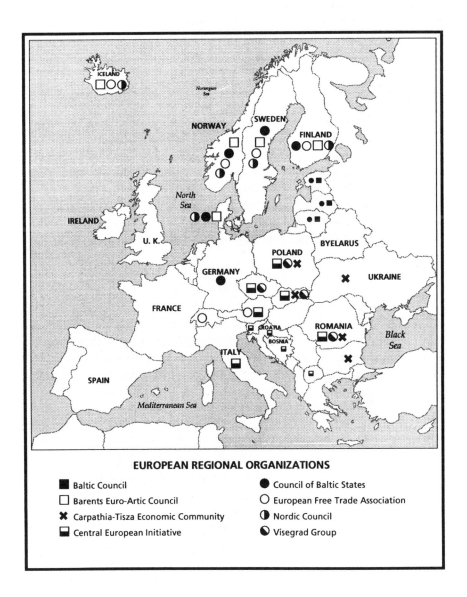

EUROPEAN REGIONAL ORGANIZATIONS

■ Baltic Council

● Council of Baltic States

□ Barents Euro-Artic Council

○ European Free Trade Association

✖ Carpathia-Tisza Economic Community

◑ Nordic Council

▱ Central European Initiative

◐ Visegrad Group

The third follow-up meeting was held in Vienna and lasted from November 1986 to January 1989. The Soviet Union, by this time beginning to seriously weaken, agreed to the concluding document which provided for a continuous monitoring mechanism on human rights issues, eliminating a signatory government's ability to raise the claim that such issues amounted to interference in their internal affairs. Premier Gorbachev of Russia, whose shift in position had enabled the Madrid meetings to be concluded successfully, took a further step in his hope to balance liberalization within the USSR and the Soviet empire and the continuation of Communist control in that part of the world. For the first time individuals were recognized as having the right to seek remedy against injustices by states.

What followed were a series of subsidiary meetings to negotiate reduction of conventional armed forces in Europe (CFE) and to develop confidence- and security-building measures.

NATO

In the meantime, the WEU, the Council of Europe, the CSCE, and NATO, which goes beyond Europe, are all becoming anchored on the EU which sustains them and gives them strength that goes beyond that of mere treaties. In the case of the North Atlantic Treaty Organization, it has two anchors, one in North America and the other in Europe, giving it even greater strength.

Originally a defensive alliance of the North Atlantic democracies led by the United States, NATO always had possibilities built into its charter for more, but never really exercised or developed any of those possibilities. Now NATO is undergoing a reevaluation as to its security role and with regard to activating at least some of those other possibilities. The halting, yet perhaps effective in the end, intervention of NATO, the Western European Union, and the CSCE in the republics of the former Yugoslavia may be a major event stimulating further moves in that direction.

In part, confederal arrangements in Western Europe were made possible by the existence of NATO, established under the aegis of the United States as a superpower. Its "umbrella" provided for Western European security and eliminated the necessity for agreement between initially hesitant partners on defense matters. Indeed, the effort to establish a Franco-German defensive union collapsed very early on but did not particularly affect the development of the European Community even then. Now, the members of the EU are beginning to concern themselves with security matters through the Western European Union, a separate body that can be used to extend its reach as a "security community" (in Karl Deutsch's terms) or, more accurately, subcommunity, considering that NATO continues to exist as the dominant body beyond the limits of the EU.

With the collapse of the Soviet Union and the Communist empire in Eastern Europe, the newly freed Eastern European states, as part of their drive for democratization and civil society, wanted to gain membership in NATO, which they saw as providing them with protection against a resurgent Russian imperialism. NATO at that time was undergoing a change in the definition of its purposes in light of the Soviet collapse, shifting from defense of the Western European and North Atlantic countries to the protection or achievement of stability throughout the world as an act of self-protection. Hence, the NATO members welcomed the initiative of the Eastern European states, but hesitantly, fearing to antagonize the Russians and to get themselves involved in an unmanageable thicket.

Their interim solution was to establish the North Atlantic Cooperation Council (NACC) as an adjunct to NATO to which twenty-two non-NATO members in Eastern Europe could adhere and be represented, and thereby be in close contact with NATO itself and its policies. As pressures for membership grew, NATO also established the Partnership for Peace (PFP) to extend a kind of associate membership of NATO eastward. This has offered a somewhat more intensive associate membership to the former Communist states, but pressures are still there for fuller membership, at least west of the old Soviet border.

Full integration involves three questions: (1) The extent to which it is useful to extend security guarantees eastward in the face of Russian opposition. (2) The political willingness, military needs and capabilities of the potential member. (3) The willingness of present NATO members to extend themselves by taking on these additional responsibilities. Signatories to the PFP participate at their own expense and in turn gain a certain access to NATO data plus military and political coordination at NATO headquarters. As of May 30, 1995, twenty-six states had become signatories to the framework document including such former neutrals as Finland and Sweden and the former Soviet Central Asian states as well, thus really making NATO and its auxiliaries extend around the world from Alaska to eastern Siberia, albeit in a very limited way. Only Switzerland has refrained from joining any of these arrangements, while Serbia apparently has not been asked. All PFP expenses are borne by the subscribing states, while NACC members' expenses are paid by NATO. While there are confederal dimensions to NATO, the NACC is an international treaty, while the PFP provides for bilateral relations between NATO and each subscribing state.

The Commonwealth of Independent States

Elsewhere in Europe, the Commonwealth of Independent States (CIS) was formed from the residue of the Union of Soviet Socialist Republics. The USSR formally was a federation based on the various ethnic/nationality groups within it, but in fact was a consolidated empire under Communist dictatorship. Hence, when the empire disintegrated, there was no will to retain the federation. Quite to the contrary, each ethnic-based union republic sought to escape the overweening power of Russia and to become independent. For that matter, most of the ethnic groups *within* Russia proper wanted to become meaningfully autonomous and were limited only by the practical need to recognize that Russia would require them to remain within a Russian federation.

On the other hand, these newly independent republics also recognized that they had certain arrangements and needs in common. The fact is that they were all part of a common ruble area and were affected by the economic fallout from that, their security needs were at least partly accommodated under the umbrella formerly provided by the USSR, and that certain other formerly imperial transactions had to be preserved, at least in a weakened way. So the Commonwealth of Independent States (CIS) was established to be formally something less than a confederation but in fact considerably more than merely a league or international treaty.[12]

As in Western Europe, the Commonwealth of Independent States consists of several joint authorities where agreement has been reached among the ex-Soviet republics, with two departures from the model of the European Community. The first is that, while general membership forms the basis of the CIS, not all states are members of the same functional authorities. Also, some functional authorities extend beyond the general membership. The second is the existence of agreed-

upon sharing arrangements that have not been formally constitutionalized. Most are survivals from the previous regime, for example, the role of the ex-Soviet, now Russian, army in the various
republics, or the existence of a common currency, or other shared
economic arrangements. In some cases, these are destined, at least in
the short term, to decline, but, in others, new constitutional arrangements are likely to emerge in due time, each on an individual basis.

The role of the Russian army, for example, has become important
in two ways. One is to guard the borders of CIS countries against
outside intervention. This is particularly a problem in Central Asia
where the CIS republics bordering on Iran have been threatened with
infiltration from that country. The other cases are where internal civil
wars within the newly independent republics have gotten out of hand
and the Russian army has intervened to halt the conflict, as in Moldova
and Georgia. Since it is not clear that the Russian leadership has made
its peace with the breakup of the old Russian empire, it may be that in
some of these latter cases Russian intrigues have led to the crises in the
first place and then Russian intervention conditioned upon the formal
adherence of those republics to the CIS has followed. This was the
case with regard to Georgia.

What is particularly interesting is that while there are civil wars
taking place within the CIS, almost all are within the newly independent republics and between ethnic groups within those republics. Only
in one case (Armenia and Azerbaijan) is a war being waged between
two independent republics over territory within Azerbaijan taken from
Armenia during the Soviet years. Despite charges and countercharges
about Russian involvement, with the latter exception, these do not
involve major inter-republic conflicts.

One potential conflict may be in the offing between Russia and
Ukraine over the Crimean peninsula. When the USSR was at the
heyday of its strength, the Soviet leadership transferred Crimea from
Russia to Ukraine. Under Communist dictatorship, this was merely a
nominal transfer. Subsequently, when Ukraine became independent,
the heavily Russian Crimea pressed for autonomy, which was granted
to it, but in a less than satisfactory (to them) way so that the Crimean
majority has continued to press for their territory to be returned to
Russia. Ukraine, of course, adamantly refuses and has countered by
revoking its grant of autonomy. To date, both sides have indicated that
whatever the problem, it should be settled by peaceful means, and have
refrained from any kind of armed intervention, but the matter is a
volatile one.

The one case where there has been an effort to actually secede from Russia itself is Chechnya. There Russia intervened militarily to bring the Chechens back into line and suffered a terrible setback. This situation remains even more volatile than any of the others, but it is an internal Russian rather than a CIS problem.

Most recently, Russian President Boris Yeltsin has announced that Russia sees its "near abroad," that is to say, the former territory of the USSR, most of which is now in the CIS, as within its special sphere of influence. This may portend additional movement either for strengthening the CIS or for reunification of some of those states with Russia itself. As of late 1994, Yeltsin's claims had not been recognized by the United States.

Meanwhile, the independent member states of the CIS have felt the necessity to resort to federalism to deal with certain of their internal ethnic problems with varying degrees of reluctance since in no case can there be found a federal political culture to make federalism attractive as an option and not just a tactical or strategic necessity. Russia, by far the largest of the CIS states, is a full-fledged federation, with 89 constituent polities, but one that seems to be trying to impose ever greater centralization with very mixed results. Other states such as Georgia and Ukraine have made provision for the constitutional autonomy of ethnic minority regions within them, three in Georgia and one in Ukraine. Belorus, on the other hand, which reluctantly accepted independence and whose people see themselves as Russians, seems to be seeking even closer ties with the Russian Federation.

The CIS represents a new departure in postmodern confederal arrangements in several ways. It is concerned with security as well as economics. Indeed, the security card has been one of the strongest cards that the Russian Federation has been able to play to get its sister republics to join the CIS. For example, Russia forced Georgia into the CIS after Georgia had refused to join. In 1993, Georgia was faced with two substantial revolts within its territory, one ethnic and one based on political rivalries. The Russians maneuvered the legitimate Georgian government under Shevardnadze into a position whereby it needed Russian military assistance, which the latter provided at the price of Georgia joining the CIS. Georgia did, and thereby, Shevardnadze and his government were saved.

The Russian presence in the central Asian republics, to the extent that it exists, also rests on Russian provision of military security against Islamic fundamentalists from Iran and Afghanistan. On the basis of that service, in 1994 Russia demanded that the ethnic Russian citizens of those republics be allowed dual citizenship, a demand which was rejected.

The precise character of the CIS is not yet clear. The Baltic states, for example, have refused to join. The government of Ukraine has been resisting Russian involvement with it, even in the economic sphere, rejecting the ruble zone and its joint currency insofar as it has been able to do so. But Ukraine itself is sharply divided between its western regions which are ethnically more purely Ukrainian and were not even part of the Soviet Union until after World War II; its eastern regions which have large ethnic Russian populations settled in them by the Soviets in an effort to consolidate their hold on Ukrainian territory; and the Crimea, a Russian territory inhabited by ethnic Russians which was only attached to the Ukrainian union republic after World War II. The latter was given autonomous status as a region within Ukraine but is struggling to make that status more than a formality. The 1994 elections in both brought to power leaders reflecting a popular desire to move closer to Russia. The consequences of their victory are yet to unfold.

The CIS continues to have its ups and downs. Two actions involving the Russian Federation, its dominant partner, in March 1996 are indicative. The Russian Parliament turned nationalist after the 1995 elections and enacted a resolution unilaterally disqualifying the 1991 breakup of the Soviet Union, a resolution with no immediate practical effect since President Yeltsin rejected it out of hand, but a sign as to which way the wind was blowing in Russia.

Three weeks later, the leaders of Russia, Belorus, Kazakhstan, and Kyrgyzstan signed an agreement providing for further integration and cooperation while promising to keep their respective states sovereign. The essence of the agreement was to create a tighter community within the CIS, one that would allow freer movement of people, services, goods, and capital, and might even lead to the introduction of a single currency. On the signing of the agreement, Yeltsin said, "The person who does not regret the dissolution of the Soviet Union does not have a heart, but the one who wants to reproduce it in full does not have a head."

Nevertheless, the pact calls for closer political, economic, trade, and cultural ties, and envisages a common market of goods and services, unified transportation and communication, and a common currency. These goals are hardly different than the stated goals of the CIS, but whereas the twelve CIS members cannot agree to the steps required to reach them, the four inaugurated a new inner circle. It also leaves the door open for other CIS members to join. Three days later, at the beginning of April, Russia and Belorus signed an even more far-reaching agreement providing for even greater integration of the two countries while proclaiming that each will keep its sovereignty and independence.[13]

Notes

1. Daniel J. Elazar, *Exploring Federalism* (Tuscaloosa, Ala.: University of Alabama Press, 1987); Forsyth, *Unions of States, op. cit.*

2. Andrew C. McLaughlin, *The Foundation of American Constitutionalism* (Greenwich, CT: Fawcett Publications, 1961); Donald Lutz, *The Origins of American Constitutionalism* (Baton Rouge: Louisiana State University Press, 1988); D.W. Meinig, *The Shaping of America* (New Haven: Yale University Press, 1986).

3. Raymond Breton, *Cultural Boundaries and the Cohesion of Canada* (Montreal: Institute for Research on Public Policy, 1980); *idem., The Governance of Ethnic Communities: Political Structures and Processes in Canada* (New York: Greenwood Press, 1991); Ivo Duchacek, "Antagonistic Cooperation: Territorial and Ethnic Communitites," *Publius*, vol. 7, no. 4 (Fall 1977).

4. Jurg Steiner, *Gewaltlose Politik und Kulturelle Vielfalt* (Bern: P. Haupt, 1970).

5. Derek Urwin, *The Community of Europe: A History of European Integration Since 1945* (London: Longman, 1991); David Weigall and Peter Stirk, eds., *The Origins and Development of the European Community* (Leicester: Leicester University Press, 1992).

6. Michael Burgess, ed., *Federalism and Federation in Western Europe* (London: Croom Helm, 1986); Urwin, *ibid.*

7. House of Commons Debate, 4 November 1992, column 288.

8. Frederick K. Lister, *The European Union, the United Nations and the Revival of Confederal Governance* (Westport, CT: Greenwood Press, 1996), pp. 85-86.

9. *Ibid*, p. 86

10. Andrew Duff, "The Main Reform," in Andrew Duff, John Tinder, and Roy Pryce, *Maastricht and Beyond* (London and New York: Routledge, 1994), pp. 26-27.

11. Duff, p. 27.

12. Timothy J. Colton and Robert Legvold, eds., *After the Soviet Union: From Empire to Nations* (New York: Norton, 1992); John B. Dunlop,

The Rise of Russia and the Fall of the Soviet Empire (Princeton: Princeton University Press, 1993).

13. "Russia and Three Ex-Republics Seal Closer Ties," *International Herald Tribune*, March 30-31, 1996, p. 2.

Chapter 6

OTHER CONFEDERAL ARRANGEMENTS

The Caribbean Area

Perhaps the second most developed confederal arrangement, after the EU, is the Caribbean Community, embracing islands in what were formerly the British West Indies. They tried federation in the 1960s as the West Indies Federation while they were still under British rule, under pressure from Great Britian. It failed, perhaps because islands are by definition insular.[1]

However, as the West Indies Federation failed, those same islands retained, established, or preserved a congeries of functional authorities that united them for the purposes of economic development (e.g., CARICOM, the Caribbean Common Market), education (a common University of the West Indies), currency, administration of justice (a common supreme court), defense, and foreign relations that are slowly evolving into a new-style confederation in that region. These important confederal elements survived because the same islands, however insular, could not support a full range of governmental institutions nor could such institutions effectively serve such small territories by themselves. The best known of those institutions is CARICOM, an economic community that was to be like the EC. It also has been perhaps the least successful. Far less well known and far more successful have been the common university, the common supreme court, and the common monetary system.

As the islands became independent one by one or group by group, these and similar links between them were strengthened, so that today the Caribbean Community is a confederation in all but name and even

CARICOM is gaining in strength. Here, too, security concerns have been in the hands of outsiders, first Great Britain and then the United States, although there has been inter-island cooperation in security matters at least nominally, as in the case of the U.S. invasion of Grenada at the request of other member states of the region.[2]

The treaty establishing the Caribbean Community included the establishment of CARICOM with a common external tariff. It was signed by the prime ministers of Barbados, Guyana, Jamaica, and Trinidad and Tobago in Trinidad in July 1973 and entered into force at the beginning of August of that year. In April 1974, Belize, Dominica, Grenada, St. Lucia, and St. Vincent and Montserrat signed the treaty, and in July 1974 Antigua and the Associated State of St. Kitts-Nevis-Angula joined. The Bahamas became a member of the Community but not of the Common Market in July 1983. The Caribbean Community is concerned with economic cooperation, foreign policy coordination, and functional cooperation in various fields including health, education, culture, sports, science and technology, and tax administration. The Common Market has been slow to develop, but cooperation in other areas has progressed in various ways.

The Community's principal organ is the Conference of Heads of Government. Second to it is the Caribbean Community Council of Ministers, with each government designating its minister member. In January 1993 the Bureau of Heads of Government was established with a secretary general and the chairman rotating on a six-month basis. The Community also has a secretariat, a conference of health ministers, and standing committees on education, tourism, labor, foreign affairs, finance, agriculture, energy, mines and natural resources, industry, science, technology, transport, and legal affairs. The Caribbean Development Bank, Caribbean Examinations Council, Council of Legal Education, University of the West Indies, University of Guyana, and the Caribbean Meteorological Organization are associate institutions. The Community also has its own flag.

These arrangements embrace the English-speaking islands. The French-speaking islands have gone in a very different direction, to become self-governing departments of France, and as such are parts of the European Union. The Dutch-speaking islands developed in a third way, as separate self-governing entities within a common Kingdom of the Netherlands that is formally federal and further linked by informal political and economic connections.

ASEAN

The Association of Southeast Asian Nations (ASEAN) is another potential confederation. Already more than a league, ASEAN was established in response to the military threat to Southeast Asia in the 1960s as a result of the Vietnam War. ASEAN is constituted by six independent states: Thailand, Malaysia, Singapore, Indonesia, Brunei, and the Philippines, each of which (with the possible exception of Brunei, which Great Britain forced to accept independence) is known for jealously guarding its independence, but all understand that they have a common defense interest at the very least and growing common interests in the economic and social realms as well.

ASEAN was founded through the Bangkok Declaration in August 1967. The original five member states were joined by Brunei in 1984. Laos, Papua New Guinea, and Vietnam have observer status. Its main objectives are to accelerate economic growth, social progress, and cultural development, to promote active collaboration and mutual assistance on matters of common interest, and to ensure the stability of the Southeast Asian region. ASEAN maintains close cooperation with existing international and regional organizations with similar aims.

Since ASEAN is not a confederation but a confederal arrangement, it is less well developed institutionally than the European Union. Its highest authority is vested in the heads of governments of the member countries. Its highest policy-making body is the annual meeting of the foreign ministers, which has a standing committee that rotates between countries and is headed by the foreign minister of the annual host country. Work is conducted through five economic committees and five noneconomic committees, and an ASEAN national secretariat located in the capital of each member state. There is a central secretariat headed by a Secretary General, a post that revolves among the member states in alphabetical order every three years. In 1991 the ASEAN Free Trade Area (AFTA) was established with the aim of creating a common market by 2006, beginning with a Common Effective Preferential Tariff (CEPT) that went into effect at the beginning of 1993.

Although established originally as a defensive alliance against the potential expansion of Communism through Vietnam, ASEAN has shifted to social and economic pursuits while defense tasks have moved elsewhere. As in the case of the European Union, this seems to be very helpful in enabling ASEAN to pursue an agenda of peace and not to need to worry much about a common security agenda. For the ASEAN area, the five-power defense arrangement established in 1971 involving Australia, Britain, Malaysia, New Zealand, and Singapore is the key defensive factor. It is not a military pact like NATO and does not require the stationing of multinational forces within ASEAN, but the FPDA regularly holds maneuvers in the area. These defense exercises include naval, land, and air defense.

Not only are the ASEAN states exploring new forms of economic integration, but the states of former French Indochina—Vietnam, Laos, and Cambodia—now are seeking admission to ASEAN and early in 1994 received the backing of the United States for taking that step. ASEAN itself is exploring ways in which it as a unit can become part of the emerging greater Asia-Pacific trading and security leagues.[3]

New Constitutional Techniques

The revival of confederation as a viable option seems to have been made possible by the development of a new constitutional technique. Federations and confederations alike must rest on written constitutional agreements that establish the terms of the federal bargain and the rules of the game. In the past, founders of both have written single comprehensive constitutional documents to do just that.

New-style confederations, on the other hand, have been established through limited constitutional agreements among the partners on specific topics. The European Union pioneered this technique, beginning with the various Treaties of Rome, first establishing a coal and steel community, and then adding other areas of first economic and then political integration, culminating so far in the Single Europe Act and the Maastricht Treaty. Thus, the constituting states needed only to agree on which functions they wanted to provide in common as they reached consensus, enabling them to maintain more reserved powers than in a federation.

The same arrangement holds true for the Caribbean Community. The ex-Soviet republics have embarked on the same course, initialing an agreement on economic union that now has to be fleshed out constitutionally, and entering into multilateral and bilateral negotiations and agreements with regard to some kind of defense or military union as well. On the other hand, Yugoslavia, which tried to build confederation without establishing the necessary constitutional arrangements in this manner, has slid into civil war and again has dissolved into its original form. Senegambia dissolved without war and Canada has been seeking to avoid dissolution by political means. All of the leagues and common markets on the list can be found to have some arrangements that seem confederal, but all are at the early stages of the confederal linking process.

This "functional" technique seems to resolve the problems of constitutional design in confederations. We have yet to see whether it can solve the problem of governance. While there is even less of a set institutional designs for these confederations or incipient confederations, we are beginning to note patterns. In the first place, the principal institutions tend to be collegial rather than executive or parliamentary. Councils of ministers of the member polities are the most prominent institutions. This is true in the European Community, on one end of the spectrum. On the other end, as Canada has moved in the direction of confederalizing its federation, the First Ministers' Conference, consisting of the federal prime minister and the premiers of the provinces, became the most significant policy-making body for that country. Obviously, where confederal arrangements are even more limited than in the EU, councils of ministers or their equivalent have an even greater share of the authority and powers vested in the confederal entity.

The other institutions can be seen to be more developed, the more integrated the confederal polity becomes. Thus, for example, there are executive institutions with varying degrees of importance, ranging from secretariats with relatively little power to the European Commission which represents the executive power for the European Union. By and large, these are mainly bureaucracies manned by professional civil servants, presumably with little discretionary decision-making power beyond the strictly administrative. In the case of secretariats this is normally true. In the case of a body such as the European Commission which presides over a massive and powerful bureaucratic structure, it is less so. That is why as the executives of the confederal polities are strengthened, an appropriately confederal policy-making structure headed by political figures is added to them. In the case of the European Union, the European Commission constitutes the plural political executive that is meant to control the bureaucracy. It includes political representatives of every member state and is headed by a president elected by the commission as a whole from among its members who, while not a full executive president, does have certain executive powers.

A parliamentary arm is one of the last additions in these new-style confederal arrangements, since it requires a much higher degree of political integration of the confederal polity and its member states. Often, it is established as an advisory body, and even if it becomes an elected parliament as in the EU, its powers are very limited and its role is more advisory or modificatory than original or initiatory. It becomes more of a forum for the various member-state parties to coalesce with their equivalents from other member states into accepted parliamentary blocs, i.e., social democratic, conservative, liberal, green, fascist, or whatever. In essence, there is a competition between the council of ministers and the parliamentary body for the same powers.

It is particularly important to note the expanded role of constitutional courts in these new-style confederacies. The reliance on constitutional courts is a federal device originally developed for the United States of America under the Constitution of 1787. (Although judicial review was not explicitly authorized by that constitution, it was asserted by the Supreme Court within fifteen years of the constitution's adoption.) The reliance upon constitutional courts to settle disputes within the spheres of competence of the confederacy is one of the principal inventions or adaptations in new-style confederations. Hence, constitutional courts often are second in power only to councils of ministers. Normally, they, too, are constituted on a confederal basis with judges appointed from all of the confederal units.

Normally, federations are designed on a tripartite basis—the classic legislative, executive, judicial division of powers—and on a tri-arena basis—federal, state, and local. New-style confederations, on the other hand, are more likely to be based upon a quadripartite and quadra-arena structure. The EU is a good example. The Council of Ministers has the primary legislative function, the Commission the primary executive function, and the Constitutional Court the primary judicial function, but there also is a Parliament which has a consultative-advisory function.

With regard to arenas, there is the state arena consisting of the national states that are members of the EU. The EU constitutes another arena that embraces those states. Within those states are the federated states/regional arenas—the *länder* of Germany, the federated regions of Belgium, the autonomous communities of Spain, the four countries of Great Britain, etc., and within them are the local arenas. The national state arenas are the least flexible; the EU arena more so because new members can be added (or, in theory, members can secede); the federated states/regional arena has about the same degree of rigidity and flexibility as the EU; while the greatest flexibility exists in the local arenas.

The governance of the EU is predominantly collegial, rather than single-headed or parliamentary, that is to say, in the hands of small groups of individuals with equal standing because of whom they represent. This has advantages and disadvantages, but may very well be one of the hallmarks of confederations and confederal arrangements. As a result, institutional functions differ between federations and confederations nearly as much as they do between confederations and modern-style states.

Figure 6.1

THE EUROPEAN COMMUNITY AS A MATRIX

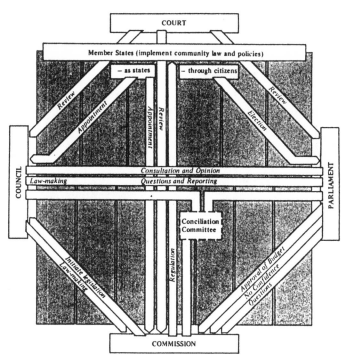

The other difference between earlier and contemporary confederations is that the primary purpose of earlier confederations was military security, while in postmodern confederations it is economic. This shift from a concern with peace to a concern with prosperity reflects the change in the world's security situation whereby security umbrellas are provided through separate leagues and alliances led by dominant "great powers," in most cases, which themselves may embody certain confederal arrangements, though, because they are not perpetual, are not confederations. The CIS experiment may be the exception to this. Even there, the economic issue has been placed first in the confederation process, with security second.

Confederal Interconnections in the New International System

Meanwhile, in a third arena, the interconnections that are not quite confederal but have more constitutional substance than mere treaties or alliances are spreading. The North American Free Trade Association (NAFTA) linking Canada, the United States, and Mexico; the General Agreement on Tariffs and Trade (GATT) for almost the entire free-market world (166 member states), now the World Trade Organization (WTO); the ties between the "Group of Seven" and the desire of other states to be admitted into that company, each in its own way, are an example of this. What is characteristic of them all is that, even when they seem to be no more than treaties, they are not treaties that any one state can abandon without incurring severe costs.

On the contrary, their member states want to be part of those frameworks because they have found them advantageous. This means that when crises occur, usually around renegotiations to resolve outstanding problems and to expand the scope of the association, in the end, the negotiations are successfully completed. Not only are the specific problems resolved, but there often is movement in the direction of further expansion as well.

Free Trade Areas

Other potential confederal arrangements may be emerging in the form of constitutionalized leagues in conjunction with regional economic arrangements in other parts of the world, particularly free trade areas. This, indeed, was one of the key elements in the formation of the European Community in the 1950s. The most advanced of these emerging new arrangements is to be found in the relationship between Australia and New Zealand that dates back to the Canberra Pact of 1944 which provided the constitutional basis for the two to continue to work together on the security and economic spheres as they had as British colonies and dominions during the previous one hundred years.[4]

Originally, these arrangements dealt primarily with security issues. It should be remembered that Australia and New Zealand fought under joint commands in both world wars. The famed ANZACS not only were well-publicized, but covered themselves with glory at Gallipoli, in France, and in North Africa, as well as on other fronts in both wars.

It was not until the 1960s that pressures emerged in New Zealand for effective economic cooperation. In 1965, the partial free trade agreement establishing the New Zealand and Australia Free Trade Area (NAFTA) was signed between Australia and New Zealand. Perhaps because New Zealand, rather than the far larger Australia, was the principal initiator of NAFTA, the actual implementation of the agreement became bogged down in endless negotiations. At that point, another round of discussions between Australia and New Zealand began and lasted for four years. The result was the ANZCER agreement signed in 1983 whose purpose was to broaden the free trade agreement and build a new timetable for it to be fully effective by 1995. At the same time, free trade arrangements were negotiated with the other South Pacific nations, leading to SPARTECA.

A five-year review of ANZCER followed where difficulties ranging from dumping to state preferences were resolved and the 1995 final date was brought forward to 1990. Plans for harmonization under ANZCER include banking, business law, broadcasting, civil aviation, communications, competition policy, currency, customs, industry assistance, insurance, investment services, shipping, standards, taxation, and tariffs. Transportation and communications are already far along the way toward harmonization. At the same time, there are now regular meetings of the state ministers of both countries to build up connections between executives. Predictions are already being made as to what this will do to the sovereignty of each country. Supporters of Australian-New Zealand economic union are also concerned about the development of the South Pacific regional grouping.

Meanwhile, in North America, the United States has taken the lead in developing the North American Free Trade Area (NAFTA) to include the U.S., Canada, and Mexico. A treaty establishing the free trade area was signed and ratified by all three and went into effect on January 1, 1994. Not as far-reaching as the Australian-New Zealand arrangements, it still is a major step in the direction of a new relationship between the three countries, again, initiated through economic arrangements.

Within its first few months the agreement produced movement of firms from Canada and the United States to Mexico, to the great dissatisfaction of Canadian and American workers, and helped precipitate a peasant revolt in the state of Chiapas in Mexico to which the response by the Mexican government was to agree to greater democratization, fearful of the revolt's impact on NAFTA.[5] Mexico, indeed, seems to be very serious in its efforts to join the North American democratic "club," seeing NAFTA as more than an economic pact but also as a chance for Mexico to pull itself up politically and socially as well. One sees these efforts not only with regard to dissident groups, but with regard to honesty in elections and increasing the real power of state and local governments in what always has been a very highly centralized federal system.

The five independent states of Central America have attempted to establish a common market, or at least something between that and a free trade area, reviving old ideas of Central American confederation that go back to the nineteenth century. Indeed, the five started as a confederation when they gained their independence from Spain, one of the nineteenth-century experiments in that line. However, social and cultural localism coupled with local political ambitions and the ideology of modern statism and nationalism led to the failure of that Central American confederation after thirteen years (1825-1838) of nominal existence. Other common markets or free trade areas have been initiated in South America, all of which function principally on paper to date.[6]

In the wake of the establishment of NAFTA, the two very large states of South America—Argentina and Brazil and their smaller neighbors, Paraguay and Uruguay—came to the conclusion that they had no choice but to organize their own trading arrangement, so in 1994 they established MERCOSUR, the fourth largest regional body after NAFTA, the EU, and ASEAN. MERCOSUR came into existence on June 1, 1995, as a customs union more than a true free trade zone. MERCOSUR embraces 195 million people and covers an area of twelve million square kilometers, with a combined domestic product of over $800 billion and a total foreign trade of $100 billion, almost 60 percent of the total economic output of Latin America. While the members of MERCOSUR have made substantial strides towards freer trade across their common borders, they themselves claim that the most important service MERCOSUR has provided has been to serve as a successful forum for dispute resolution and policy coordination, especially in the wake of the Mexican peso crisis. MERCOSUR has proclaimed the European Union as its model and has also signed an agreement with it to work toward the first interregional free trade agreement, thereby continuing the traditional European-Latin American ties.[7]

A good example of how rapidly this idea has become not only accepted but viewed as necessary among the world's states is the rapid emergence of the Southern African Development Community on the heels of the collapse of the apartheid regime in the Republic of South Africa. For many years, the states of southern Africa have realized that their economies were interdependent, whether with regard to railroads, ports, and the transportation of goods throughout the region, or with regard to the labor force which involved considerable interstate migration into the Republic of South Africa from the states to the north of it, or in the matter of trade. The RSA wanted to develop some kind of regional arrangement even under the old regime, but for obvious reasons the black majority states to the north of it were reluctant to move too far.

Once the new regime was installed in South Africa, it became possible to move ahead and under President Nelson Mandela's leadership, serious steps were taken, leading to the convening of the Southern African Community Development Summit in Johannesburg on August 25, 1995, which was hailed in the South African black press as the climax of a "tireless fifteen-year-long struggle of the region for the economic emancipation of its people."

The pattern is similar to other such regional arrangements. A developed core state, in this case the Republic of South Africa, serves as a magnet and convener for economically weaker adjacent states. The core state itself has incorporated federal principles within its internal structure, opening it up to looser arrangements with the other member states in the economic sphere.

The summit decided to move toward a free trade area embracing the twelve member-states of Southern Africa.[8] More than that, at an earlier meeting in Harare, Zimbabwe, in March 1995, the SADC foreign ministers drew up a proposal for an association to promote regional peace, democracy, and security, to be known as the Association of Southern African States (ASAS). This association needs to be endorsed by SADC, but since it involves common security arrangements, there have been second thoughts and formal steps are now expected to take somewhat longer, although the direction is clear. Thus Southern Africa will enter into the block of regional economic associations that are concerned with economics plus. It is already talking about closer relations with its two neighbors in the Southern Hemisphere, ASEAN and MERCOSUR, its southern Latin American counterpart.

It is through this third arena that the merging of the two state systems of the modern world is taking place. The "politically sovereign" states, of which there are over 180, and the constituent or federal states, of which there are over 350 or twice as many, are merging into a single international system for most purposes. We already have discussed how the politically sovereign states are being linked, but it is also important to note that the federal states, which under the constitutions and terms of reference of modern federations were confined to internal matters (if there was anything that was certain about modern federations it was that foreign affairs were entrusted to the federation government and were forbidden to the constituent states), slowly began to acquire formal or informal powers in matters of transborder and international relations, especially when they had other federal states attached to other federations along their borders.[9]

Thus, federal Switzerland has developed closer transborder relations with federal Germany than with unitary France. In the 1970s, when the executive director of the Regio Basiliensis, which serves the Basel region, including southeastern France, southwestern Germany, and northwestern Switzerland, would negotiate with France, he was received on the seventh floor of the Quay D'Orsai (the French Foreign Ministry), while the Swiss ambassador was only received on the fifth floor. On the other hand, when he had to arrange any transborder arrangement with Alsace, he had to go to Paris, while with regard to Baden-Württemberg (the German state bordering Basel and the other northwestern Swiss cantons) he went to Stuttgart, the *land* capital.

By the 1960s, the revolution in international economics had put the federal states, even in the United States and other large federations, in the position of beginning to market the products produced within them or to seek outside investment for economic development by extending themselves worldwide, at least to the major cities of the principal trading partners of their federations. One by one, the states of the United States opened offices in Brussels for the European Community, then in Japan for that country and east Asia, and often elsewhere as well. The American federal government, recognizing that it could not do as well in either encouraging sales or investments, encouraged the states in that direction as early as the Kennedy administration (1961-1963).

In its struggle with Canada for greater cultural integrity and political independence, the Canadian province of Quebec developed its own foreign relations activities with the blessings, however reluctant, of the Canadian federal government. Its efforts were primarily cultural and economic, and were encouraged by President Charles de Gaulle of France as part of his conception of the cultural alliance of all Francophone polities to strengthen the position of France in the world. After Quebec's successful sorties abroad, other provinces also began to be active in foreign affairs. To keep on top of matters, the Canadian government decided to establish a division for provincial activities within its foreign ministry and to provide a formal place for those provinces that sought it in Canada's foreign policy activities. Examples like this can be multiplied in country after country.

In most cases, where the federal states are proactive, they do not act through comprehensive foreign ministries but through focused functional authorities, rarely given a separate designation as responsible for foreign affairs of any kind. (Canada is somewhat of an exception in this.) But, however undertaken, this puts the federal states that are augmenting their presence in foreign affairs more on a par with the politically sovereign states that are losing their powers of independent action in that sphere.

The phenomenon has been helped along by the development of institutionalized interest groups around each of these regional, interregional, and international bodies that have a stake in making those bodies stronger, just as other interest groups that have a stake in making more formally federal bodies stronger in various countries and regions. The strengthening of these constitutionalized arrangements is in no small measure due to the work and support of these interest groups.

This is also beginning to lead—slowly—to the development of a cadre of international civil servants and diplomats who have had to learn to work federally, using very different diplomatic techniques than those of foreign relations among states in the modern epoch, just as the latter were so different from the foreign relations among rulers in premodern times. Little, if any, attention has been paid to this latter phenomenon, neither in studying it nor in helping these new cadres to prepare themselves.

In the last analysis, confederation and confederal arrangements are not only being revived as a species of federalism but are transforming world affairs. We have yet to explore this dynamic process of change or to understand its ground rules. We are just scratching the surface.

Unfolding Possibilities

One of the most prominent possibilities for new confederal arrangements is to be found in the Middle East now that Israel and the Palestinians have signed two agreements to make peace. Suggestions for using federal arrangements to solve the problem of the territory embraced by British Mandatory Palestine between 1921 and 1948 were not infrequent and came in many varieties. Rarely were they ever spelled out beyond the idea itself. Indeed, the partition plan proposed and adopted by the United Nations in 1947 provided for such confederal arrangements between the Jewish and Arab states that were to be established by it, without using the term, since that was even before the EC. The Arab rejection of the plan led to its rapid demise, and when it is recalled at all today, it is thought of only in terms of the partition of western Palestine between the two states and almost never with regard to the arrangements the plan required to be established linking them.

Partition (separation) as the basis for a solution to the conflict was the order of the day from 1921 (when Transjordan was separated from western Palestine) to the 1970s when serious talk of federal solutions was revived and at least partly embodied in the Camp David agreement between Egypt and Israel (1979). The 1993 Israel-Palestinian agreement rests on the idea that, minimally, the Palestinian entity that will emerge will be confederated with Jordan and that it will have a variety of confederal linkages with Israel through joint authorities and shared functions.[10] When Jordan publicly joined the peace process a year later, it included an apparent willingness to develop joint authorities with Israel in a number of spheres with or without the Palestinians, thereby strengthening the possibility that some set of confederal arrangements will form the basis for a constitutionalized linkage between Israel, the Palestinians, and Jordan when the peace process comes to a successful conclusion. All of this needs to be worked out in practice with powerful voices on both sides seeking maximum separation. There will be great problems ahead in devising joint arrangements, but as was predicted by some in the aftermath of the Six-Day War of 1967, such arrangements, particularly their confederal variations, seem to be almost inexorably the only way to achieve peace.[11]

A very different arrangement has been suggested for Northern Ireland. The Ulster Protestant majority is committed to remaining firmly a part of Great Britain, while the Catholic minority feel that they can only achieve a safe future through unification with the Republic of Ireland. The major interest of the two states involved lies in establishing peace in the area. Among the proposals bruited about for doing so is to make Northern Ireland internally autonomous under joint British-Irish rule, a condominium, essentially following the pattern established centuries ago for Andorra which is de facto independent, limited only by the joint suzerainty of the president of France and the Bishop of Urgel in Spain. Many obstacles lie in the path of this solution, but to date, it remains the most promising of any suggested.

The New Paradigm

It is still too early to predict whether these confederations and confederal arrangements will succeed as such, but the chances are that the development of worldwide, multilateral, overlapping, linking institutions embracing formally sovereign states, to which all nations will have to be attached in one way or another, offers the opportunity for and will place demands on smaller nationalisms and localisms to find their place in the sun through confederal political arrangements of one sort or another. These may still be called "statehood" and "sovereignty," but with a very different meaning than those terms had during the modern epoch. The modern terms may survive, but implicit within them will be federal limitations of one kind or another, somewhere between the constituent states of federations and the sovereign states defined and recognized by modern international law.

Even international law is beginning to reflect this paradigm change. Modern international law was born in the years following the Treaty of Westphalia to embody the new statist system and to anchor it juridically and philosophically as well. In time, it became one of the greatest barriers to the introduction of a federalist paradigm because practitioners in the international arena were trained, formally or informally, to think and talk in terms of state sovereignty as defined by international law and to insist on those terms for their states.

Now this is changing. Students of jurisprudence are beginning to note how many provisions for combining self-rule and shared rule are finding their way into international law and are embodied within it in the formalistic ways that law requires. To give but one example, the Vatican is a politically sovereign state in international law and, indeed, was given that status after the unification of Italy and the annexation of the medieval Papal States by the latter, so that the pope would not have to be under the temporal sovereignty of anyone else. However, police powers in Vatican City are, by international law, in the hands of the Italian government, as are the provision of most ordinary domestic functions of government, making Vatican City an associated state. There is an interesting twist in this. In most similar arrangements, associated states retain full or very substantial powers over their domestic affairs but are bound to larger states for their foreign affairs and defense; but in the case of the Vatican, its foreign affairs are precisely its major powers, while domestic and police powers are in the hands of the Italian state. The growing expression of these new arrangements in international law with all their complexity is just beginning to be recognized.[12]

While the ties that increasingly bind the nations of the world are not yet confederal, it is becoming increasingly difficult for any of the existing states to think of withdrawing from the international bodies in which they are united and "going it alone," whether we are speaking of the International Postal Union, the World Trade Organization, or the United Nations itself.[13] Indeed, once the bipolarization of the world evaporated in the wake of the collapse of the Communist bloc, the United Nations began to acquire an ever greater role and may someday become the basis for a new world order. This will probably be a slow process and, in the process, may require the strengthening of such regional bodies as NATO or bodies of especially powerful states such as the G-7 Group. In many respects, the growth of regional trading blocs in recent years are counterbalances to the United Nations and other worldwide international organizations.[14]

The Communist bloc collapsed in 1989, making it possible for the UN to expand its ability to make decisions on worldwide peace-keeping efforts. The result was that, by 1993, the United Nations had

80,000 troops seconded to it by its member states serving in peace-keeping missions under the UN flag in various parts of the world and talks were under way that could involve somewhere between 50,000 and 75,000 more in the near future.[15]

By 1994 the more powerful states of the world began to see the UN as overreaching itself in its peace-keeping efforts. Together they halted this trend and instead either took responsibility upon themselves to intervene directly (as France did in Rwanda in the summer of 1994) or took the lead in securing troops from various countries under UN authorization (as the United States did in the case of Haiti in the fall of 1994). In some cases, such as Bosnia and other parts of ex-Yugoslavia, national, regional, and UN peace-keeping forces all intervened, leading to jurisdictional disputes between them from time to time. To date, these have been kept under control, but the potential for greater problems remains.

There are real dangers in this trend as well as much promise. Political and institutional arrangements should not progress faster than agreement on the norms and values underlying them. Moreover, it is not at all clear that such agreement is desirable, given the present state of the world. The idea of confederal arrangements is that they do not require the same level of agreement on values or basic moral principles that more far-reaching linkages of people and peoples do, but they still require some.

Experience should teach us that concentrations of potentially coercive power, where they exist, can be brought to bear against dissidents—dissident polities as well as individuals—whether justified or not, and that great care must be taken before entrusting power to anybody to secure control over its invocation, exercise, and consequences. We have already heard echoes of this problem in the specific debates over the changes that have taken place. Does NAFTA help Canada, Mexico, and the United States to advance economically, or does it help make a few corporations wealthier at the expense of many workers who lose their jobs in the name of economic "progress"? Will Mexico become more democratic as a result? Will Quebec be encouraged to secede from Canada because it will have an alternative economic umbrella? Will the U.S. federal government further preempt state powers to "fulfill" NAFTA agreements?[16]

Are Western standards of human rights always applicable to non-Western peoples no matter what their customs and cultures call for? Are the premises of radical individualism that underlie so many of the new international efforts at influence, if not control, of the domestic policies of states and peoples always appropriate? Is there a place for group rights? Conversely, how do group rights affect the liberty of individuals to be themselves, and how much should a massive set of multinational orders impose group authority on "deviant" individuals?

These are all very serious questions, indeed, that strike at the very heart of what seems to be happening on a piecemeal basis without advanced strategic planning. That is probably to the good since the good things that are happening in this sphere probably would not have, had advanced strategic planning been required from the first. Nevertheless, it may be asked, when does ad hocery and its results reach its limits and strategic planning become necessary.

In essence, the Maastricht Treaty bringing into existence the European Union is an example of a step beyond ad hocery into an effort at strategic planning, but it was an effort already limited by the "facts" established through ad hoc developments. What does that tell us about the limitations of humans, including human institutions, to develop and grow? The federal convention that wrote the United States Constitution in 1787 also can be seen as a form of strategic planning. Its members assumed that the existing confederation had to be scrapped and that an entirely new edifice had to be erected. Americans are used to celebrating the virtues of that choice. Now we need to look at its drawbacks and misassessments as well.

Failures and Partial Efforts

This record of movement to new-style confederation is not unidirectional or unblemished. One precursor of new-style confederation, the East African Community, developed in the twentieth century under British colonial rule to link Kenya, Tanganyika, and Uganda, collapsed after each of those colonies became independent states, despite the fact that it had tangible functions, such as the East African Railroad, that were useful to all three. As we know, almost any irrational political ambitions and passions can overcome even the most sensible and rational political behavior, in a very wide variety of ways, anywhere.[17]

Another confederal effort that failed more recently was that of Senegambia, the formal confederation of Senegal and Gambia, which is almost dictated by geography and which was tried for all of the classic reasons for confederal arrangements, principally security. It was based upon a comprehensive confederal government and the transfer, at least on paper, of substantial powers to it by the constituent states in one fell swoop. It was disbanded in 1989. Nevertheless, confederal arrangements more along the lines of the postmodern experiments still link Senegal and Gambia. Indeed, faithfulness to classic models may have been why the original confederation did not succeed. It had too little of the new-style confederal arrangements in its composition and purposes so it may have aspired to be too comprehensive. Now, in the wake of its collapse, the two states are trying to form joint authorities to handle those tasks that must be shared.[18]

Yugoslavia, established by Josef Broz Tito after World War II as a Communist-dominated federation, drifted from federation to de facto confederation after Tito's death. The combination of Slovenian and Croatian demands to formally constitutionalize this shift and the unwillingness of the Serbs to acknowledge the change and embody it in a new constitution led to the present crisis in that polity (or congeries of polities) whose seceding republics all indicated initially that they were prepared to remain linked confederally, but not by federation. Slovenia and Croatia, seceded, apparently encouraged by Germany, their old ally. Serbia's ex-Communist leaders, seeking to hold onto their power as Communism dissolved, used deeply entrenched Serbian national grievances to initiate a power play to unite all Serbs in one Serbian state through invasion and "ethnic cleansing" of the neighboring republics, leading to a bloody ethnic-based civil war.[19]

Yugoslavia survives as a kind of greater Serbia and even survives formally as a federation, linking Serbia and Montenegro, with the possibility that the Serbian-occupied sections of Bosnia and Croatia will be federated with the other two as separate republics as well. Slovenia, Croatia, and Macedonia have become independent states. As of this writing, Bosnia is the principal battleground in the civil war, with Serbs and Croats, contesting with the Bosnian authorities for control. Proposed solutions revolve mainly around the establishment of a federation or a confederation in Bosnia that would give the Serbs, Croats, and Bosnian Muslims each a piece of the former republic as political entities of their own. At this writing, Croatia and Bosnia formally have established a two-state confederation.[20]

At the same time, there may be other decentralizing developments in existing federations that may lead to more confederal arrangements. Quebec has been demanding a special status in Canada that it has called "sovereignty-association" and, while English Canada has been standing fast in opposition to that arrangement in principle, in fact, a certain recognition of Quebec's special place in Canada has been granted on an issue-by-issue basis, even as sovereignty-association has been rejected as a general principle.[21] In the United States, where no such open demands have been made, the six states of New England and the thirteen states of the South have developed institutionalized interstate ties that may, in time, point in the direction of sectional confederal arrangements within the larger Union.

Notes

1. Amitai Etzioni, *Political Unification* (New York: Holt, Rinehart and Winston, 1965); Robert D. Crassweiler, *The Caribbean Community* (London: Pall Mall Press, 1972); Franklin W. Knight, *The Caribbean: The Genesis of a Fragmented Nationalism* (New York: Oxford University Press, 1978).

2. William C. Gilmore, *The Grenada Intervention* (New York: Facts on File, 1984); Anthony Payne, Paul Sutton and Tony Thorndike, *Grenada: Revolution and Invasion* (New York: St. Martin's Press, 1984).

3. Daniel J. Elazar, ed., *Federal Systems of the World,* 2nd ed. (Harlow, Essex, UK: Longman, 1994); Amitav Achaya, *A New Regional Order in South-East Asia: ASEAN in the Post Cold-War Era* (London: Brasseys, 1993); Ronald D. Palmer and Thomas Reckford, *Building ASEAN: 20 Years of Southeast Asian Cooperation* (New York: Praeger, 1987).

4. Thomas B. Millar, ed., *Australian-New Zealand Defense Cooperation* (Canberra: Australian National University Press, 1968); Douglas H. Pike, *Australia: The Quiet Continent* (Cambridge: Cambridge University Press, 1966); Frederick L.W. Wood, *This New Zealand* (Hamilton, New Zealand: Paul's Book Arcade, 1958).

5. Charles F. Bonser, ed., *Toward a North American Common Market* (Boulder: Westview Press, 1991); M. Delal Baer and Sidney Weintraub, eds., *The NAFTA Debate* (Boulder: Lynne Rienner, 1994).

6. Karel Holbik, *Trade and Industrialization in the Central American Common Market* (Austin: University of Texas at Austin, 1972); William R. Clive, ed., *Economic Integration in Central America* (Washington: Brookings Institution, 1978); Robert T. Brown, *Transport and the Economic Integration of South America* (Washington: Brookings Institution, 1966).

7. *International Herald Tribune,* 24 March 1996, pp. 18-20.

8. Angola, Botswana, Lesotho, Malawi, Mozambique, Namibia, Swaziland, Tanzania, Zambia, and Zimbabwe as well as South Africa, and a newly admitted member, Mauritius.

9. Susan A. Koch, "Toward a Europe of Regions: Transnational Political Activities in Alsace," *Publius,* vol. 4, no. 3 (Summer 1974); James W. Scott, "Transborder Cooperation, Regional Initiatives, and Sovereignty Conflicts in

Western Europe: The Case of the Upper Rhine Valley," *Publius*, vol. 19, no. 1 (Winter 1989).

10. Daniel J. Elazar, ed., *Governing Peoples and Territories* (Philadelphia: Institute for the Study of Human Issues, 1982); William B. Quandt, *Camp David* (Washington: Brookings Institution, 1986); Daniel J. Elazar, *Two Peoples, One Land: Federal Solutions for Israel, the Palestinians and Jordan* (Lanham, MD: Jerusalem Center for Public Affairs and University Press of America, 1991).

11. Elazar, *Two Peoples, op. cit.*

12. Sergio Minerbi, "Two Steps Forward, One Step Back: The Vatican, The Jews and Israel," unpublished research paper, Jerusalem Center for Public Affairs, 1993.

13. Margaret P. Karns and Karen A. Mingst, eds., *The United States and Multilateral Institutions* (London: Routledge, 1992).

14. Leland Goodrich, *The United Nations* (New York: T.Y. Crowell, 1959); Even Luard, *A History of the United Nations* (New York: St. Martin's Press, 1982-1989), 2 vols.

15. Philippe Manin, *L'Organisation des Nations Unis et la Maintien de la Paix* (Paris: Librairie Generale de Droit et de Jurisprudence, 1971); James M. Boyd, *United Nations Peace-Keeping Operations* (New York: Praeger Publishers, 1971).

16. Conrad Weiler, "GATT, NAFTA and State and Local Powers," in Daniel J. Elazar, ed., *American Confederal Experiences, Past and Present*, (forthcoming).

17. Christian P. Potholm and Richard A. Friedland, eds., *Integration and Disintegration in East Africa* (Lanham, MD: University Press of America, 1980); Arthur Hazlewood, *Economic Integration: The East African Experience* (New York: St. Martin's Press, 1975).

18. Lucie Gallistel Colvin, "Theoretical Issues in Historical International Politics: The Case of Senegambia," in Daniel J. Elazar, ed., *Community and Union: The Rebirth of Confederal Arrangements in Europe and Beyond* (forthcoming); Robert Fatton, *The Making of a Liberal Democracy: Senegal's Passive Revolution, 1975-1985* (Boulder: Lynne Rienner Publishers, 1987); Robert N. Bates, *Patterns of Uneven Development: Causes and Consequences in Gambia* (Denver: University of Denver, 1974); Arnold Hughes, "The Collapse of the Senegambian Confederation," *Journal of Commonwealth and Comparative Politics*, vol. 30, no. 2 (July 1992); Halifa Sallah, *The Sene-Gambia Confederation: Facts, Fears, Myths, Doubts and the Truth* (Banjul, Gambia: n.p., 1985).

19. Jonathan Eyal, *Europe and Yugoslavia: Lessons From a Failure* (London: Royal United Services Institute for Defence Studies, 1993); Frederick B. Singleton, *A History of the Yugoslav People* (Cambridge: Cambridge University Press, 1985); Leonard J. Cohen, "The Disintegration of Yugoslavia," in Daniel J. Elazar, ed., *Community and Union, op. cit.*

20. Cohen, *ibid.*; Jim Seroka, "The Dissolution of the Czechoslovak and Yugoslav Federations: Comparisons and Contrasts," in Daniel J. Elazar, ed., *Community and Union, op. cit.*

21. Michael K. Oliver, *The Passionate Debate* (Montreal: Vehicule Press, 1991); Daniel Latouche, "Problems of Constitutional Design in Canada: Quebec and the Issue of Bicommunalism," *Publius*, vol. 18, no. 2 (Spring 1988); Peter M. Leslie, "Bicommunalism and Canadian Constitutional Reform," *Publius, ibid.*; Pierre Fournier, *A Meech Lake Post-Mortem* (Montreal: McGill-Queen's University Press, 1991).

Chapter 7

CONFEDERAL ARRANGEMENTS AND THE EMERGING WORLD ORDER

The paradigm shift now taking place has consequences worldwide that are leading slowly to the application of federal principles and even more to the emergence of federal arrangements worldwide in their confederal form. The statist paradigm led to the emergence of a world order based upon the international state system whose apotheosis was the balance of power among states that served as major power centers. One reason for the paradigm shift was that reliance on the balance of power internationally became too dangerous in the nuclear age. At the same time, the necessity of greater economic cooperation and the need to enable competition to function within a cooperative framework rather than on a cut-throat basis lay at the basis of the shift in international economic arrangements that has led to the paradigm shift.

The first steps toward this new world order were taken during World War II to establish economic and political foundations that would safeguard the world against the agonies of another great depression. These led to the development of the network of economic arrangements and institutions to implement them presently in place and expanding all the time. In the case of economics, the worldwide arrangements preceded regional ones, initially seen as sustaining the old state system through a new kind of balance of power. Only in the second generation of the postmodern epoch, that is to say, sometime after the mid-1970s did it become apparent that irrevocable steps had been taken in the establishment of worldwide economic connections and that powerful institutions had emerged within that functional

155

sphere in which all states had to participate if they wished to survive and prosper economically. The extent to which this had happened did not reach public attention until a decade later.

Meanwhile, a similar effort on the security front had run headlong into the sovereign interests of established states and the confrontation between the West and the Communist Bloc. At the same time, it also ran into the decolonization movement that was a preoccupation of international affairs during the first postmodern generation, as colonies sought state sovereignty in the same measure as their colonial masters. The political organs of the UN often were paralyzed, while the economically-oriented functional agencies surrounding the UN gained in power. The collapse of the Soviet empire brought an end to the Cold War. Instead of two competing security communities in the world in a standoff, there came to be one great security community with pockets of conflict representing either unsettled conflicts of the past or certain regional and local perversities that increasingly were contained by the dominant powers in the security community, even if the conflicts themselves could not be extinguished.

What, then, is the situation today? A new world order has developed, based primarily on the same functional foundations as the European Union developed, only much weaker. Its functional achievements are primarily economic, but also include a growing number of social and environmental concerns. Thus, the world is moving toward a minimum floor on matters of health (e.g., eradication or containment of communicable diseases), communications (e.g., a world completely interconnected through postal and telecommunications and increasingly through cybernetic ones as well), protection of common properties (e.g., the international law of the sea, the internationalization of Antarctica, and, more recently, stronger protections for intellectual property worldwide), and even an agricultural floor that provides sufficient nourishment for all of the planet's inhabitants achieved through the Green Revolution. Much of this has been achieved through the old state system and institutions designed to serve it, but increasingly those institutions are shifting to the new federalist paradigm and their member states are falling into line out of necessity if not out of choice.

The institutional framework that has evolved in itself is telling (Tables 7.1 and 7.2).

Table 7.1

INTERNATIONAL ORGANIZATIONS

Organization	Founding Date	Members
Governmental Organizations		
Universal Postal Union (UPU)	1875	185
International Labor Organization (ILO)	1919	167
International Telecommunication Union (ITU)	1932	166 (1991)
United Nations (UN)	1945	184
Food and Agriculture Organization (FAO)	1945	160
International Monetary Fund (IMF)	1945	178
International Bank for Reconstruction and Development (IBRD)	1946	176
International Civil Aviation Organization (ICAO)	1947	180
World Health Organization (WHO)	1948	187
General Agreement on Tariffs and Trade (GATT)/ World Trade Organization (WTO)	1948/1995	111/117
World Meteorological Organization (WMO)	1951	167
United Nations Educational, Scientific and Cultural Organization (UNESCO)	1956	179

International Finance Corporation (IFC)	1956	143
International Atomic Energy Agency (IAEA)	1957	114
International Maritime Organization (IMO)	1958	147
Organization for Economic Cooperation and Development (OECD)	1961	24
World Intellectual Property Organization (WIPO)	1970	140
International Fund for Agricultural Development (IFAD)	1977	147

Worldwide Nongovernmental Organizations

Bank for International Settlements	1930	80 central banks
World Federation of Trade Unions (WFTU)	1945	105 orgs. in 83 countries (mainly Communist or formerly so)
World Confederation of Labor	1945	orgs. in 90 countries, mainly Roman Catholic, with Protestant, Buddhist and Muslim member confederations
World Council of Churches	1948	320 churches from 100 countries
International Confederation of Free Trade Unions (ICFTU)	1949	154 orgs. in 109 countries

Table 7.2

REGIONAL ORGANIZATIONS

Organization	*Date*	*Members*
The League of Arab States	1945	Algeria, Bahrain, Comores, Djibouti, Egypt, Iraq, Jordan, Kuwait, Lebanon, Libya, Mauritania, Morocco, Oman, PLO, Qatar, Saudi Arabia, Somalia, Sudan, Syria, Tunisia, United Arab Emirates, Yemen
Western European Union (WEU)	1948	Belgium, France, Germany, Greece, Italy, Luxembourg, Netherlands, Portugal, Spain, United Kingdom; Observers: Denmark, Ireland; Associate Members: Norway, Turkey
Organization of American States (OAS)	1948	34, with 30 permanent observers
South Pacific Commission	1949	27
North Atlantic Treaty Organization (NATO)	1949	16 (38 in the North Atlantic Cooperation Council)
Council of Europe	1949	31 European democracies
Organization of Petroleum Exporting Countries (OPEC)	1960	Algeria, Gabon, Indonesia, Iran, Iraq, Kuwait, Libya, Nigeria, Qatar, Saudi Arabia, United,
European Trade Union Confederation	1973	21 European countries Arab Emirates, Venezuela

Regional Groupings/Institutions

Nordic Council	1952	Denmark, Finland, Iceland, Norway, Sweden

Inter-American Development Bank (IDB)	1959	44
European Free Trade Association (EFTA)	1960	Austria, Finland, Iceland, Liechtenstein, Norway, Sweden, Switzerland
Latin American Integration Association (LAIA)	1960	Argentina, Bolivia, Brazil, Chile, Colombia, Ecuador, Mexico, Paraguay, Peru, Uruguay, Venezuela
Central American Common Market	1960	El Salvador, Guatemala, Honduras, Nicaragua, Panama
Organization of African Unity	1963	52
Association of South East Asian Nations (ASEAN)	1967	Brunei, Indonesia, Malaysia, Philippines, Singapore, Thailand; Observers: Laos, Papua New Guinea, Vietnam
The Andean Pact	1969	Bolivia, Colombia, Ecuador, Peru, Venezuela
South Pacific Forum (including South Pacific Regional Trade and Economic Cooperation Agreement)	1971	Australia, Cook Islands, Federated States of Micronesia, Fiji, Kiribati, Nauru, New Zealand, Niue, Papua New Guinea, Republic of the Marshall Islands, Solomon Islands, Tongu, Tuvalu, Vanuatu, Western Samoa
Senegal River Development Organization (OMVS)	1972	Mali, Mauritania, Senegal
Caribbean Community (CARICOM)	1973	13; Associate Members: British Virgin Islands, Turks and Caicos Islands
Mano River Union	1973	Guinea, Liberia, Sierra Leone
Permanent Interstate Committee on Drought Control in the Sahel (CILSS)	1974	Burkina Faso, Cape Verde, Chad, Gambia, Guinea, Guinea-Bissau, Mali, Mauritania, Niger, Nigeria, Senegal

Group of Latin American and Caribbean Sugar Exporting Countries (GEPLACEA)	1974	Argentina, Barbados, Bolivia, Brazil, Colombia, Costa Rica, Cuba, Dominican Republic, Ecuador, El Salvador, Guatemala, Guyana, Haiti, Honduras, Jamaica, Mexico, Nicaragua, Panama, Peru, Philippines, Trinidad and Tobago, Uruguay, Venezuela
Office for Security and Cooperation in Europe (OSCE)	1975	53
Economic Community of West African States (ECOWAS)	1975	Benin, Burkina Faso, Cape Verde, Gambia, Ghana, Guinea, Guinea-Bissau, Ivory Coast, Liberia, Mali, Mauritania, Niger, Nigeria, Senegal, Sierra Leone, Togo
Latin American Economic System (SELA)	1975	Argentina, Barbados, Bolivia, Brazil, Chile, Colombia, Costa Rica, Cuba, Dominican Republic, Ecuador, El Salvador, Grenada, Guatemala, Guyana, Haiti, Honduras, Jamaica, Mexico, Nicaragua, Panama, Paraguay, Peru, Spain, Surinam, Trinidad and Tobago, Uruguay, Venezuela
Economic Community of Great Lakes Countries (CEPGL)	1976	Burundi, Rwanda, Zaire
Amazon Pact	1978	Bolivia, Brazil, Colombia, Ecuador, Guyana, Peru, Surinam, Venezuela
Alpen-Adria Grouping	1978	5 Austrian *länder*; 3 western Hungarian regions; 4 northern Italian regions; Bavaria, Croatia, Slovenia
Organization of Eastern Caribbean States (OECS)	1981	Antigua and Barbuda, Dominica, Grenada, Montserrat, St. Christopher and Nevis, St. Lucia, St. Vincent and

		the Grenadines; Associate Members: British Virgin Islands
Gulf Cooperation Council (GCC)	1982	Bahrain, Kuwait, Oman, Qatar, Saudi Arabia, United Arab Emirates
Economic Community of Central African States (CEEAC)	1983	Burundi, Cameroon, Central African Republic, Chad, Congo, Equatorial Guinea, Gabon, Rwanda, Sao Tome and Principe, Zaire; Observer: Angola
South Asian Asso- ciation for Regional Co-Operation (SAARC)	1985	Bangladesh, Bhutan, India, Maldives, Nepal, Pakistan, Sri Lanka
Inter-Governmental Authority on Drought and Development (IGADD)	1986	Djibouti, Ethiopia, Kenya, Somalia, Sudan, Uganda
Group of Rio	1987	Argentina, Bolivia, Brazil, Chile, Colombia, Ecuador, Mexico, Paraguay, Peru, Uruguay, Venezuela
Arab Maghreb Union	1989	Algeria, Libya, Mauritania, Morocco, Tunisia
Asia-Pacific Economic Cooperation	1989	Australia, Brunei, Canada, China, Hong Kong, Indonesia, Japan, South Korea, Malaysia, Mexico, New Zealand, Papua New Guinea, Philippines, Singapore, Taiwan, Thailand, U.S.A.
Central European Initiative	1990	Austria, Bosnia-Hercegovina, Croatia, Czech Republic, Hungary, Italy, Macedonia, Poland, Slovakia, Slovenia,
Baltic Council	1990	Estonia, Latvia, Lithuania
Latin American Integration Association (ALADI)	1990	Argentina, Bolivia, Brazil, Chile, Colombia, Ecuador, Mexico, Paraguay, Uruguay, Venezuela; 11 Observer states

Visegrad Group	1991	Czech Republic, Hungary, Poland, Slovakia
European Bank for Reconstruction and Development (EBRD)	1991	59
Central American Parliament (Parlacen)	1991	El Salvador, Guatemala, Honduras, Panama; Observers: Costa Rica, Nicaragua
Council of Baltic States	1992	Denmark, Estonia, Finland, Germany, Latvia, Lithuania, Norway, Poland, Russia, Sweden
Southern African Development Community (SADC)	1992	Angola, Botswana, Lesotho, Malawi, Mauritius, Mozambique, Namibia, South Africa, Swaziland, Tanzania, Zambia, Zimbabwe
Black Sea Economic Cooperation Project	1992	Albania, Armenia, Azerbaijan, Bulgaria, Georgia, Greece, Moldova, Romania, Russia, Turkey, Ukraine
Carpathia-Tisza Economic Working Community	1992	Hungary, Poland, Romania, Slovakia, Ukraine
Carpathians Euroregion	1993	Border regions of Hungary, Poland, Ukraine
Barents Euro-Arctic Council	1993	Denmark, Finland, Iceland, Norway, Russia, Sweden
Common Market for Eastern and Southern Africa (COMESA)	1993	Angola, Burundi, Comoros, Djibouti, Eritrea, Ethiopia, Kenya, Malawi, Mauritius, Mozambique, Namibia, Rwanda, Seychelles, Somalia, South Africa, Sudan, Swaziland, Tanzania, Uganda, Zaire, Zambia, Zimbabwe
Association of Caribbean States	1994	G-3; 5 Central American countries; 13 members of CARICOM; Cuba, Dominican Republic, Haiti, Surinam; Associate Members: 12 regional dependent territories

Group of Three (G-3)	1994	Colombia, Mexico, Venezuela
North American Free Trade Agreement (NAFTA)	1994	Canada, Mexico, United States; Chile due to join
Economic and Monetary Community of Central Africa (CEMAC)	1994	Cameroon, Central African Republic, Chad, Congo, Equatorial Guinea, Gabon
Union economique et monetaire ouest-africaine (UEMOA)	1994	Benin, Burkina Faso, Ivory Coast, Mali, Niger, Senegal, Togo
South American Common Market (MERCOSUR)	1995	Argentina, Brazil, Paraguay, Uruguay

These institutions are almost all functional ones, served by secretariats and international civil service. They have not developed the kind of authoritative institutions that brought about the transformation of the European Community into the European Union, i.e., from loose confederal arrangements into a confederation. Nor is there any real effort on the part of their members to give them stronger institutions. In that sense, these confederal arrangements are more appropriately leagues, but confederal arrangements they are, nonetheless, in the sense that they limit the "sovereignty," i.e., independent action, of their member states, and in most cases it is impossible for any of those member states to secede from them without suffering considerable damage.

The United Nations and Its Network

The United Nations (UN), formally an association of states that, by signing the UN Charter, have pledged themselves to maintain international peace and security, and to cooperate in establishing political, economic, and social conditions under which this task can be securely achieved, is the most comprehensive of the international organizations in scope and because of that, also the most limited in powers. In February 1994 it had 184 members. Its charter does not authorize it to intervene in the internal affairs of any state, although the line between internal and external affairs, as we have seen, is becoming harder to define.

The UN is also the first of the postmodern international organizations. Its charter was formulated in a series of multilateral discussions that began at the Dumbarton Oaks meeting in Washington, D.C., in 1944 and was adopted at the United Nations conference on international organization held in San Francisco in the spring of 1945. It was signed on 26 June 1945 by the delegates of fifty countries, all of which ratified the document by the end of that year. It officially came into existence on 24 October 1945 when the notification of the requisite number of ratifications had been deposited with the U.S. State Department. As all these venues indicate, the United States was the midwife or the godfather of the UN, as is further evidenced by the decision to locate its headquarters in New York.

From the very first, the UN adopted several features of contemporary confederal arrangements such as:

1. It was a league of sovereign states bound by a charter technically renounceable unilaterally by any member state, but in fact, no member can afford to do so.

2. It had multiple official languages, now six (Arabic, Chinese, English, French, Russian, and Spanish).

3. Its powers were divided among four principal and two secondary bodies. The General Assembly, the Security Council, and the Secretariat serve as the legislative and executive arms of the UN, with "legislation," mostly policy pronouncements, not enforceable except by its members. The International Court of Justice is the limited judicial arm, and the Economic and Social Council and the Trusteeship Council each have relatively broad functional responsibilities within their areas of concern.[1] Supplementing these are a network of committees, commissions, and other special bodies.

The International Court of Justice was established by a separate international treaty, the Statute of the Court, which forms an integral part of the United Nations Charter. All members of the UN are parties to the Statute of the Court by virtue of that treaty.

The powers of all of these bodies are in fact limited by the willingness of the member states to accept their involvement and most especially by the willingness of the permanent members at the Security Council to use the UN or its institutions to advance shared purposes. During the years of the Cold War the UN was very limited in what it could do, serving essentially as a mediating institution and a bridge in certain limited ways that both sides plus the Third World could agree upon. Since the fall of the Soviet empire the UN has gained power as an instrument of a far less divided world. Moreover, its present Secretary General, Bhutros Bhutros Ghali, himself ideologically a federalist, has been pushing for a greater UN world role, especially in matters of peace-keeping; but after a few years of expansion, the United States and other powers have pulled back in their support for Ghali's efforts and the UN mission has become a more modest one. Still, there has been a significant step forward from the Cold War years.[2]

The United Nations also includes independent specialized agencies and some fourteen major programs and funds principally serving the developing countries. The latter include UNICEF, the Population Fund, UNRWA, and the Office of the United Nations High Commissioner for Refugees.

In addition, there are sixteen specialized intergovernmental agencies within the terms of the UN Charter that report annually to the Economic and Social Council. These include the International Labor Organization (ILO), originally established in 1919 as an autonomous part of the League of Nations, and the Food and Agricultural Organization of the United Nations (FAO), established in 1943 on an interim basis after the International Conference on Food and Agriculture held in Hot Springs, Virginia, that year and formally organized in October 1945. The United Nations Educational, Scientific, and Cultural Organization (UNESCO) may be the most visible of these agencies and the most controversial. As UNESCO became dominated by the Third World, it suffered from waste, bias, and probably uses of funds bordering on corruption, which led to a United States pullout, which had contributed one-third of UNESCO's budget, and a cooling on the part of the other Western states, that have led the agency to substantially reduce its profile and make some attempt at reform.

On the other hand, the World Health Organization (WHO) is one of the most successful of the independent agencies since every member state has an interest in its activities. It tends to be technical and ministerial rather than political. The World Health Organization adopted a constitution in April 1948. Presently, it has 187 members.

The International Monetary Fund (IMF) was established as an independent organization in December 1945. It became operational in March 1947 and through an agreement of mutual cooperation became linked with the United Nations in November 1947. Its purpose is to promote international monetary cooperation, the expansion of international trade, and exchange rate stability, to eliminate exchange restrictions and establish a multilateral system of payments so as to alleviate any serious disequilibrium in members' international balance of payments. The IMF has grown to be a significant world power in its own right in the effort to fulfill those purposes and member states find that they are rather bound by IMF decisions and policies. Membership in IMF is by separate choice. Presently, it has 178 members. IMF may be the most powerful of the independent agencies since it controls the access of developing countries to the fiscal assistance and stability that they need to develop. Its capital resources include special drawing rights (SDRs) on member states' currencies, especially those of its industrial members, led by the major economic powers in the world. Even Switzerland has joined the IMF, a sign of its scope and power. In that respect it is like other world economic bodies.

The Bank for International Settlement, founded in 1930, was originally designed to settle the question of German First World War reparations. Since then it has become the central banks' bank that functions to promote cooperation between central banks and provides facilities for international financial operations. It also acts as agent and trustee in international financial settlements. Its assets are owned by 33 central banks on behalf of 80 central banks linked with it.

The International Bank for Reconstruction and Development (IBRD), otherwise known as the World Bank, was conceived at the Bretton Woods conference in New Hampshire in July 1944 and began operations in June 1946. It is another major link in the network of worldwide financial organizations controlled by the world's leading industrial states to establish a common world trade and development framework. It is supported by funds paid in by member countries, sales of its own securities, and earnings. Other elements in that network are the International Development Association (IDA) which came into existence in September 1960, is administered by the World Bank, and is open to all the members of that latter institution. The International Finance Corporation (IFC) was established in July 1956 to supplement the activities of the World Bank.

The International Civil Aviation Organization (ICAO) was established by a convention that was agreed upon at a Chicago meeting at the end of 1944. The ICAO was formally established in April 1947. Its convention superseded the earlier Paris Convention of the International Commission for Air Navigation which dated back to 1919. It and its subsidiary bodies engage primarily in the technical regulation of international air transport.

The Universal Postal Union was established in July 1875 and is one of the two oldest of the IGOs. It has 185 member countries and has been a specialized agency of the UN since 1948. Its tasks are purely technical and highly successful since it is in everyone's interest to stay within the UPU framework. Along with it, the International Telecommunication Union (ITU) does the same with regard to telephone, telegraph, and radio regulations. The ITU was formed in 1932 by a merger of the Telegraph Convention, which dates back to 1865, and the Radio Telegraph Convention, adopted in 1906, into a single International Telecommunication Convention, making it more comprehensive. Its present constitution and convention were adopted in 1989 and are pending ratification.

The World Meteorological Organization (WMO) is another technical body, the successor to the International Meteorological Organization established in 1873. The WMO adopted its convention in 1947 and was formally established in 1951. That same year it established a formal relationship with the United Nations. It has 167 member states and 5 member territories.

The International Maritime Organization (IMO) is the successor to the Intergovernmental Maritime Consultative Organization (IMCO), established through a convention drafted at the UN maritime conference held in February-March 1948. That convention became effective in March 1958 after 21 countries including seven of the largest shipping powers had ratified it. It was transformed into the IMO in 1982. Today it has 147 members and 2 associate members. It supervises the enforcement of nearly two dozen conventions governing maritime affairs in the world in matters of safety, health, environmental quality, international law when it comes into conflict with the law of the individual states, and the certification and training of maritime personnel. As a technical body it is led by international civil servants.

The World Intellectual Property Organization (WIPO) was established by a convention signed in Stockholm in 1967 by 51 countries and entered into force in April 1970. The WIPO became a specialized agency of the UN in December 1974, assuming the functions of the United International Bureaux for the Protection of Intellectual Property that dates back to 1893. It has a technical task, yet a difficult one, because it is often in the interests of the member states of the world to allow intellectual property to be used within their borders without compensation. By and large, it seeks protection for intellectual property through individual state action in conformity with the model laws and similar acts that it promulgates.

The International Fund for Agricultural Development (IFAD), initiated in 1974, became operational in 1977 as a means to mobilize additional funds for agricultural and rural development in developing countries. By the end of 1991 it was financing projects in 94 developing countries. The United Nations Industrial Development Organization (UNIDO), its industrial counterpart, became an autonomous organization within the UN Secretariat in 1966 and was converted into a UN specialized agency twenty years later.

The World Trade Organization (WTO) came into existence on January 1995 as the successor to the General Agreement on Tariffs and Trade (GATT), which was negotiated in 1947 and came into force on January 1, 1948. Its 23 original members were members of a preparatory committee appointed by the UN Economic and Social Council for the purpose of developing an international trade organization, but the charter of the latter was never ratified and GATT, which had originally been intended as an interim agreement, remained in force until the negotiations for the agreement that lead to the World Trade Organization were completed in 1994. In the end, GATT had 111 contracting parties and 22 other countries applying GATT rules on a de facto basis.

The development of GATT-WTO reflects the slow process of expansion and transformation. In October 1947, 23 states meeting in Geneva negotiated the General Agreement on Tariffs and Trade. President Truman signed for the United States. It went into effect in January 1948. It covered 20 percent of annual world trade. Between 1948 and 1960, four rounds of talks were held to expand GATT. Thirteen more states joined the system. In the period 1960-62, the Dillon Round took place, named after the U.S. Secretary of Treasury, C. Douglas Dillon. Tariffs on manufactured goods were cut further and six more states joined. Almost immediately the Kennedy Round began in 1963, named after President John F. Kennedy. It lasted until 1967 and at the end the membership in GATT grew by another 32 states.

In 1973 the Tokyo Round of negotiations began. GATT members negotiated rules on customs, subsidies, antidumping, and industry safeguards by 1979 when that round was completed. Eight more states joined. In 1986 the Uruguay Round began, which began in that South American country and continued in various other parts of the world. Services and agriculture were included in the negotiations, whose completion in 1994 included the agreement to transform GATT into the World Trade Organization to referee disputes. Forty more states joined GATT. In December 1994 the United States ratified the Uruguay Round, and on January 1, 1995, the World Trade Organization came into existence.

The WTO is the other pillar in the international economic order developed since World War II, in part under the aegis or with the stimulation of the United Nations, but primarily because the industrialized states of the world wanted it. The WTO came into existence after the eighth round of multilateral trade negotiations. It represents a major leap forward that formally limits state sovereignty in matters of international tariffs and trade that had previously been limited by the GATT agreement only in a de facto manner. In truth, even the de facto limitations were very real ones since, while every member state retains the right to renounce the interim agreement, none could afford to do so if it wanted to stay within the arena of world trade. The WTO is likely to become one of the most powerful of the international organizations as it develops.

Supporting Organizations

Supporting this UN-connected network are such bodies as the Organization for Economic Cooperation and Development (OECD). Founded in 1948 as the Organization for European Economic Cooperation, the OECD expanded to include Canada and the United States and then the more developed countries from throughout the world. It now has 24 members including neutral countries like Switzerland. Essentially, it works to stimulate economic development throughout the world and engages in other activities through four autonomous or semiautonomous bodies: the International Energy Agency (IEA), the Nuclear Energy Agency (NEA), the Development Center, and the Center for Educational Research and Innovation (CERI).

Supporting these formal interstate structures is a growing group of non-governmental organizations (NGOs) developed prior to or around them, many with official status in relation to them. Among these are the World Council of Churches, constituted in August 1948, uniting 320 Protestant, Anglican, Orthodox, Old Catholic, and Pentacostal churches; the World Jewish Congress, founded in 1936 by Jewish representative bodies from various countries throughout the world to protect Jewish rights and combat anti-Semitism; and, of course, the Vatican, representing the Catholic Church.

Similarly, international trade unionism includes the European Trade Union Confederation, the International Confederation of Free Trade Unions, the World Confederation of Trade Unions, and the World Confederation of Labor.

There is no better sign of the growing importance of these bodies than in the way that the United States Congress, once content to leave relations with them in presidential hands, has come to assert its own role. Nor has congressional intervention developed without international impact. Congressional skepticism of the value of the UN system as embodied in the Kassebaum Amendment of 1983 limiting the U.S. contribution to the UN and its specialized agencies to no more than 20 percent of their annual assessed costs and mandating the withholding of at least 20 percent pending the introduction of weighted voting for budgetary matters led to the UN adoption of a reform package in December 1986 that well reflects the other side of these new confederal arrangements, i.e., the possibility of powerful member states influencing the structures and processes of the arrangements themselves.

As in a confederation, Congressional mandates have instructed American representatives in IGOs to support or oppose certain actions of the latter. These efforts were particularly prominent during the Reagan administration and led to some notable changes in the IGOs affected. The Reagan administration was generally negative toward multilateralism. Nevertheless, even the powerful U.S. only withdrew from one IGO, UNESCO, where it provided 33 percent of the budget, in a situation where the excesses of those in charge had passed all reasonable expectations. Needless to say, U.S. withdrawal and the withdrawal of a third of the UNESCO budget led to some much-needed changes, but not entirely to American satisfaction.

One may look at all these institutions as part of a means to establish clearly framed "marketplaces" rather than to provide centralized direction. That is very much in keeping with the federalist paradigm. Federalism begins by recognizing the fundamental equality of all partners and only seeks to provide better networks linking them. The market analogy is by far the better one with which to begin the federalist paradigm than the hierarchical bureaucratic analogy, although federalism, in order to better stabilize markets, may introduce some hierarchical elements and bureaucracy to manage their networks.

But federalism is not merely a matter of markets; federalism is political. Some, indeed, would argue that it is the essence of politics.[3] Federalism requires noncentralization and negotiated collaboration, involving both competition and cooperation but within a political framework, i.e., one that requires normative choices. These normative choices are critical, but they must be made within a context that minimizes the use of coercion to enforce them—minimizes but does not obviate or abandon.

Federalism not only combines self-rule and shared rule, but seeks to do so on the basis of a minimum of coercion and a maximum of consent. That is why implementing federal principles or even achieving workable federal arrangements is so difficult, and can be advanced only by careful preparation of the ground to cultivate a political culture capable of sustaining those principles and arrangements, or through a mutuality of response on the part of those who are terrified by the alternative. It may very well be that much of present movement toward a federalist paradigm was stimulated by the latter reason more than the former. Terror generated by fears of massive economic depression, on one hand, and fears of nuclear holocaust, on the other, have been powerful instruments in leading the world's political leadership down paths that they otherwise might never have considered. However, they have been able to move down those paths only at the speed that the political situation can adapt to them and only after a political culture sufficiently capable of at least minimally maintaining such principles and arrangements had developed, at least among the leading countries of the world, the ones whose lead the rest of the world not only had to follow, but which they wanted, in most cases, to emulate as well.

Functional or Federal?

Margaret P. Karns and Karen A. Mingst examine the important American role in establishing international multilateral institutions in both IGOs and NGOs in the postwar period.[4] They argue that these multilateral institutions were designed to establish a loose but very real worldwide regime and were used by the United States to that end and to secure regime change, both to legitimate its own actions and to move the actions of others. In fact, they argue, other states have found IGOs even more useful than the United States because of American power and its limits. What has resulted is functionalism on a world scale. They disagree with Keohane who describes IGOs as "elements of a new international order beyond the nation state."[5]

But even they argue that IGOs are "elements of such an order, of, by, and for nation states."[6] "Integral parts of the contemporary international system and potentially important non-state actors . . . yet another international source of domestic politics."[7] They do this through rule establishing and supervisory decisions, information-sharing and surveillance, and by establishing agendas for national bureaucracies. All of these are elements that students of federalism have encountered within federations, not to speak of looser federal systems.[8]

Four explanations have been considered as to why multilateral institutions have developed the way they have:

1. The decline in the overall power of the United States.
2. The characteristics of particular issue areas.
3. The properties of specific international organizations.
4. Domestic political factors.

In fact, all of them have relevance in particular situations and together constitute most of the explanatory variables required. A fifth may be added: the sometimes latent, sometimes manifest search for world order, especially on the part of Americans, but also on the part of other Westerners and, in its own way, the Soviet Union when it existed. This is reflected in the spheres of the functional development of multilateral institutions: one, the development of a world economy, especially as economic liberalism has become more widely accepted as the right way to do so, even on the part of those who do not accept liberalism in other spheres; two, the search for peace, security, and territorial integrity; three, the assumption on the part of the United States of global responsibility as the guardian of freedom and morality, defined as democracy, freedom, equality, progress, and perfectibility of human institutions.

Perhaps the final point to be made about these new confederal arrangements is the degree to which they involve overlapping linkages of states. States or state-like polities, whether politically independent or federated, serve as the building blocks for these arrangements. Those building blocks then form groups, ranging from relatively firmly bounded ones, such as the EU, the Caribbean Community, or ASEAN, which are at the same time the strongest in terms of their powers.

Around (and including) them are more limited regional and worldwide groupings whose memberships are not clearly divided from one another or symmetrical. In other words, blocs overlap blocs, forums overlap forums, and agreements overlap agreements. Figure 7.1 maps the major such agreements by region and worldwide.

Nor can one identify a hierarchy of boundedness. For example, the World Trade Organization is a much tighter linkage for its limited functional purposes than its political equivalent, the United Nations, where older patterns of limitations based upon state sovereignty are pronounced. While, as a general rule, economic entities are more firmly bounded than others, even this is not always the case. For example, the Asia-Pacific economic community has less power than ASEAN, which has yet to enter deeply into economic affairs and whose member states are members of both.

Table 7.1

MAJOR CONFEDERAL ARRANGEMENTS WORLDWIDE

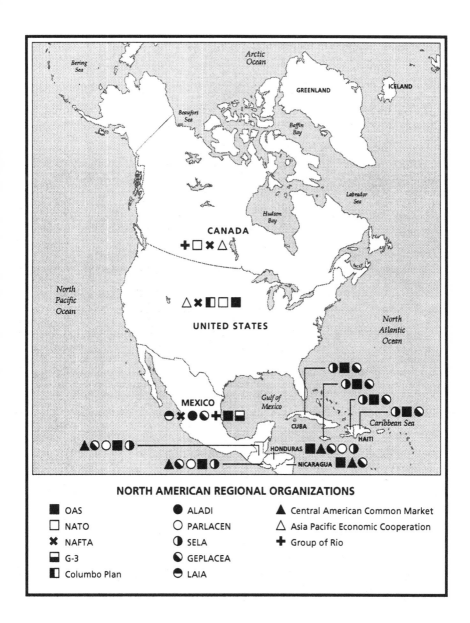

NORTH AMERICAN REGIONAL ORGANIZATIONS

■ OAS	● ALADI	▲ Central American Common Market
□ NATO	○ PARLACEN	△ Asia Pacific Economic Cooperation
✖ NAFTA	◗ SELA	✚ Group of Rio
▭ G-3	◐ GEPLACEA	
▯ Columbo Plan	◑ LAIA	

SOUTH AMERICAN REGIONAL ORGANIZATIONS

■ ALADI	● Group of Rio	▲ SELA
□ Amazon Pact	○ LAIA	△ Central American Common Market
✖ Andean Pact	◐ MERCOSUR	
◨ CEPLACEA	◗ OAS	
◧ G-3	◓ PARLACEN	

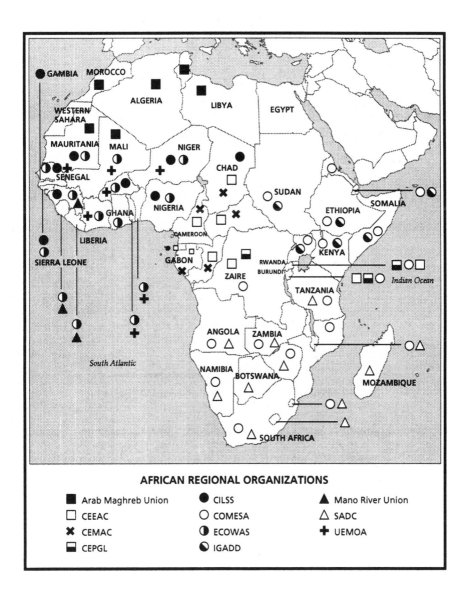

AFRICAN REGIONAL ORGANIZATIONS

■ Arab Maghreb Union	● CILSS	▲ Mano River Union
☐ CEEAC	○ COMESA	△ SADC
✖ CEMAC	◑ ECOWAS	✚ UEMOA
▭ CEPGL	◑ IGADD	

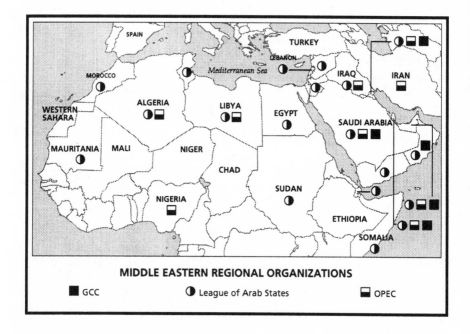

MIDDLE EASTERN REGIONAL ORGANIZATIONS

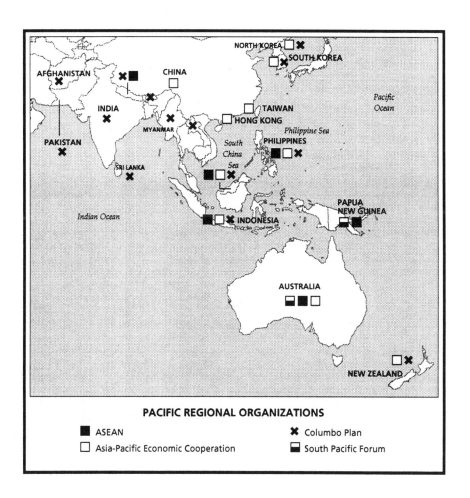

PACIFIC REGIONAL ORGANIZATIONS

■ ASEAN   ✖ Columbo Plan

☐ Asia-Pacific Economic Cooperation   ⬓ South Pacific Forum

Notes

1. As all of the eleven original trust territories have since become independent, the Trusteeship Council now has no direct responsibilities.

2. Paul Graham Taylor, *International Organizations in the Modern World* (London: Pinter, 1993); J. Martin Rochester, *Waiting for the Millennium: The United Nations and the Future of World Order* (Columbia, S.C.: University of South Carolina Press, 1993); Adam Roberts and Benedict Kingsburg, eds., *United Nations, Divided World* (Oxford: Clarendon Press, 1993); P.R. Baehr and L. Gordenker, *The United Nations in the Nineteen Nineties* (New York: St. Martin's Press, 1992).

3. Vukan Kuic, "Federalism as a Model of Political Association," *Trends in Federalism* (Greenville, N.C.: East Carolina University, 1972).

4. Margaret P. Karns and Karen A. Mingst, *The United States and Multilateral Institutions: Patterns of Changing Instrumentality and Influence* (New York: Unwin, Hyman Inc., 1990).

5. Robert O. Keohane, *After Hegemony: Cooperation and Discord in the World Political Economy* (Princeton: Princeton University Press, 1984), p. 6.

6. *Ibid.*, p. 8.

7. Peter Gourevitch, "The Second Image Reversed: The International Sources of Domestic Politics," *International Organization* 32 (Autumn 1978):881-911.

8. Morton Grodzins, *The American System: A New View of Government in the United States,* ed. Daniel J. Elazar (Chicago: Rand McNally, 1966).

Chapter 8

THE FEDERAL DIMENSIONS OF STATE-DIASPORA RELATIONS

At the far edge of the new confederal arrangements are state-diaspora relations.[1] Relative to the other relationships described in this volume, they may even be considered beyond the edge, certainly in most cases. Even where they are not, the examples are analogous to the United Nations; that is to say, quasiconstitutionalized linkages that do not compromise the political sovereignty of the states involved.

The question of state-diaspora relations is an old-new one in human history. A common phenomenon during the Hellenistic and Roman periods, it remained real, if lower key, with the rise of the modern nation-state, whose exclusivism militated against formal diaspora political expression.[2] In the interdependent world of the post-modern epoch, however, among whose principal characteristics are increasingly permeable state boundaries, the revival of ethnicity, and multiethnic states as the norm, the phenomenon has emerged once again.[3]

States and Diasporas in the Contemporary World

State-diaspora relations deal first and foremost with nations that extend beyond states and across state boundaries. The Jewish situation is perhaps the classic example of this, but it is not the only one. The Chinese, for example, have their own set of state-diaspora relations involving two or three competing states: the Peoples Republic of China, Taiwan, and Singapore.[4] The Somalis offer another example.

181

Somalia is one of the few truly homogenous nation-states in the world, with 99.9 percent of its population Somali. But about half of the Somalis live outside of Somalia in neighboring Ethiopia and Kenya, where they form a particularly troubling diaspora and, indeed, in the case of Somalia and Ethiopia, led to a brief but serious war.[5] In both of these latter cases, as in almost all other existing examples, what is lacking is a form of organized political life connecting state and diaspora.

To take an example where a state-diaspora relationship has a concrete political dimension, under French law one cannot renounce French citizenship—once a Frenchman, always a Frenchman. Accordingly, the French constitution makes provision for French citizens living outside of France to elect two members of the French Senate as representatives of the French diaspora. There are polling places in French embassies and consulates around the world where French extraterritorial nationals may go and vote, if they so choose. This is symbolic representation, no more, but it does reflect the phenomenon.[6]

Germany long has recognized a German diaspora—for example, the German colonists who settled in Russia in the eighteenth century are considered German nationals and have the right of "return" to Germany, even though their ancestors left the country over two centuries ago. Since the fall of the Soviet Union, many have exercised that right.

The United States is, in theory, a more difficult case. American political theory does not provide for unrenounceable citizenship for those Americans living outside its boundaries since the United States is very oriented toward territorial democracy. One has the right to emigrate (Americans have always stood for free emigration, if not always for free immigration), but if one does, at least in theory, he or she should become part of the body politic in the new land of settlement.

Today, however, there are several million Americans living abroad for longer or shorter periods. Willy-nilly, American diasporas have emerged around the world. Some of them are connected with American military bases or other installations, where they literally build American towns as kinds of golden ghettos, but still ghettos, in the countries in which they are located. This is what happened in Spain and Germany. Iran was a classic example before the fall of the shah. The contrast between driving into the walled-off American city north of Teheran and the rest of Iran was really extraordinary. Even in Canada and France where Americans do not live apart, the vast majority remain Americans by choice, retaining citizenship and other ties to "back home."

Not surprisingly, American political institutions have begun to adapt to this situation. There now are organized groups of Democrats and Republicans Abroad. They select delegates to their respective national conventions, and they seek better ways to secure absentee voting rights in federal and state elections for Americans living abroad. Congress has enacted legislation to further that end.[7] American corporations provide other kinds of links, and there are American-owned and operated English-language newspapers throughout the world to serve them as well as other American transients.

On another level, the Arabs have considered themselves a nation with many states since the breakup of the first Muslim caliphate. That condition has intensified with the decolonization of the Arab world in the twentieth century.[8] Now an Arab diaspora is emerging outside of the Arab world as a result of emigration. The 1980s effort to secure recognition of the PLO by the City of Berkeley in a referendum is an example of the Arabs successfully mobilizing an Arab diaspora on behalf of an issue. They failed on the issue, but they were successful in the mobilization.[9]

In this respect, politically sovereign states are becoming more like federated or constituent states, serving both as polities and as receptacles and service providers for a variety of enduring groups, some of which may be transnational in scope. Some of those groups may identify exclusively with their state. Others may identify with that state plus another people or may not identify with their state at all. One doubts if Somalis in Ethiopia identify with Ethiopia in any way, manner, or form. Jews, on the other hand, clearly prize their citizenship in the states in which they are located and, increasingly, not only identify with those states but with their people. This is a new reality for the Jewish people.

Nevertheless, while so-called "sovereign states" may not be as "sovereign" as they like to think they are, the state system remains the foundation of such international order as exists, and states have become crucially important in the state-diaspora relationship. To put it another way, in the contemporary world, diasporas without states do not seem to be able to do very well; ultimately, a people must have a state in order to have a diaspora. The Gypsies, for example, have never been able to transcend a narrow tribalism. They continue to exist as a scattered tribe, but today great numbers of Gypsies seem to be assimilating, at least in those states in which individualism rather than tribal or ethnic identity is a commanding value.

The Armenians offer a good example of both sides of this phenomenon. Before the dissolution of the USSR, both in their land and outside of it, the Armenians had to use Soviet Armenia as their state, with all their reservations about it. Even Armenians who were anti-Communists related to Armenia as their state. In the last decades of the USSR, there was something of a reconciliation between the anti-Communist Armenians and the Armenian Soviet Socialist Republic, which had two effects. On one hand, it connected them with the Soviet Republic, but on the other hand, it also strengthened the independence of the Armenian SSR within the USSR, which undoubtedly helped Armenia to become one of the leaders in the dissolution of the Soviet Union.[10] With the fall of the USSR the newly independent Armenia, now formally rejecting a Communism that it did not want in the first place, was able to openly reforge ties with Armenians throughout the world to gain the benefits of their economic and political assistance, opening a new page in Armenian history. In rare cases, a historical state may do, if it is not likely to be restored, but there must be a state in some form.

In sum, unless there is some possibility of achieving territorial statehood for at least some part of a people, it is becoming increasingly difficult to maintain intergenerational diaspora links. It may not be impossible—we do not know that yet. Hence, the importance of states should not be entirely denigrated, even though the idea and reality of state sovereignty have diminished in other respects.

Hellenistic and Roman Models

We have no appropriate theory for the present condition of state-diaspora relations. We do have some antecedent theories going back to Hellenistic and Roman times. As in most cases, the Greeks had a word for it. In the Hellenistic world, the term *politeuma* was used to describe a polity within a polity—a diaspora community located within a *politaeia*. The Greeks developed at least an operational constitutional theory to enable that combination to work.[11] The Jews benefited because of this phenomenon, putting together a combination of state and diaspora, but other such groups functioned in the Hellenistic and later the Roman world. While the conditions in that world were different from those of our own, we could usefully study the constitutional arrangements of that period as we try to build a theory for this.

One principle that can be learned from that period is that active and extensive state-diaspora relations require a kind of *pax romana* in order to flourish. To the extent that today's world system, whatever its problematics, has achieved, on one level, a common world peace that enables both small states and diasporas to survive within security-communities, to use Karl Deutsch's phrase, it has enabled this kind of relationship to develop and even has provided the conditions for it.

The Jewish People as a Case Study

Both empirical research and new theory are needed in this area. For those purposes, it is possible to treat the Jewish people as a case study.

For the Jewish people, their restoration to their historic homeland in our time and their establishment there of a concrete state was probably utterly necessary, both for the sheer physical survival of many Jews and for the survival of the Jewish people as a people.[12] Until the beginning of the modern epoch in the mid-seventeenth century, Jews, even in exile, were accepted by all as a nation apart with an appropriate juridical status, communal autonomy, and communal (governmental) institutions to make that status and autonomy real. Feudal Europe and the ethnoreligiously plural Muslim world offered space for a separate Jewish corporate existence. In Europe, the Jews were viewed as a guild or an estate among other guilds and estates, and in the Muslim world as a millet among other millets.

With the coming of the modern epoch and the rise of the nation-state, the Jews lost their autonomy, just as the other separate guilds, estates-and millets did. They were transformed into subjects of the new states as individuals and formally their institutions were left with religious functions only. In due course, they were also emancipated from the restrictions on their participation as equals in modern society, transformed from subjects into citizens and given at least a formal equality with other citizens. This process was slow and erratic, beginning in the New World in the late seventeenth century and not culminating in the Islamic world until the middle of the twentieth century, as the modern epoch was passing into the postmodern one.

As individual subjects or citizens within their respective states, Jews were expected to adopt the culture and social mores of the state in which they found themselves. Thus, the only ways to preserve Jewish national identity and a meaningful Jewish culture was for the Jews to build their own state, which they did in their historic homeland beginning in the latter half of the nineteenth century and culminating in 1948 with the establishment of the State of Israel.

The reestablishment of the Jewish state has brought about a period of reconstitution for the Jewish people as a whole, now in process.[13] Hence, the Jewish people today are much involved in constitutional design, not only of their state, but also of state-diaspora relations through the State of Israel and its institutions, and the individual diaspora country communities, first and foremost, the United States. The Jewish Agency for Israel, a unique transnational body established in international law by the League of Nations in its Palestine Mandate of 1922 and founded as an institution by representatives of world Jewry, Zionist and non-Zionist, in 1929, is becoming the nexus of the network of transstate organizations that are involved in institutionalizing the state-diaspora relationship.[14]

The Jewish Agency is one of five pivotal bodies that constitute the institutional-organizational framework and core of world Jewry. Two have already been mentioned, it and the State of Israel itself. The other three are the World Zionist Organization, the World Jewish Congress, and the Joint Distribution Committee. Essentially, all other worldwide, countrywide, and local Jewish organizations, institutions, and communities are connected to one or more of these five directly or indirectly, and the five are connected with one another in interlocking leadership networks, shared function, and, in a number of cases, formal constitutional ties. As in contemporary confederal arrangements, these bodies are designed for specific functions and are not overarching or comprehensive.

These connections are particularly challenging because they involve linking a politically sovereign state with four public, nongovernmental organizations which, in the last analysis, rely upon voluntary association and support. In this sense, the whole is a variant of the civil society model that has developed in the world since the seventeenth century involving and linking governmental institutions, public nongovernmental institutions, and a private sector. This linkage on a noncompulsory basis has had its share of problems, not the least, problems of understanding and perception on the part of the different bodies. Nevertheless, it is probably the most advanced state-diaspora framework that has emerged in the world to date.

The issue that most concerns the Agency's governing bodies at this time is this process of reconstitution. While they have to give due attention to their various functional responsibilities in immigration, the absorption and settlement of immigrants to Israel, and Jewish education worldwide—all those kinds of very real, if at times mundane, tasks—what is uppermost in the minds of all of them is this problem of reconstitution, because that is what they have been involved in doing since 1969.

They are making some real progress. But it is a reconstitution of the kind of magnitude that, at least for the Jewish people, is quite like the magnitude of the reconstitution of the American Revolutionary-Constitutional period or the French Revolution for those nations at that time. Hence, it serves as an example of the kind of institution-building for a state plus diaspora relationship that reflects a constitutional design for power-sharing.

How is it possible to have power-sharing between a state and a diaspora? A state is, after all, a state. It has a certain status in international relations. More than that, it has obligations in the international arena. It does not have the freedom diaspora communities have, especially voluntary diaspora communities.

Today, for all intents and purposes, all Jewish diaspora communities are voluntary. They exist through the voluntary consent of their members, who are not only free to be involved with them or not, but can freely determine how involved they want to be, the ways in which they want to be involved, and the degree to which they will accept even that communal discipline which is consensually established. This is very different from the situation in a state, which, because it is bounded physically, can enforce legitimate demands that everybody within it must fulfill certain obligations. Whether particular citizens or residents agree with state policy or not, they have to pay taxes and serve in the army and they are bound by the whole network and system of laws. The issue before the Jewish people is how to deal with power-sharing between elements quite disparate in character, even though united by a common sense of peoplehood and a very strong sense of common fate and interdependence.

Once that is solved, how is it possible to constitutionally design the institutions and the instrumentalities for linking state and diaspora? For those who have been involved in constitutional design in a variety of contexts, there is nothing more fascinating than being involved in

this particular process precisely because of its complexity and its
many facets.

The Context of the State-Diaspora Relationship

Let us briefly examine the environment of the institutional framework, and the governance processes of this state-diaspora relationship. Israel is a state with all the characteristics of a state, with all the
expectations of total sovereignty that every state has, yet with all the
limitations on sovereignty that are real for states, especially small
states in the world today. On one hand, Israel is more dependent on
outside support than a number of other states, but, because it has a will
to be sovereign, it is probably more independent vis-à-vis its major
patron, the United States, than any U.S. ally other than France.[15]

At the same time, there are organized Jewish communities in over
80 countries of the world, ranging in population from a few hundred
people to nearly six million in the United States. Their ties, within and
between communities, in every case are voluntary. The vast majority
of Jews live in twelve countrywide communities of 80,000 Jews or
more (Table 8.1). The largest diaspora Jewish community, in the
United States, has some five Jews for every four in Israel. But it is also
the most open of the voluntary communities, the one in which choice
is most an individual matter with the least external constraints, and the
gap is closing rapidly.[16]

This next group of communities includes Russia and France, each
with over half a million Jews. Since first the opening up and then the
dissolution of the Soviet Union, the Jews in Russia and other former
Soviet republics have organized themselves into communities and
established a number of communal institutions to serve them, even
while over a million were emigrating from the FSU. The exact number
of Jews remaining in Russia and its sister republics is unclear. In part,
it depends upon the definition of who is a Jew, but even assuming a
minimum number and a subjective definition, there seem to be well
over half a million Jews remaining in Russia, with estimates ranging
to well over a million. France, whose Jewish population tripled after
the French left Algeria and Algerian and other North African Jews
followed them to France, also has over half a million.

The other major communities are considerably smaller. There are
approximately 300,000 Jews in Britain, and in the vicinity of 300,000

Jews each in Canada, Ukraine, and Argentina.[17] Brazil, Australia, and South Africa have approximately 100,000 each.[18] The other organized communities range from a high of 80,000 to a few hundred. They are players in a far more modest way. All told, however, the existence of a network of organized communities offers a whole that is invariably greater than the sum of its parts. That network both requires and generates appropriate leadership and financing.[19]

Table 8.1

LARGEST COUNTRYWIDE JEWISH COMMUNITIES*

Country	Jewish Population
1. United States	5,800,000
2. Israel	4,500,000
3. Russia	1,500,000
4. France	650,000
5. Canada	350,000
6. United Kingdom	310,000
7. Ukraine	300,000
8. Argentina	260,000
9. Brazil	110,000
10. South Africa	105,000
11. Australia	100,000
12. Hungary	80,000

* Figures are approximate and for the mid-1990s.

Components of the Contemporary Jewish Polity

Jews outside of Israel tax themselves voluntarily through the various welfare and Israel/overseas campaigns that are conducted in each community and raise substantial sums of money. According to this writer's calculations, world Jewry, including Israel, raises something like $35 billion annually for Jewish purposes. Israel has an annual budget of some $25 billion. The Jews of the United States raise voluntarily or mobilize in some way something like $5 billion a year for their local expenditures, and for their contributions to Israel and to the needs of world Jewry. Jews in other countries raise or receive the equivalent in voluntary contributions or government support for their educational and social service institutions.

A solid civil service has developed for world Jewry and the larger communities to administer these sums. Israel as a state has a full, even overblown, bureaucracy. American Jewry has created a strong professional civil service. The major world Jewish relief organizations, such as the Joint Distribution Committee, which is nominally an American Jewish voluntary organization, maintains an internationally-recruited civil service functioning in dozens of countries around the world, including Israel. So all the institutional components have developed that are needed for governance.

There are also the beginnings of an institutional framework, linking the state, the voluntary countrywide bodies, and particularly the local communities which are the real focal points of diaspora Jewish life. They are linked through the four previously mentioned mediating institutions that have developed to accommodate the problem of linking a state with what are, in the end, voluntary organizations.

The principal, if very limited, mediating institution for many years was the World Zionist Organization (WZO). The WZO was the organized expression of world Jewry that gave birth to the State of Israel. After the state was established, the WZO's functions were, for the most part, transferred to the new entity. The WZO then found itself in what has become known in the United States as the "March of Dimes situation." When polio was eradicated, the Polio Foundation had one of two choices. It could close down or it could re-adapt and find a new mission. It chose the latter course. The Polio Foundation became the Birth Defects Foundation. It had a superb fund-raising mechanism and it had a good research establishment. It is generally agreed that it has done a good job in making the transition, although it had to sacrifice much of its public visibility to do so.

The WZO made the same effort but had less success than the Polio Foundation. From the early 1950s to the present, the WZO has been in a process of adaptation, during which time it has moved, like it or not, from being the principal mediating institution to merely one of the state's links to the diaspora. The major diaspora communities have not been organized through the Zionist movement, but have built their own community organizations responsible for and controlling the major sources of funding for Jewish purposes. They control the purse, and since they control the purse, the government of Israel allied itself with them, saying in effect to the local WZO leadership: You are all nice people and we want you to come to Israel three times a year for meetings, but we are going to make our alliances with those who can provide funding for the relief and rehabilitation needs that diaspora contributions are used for in Israel.

Nevertheless, in 1952 the State of Israel regularized its relationship with the WZO through a covenant signed by the leaders of the two bodies and enacted into law by the Israeli Knesset. The covenant provided that the WZO, through its arm, the Jewish Agency, would retain responsibility for immigration to Israel and the subsequent absorption of the immigrants—as well as for Zionist education in the diaspora. This seemingly modest agenda offered the opportunity for widespread WZO involvement in both the state and the diaspora communities, limited only by its organizational competence and the counterclaims of other bodies.

Meanwhile, a parallel process was developing in the diaspora. Initially, the diaspora communities were happy to view Israel strictly as a beneficiary of their fund-raising for relief and rehabilitation needs. However, in due course, they began to perceive—without using the terms—that they were involved in reconstituting a state. Subsequently, they came to see their role as key to a peoplehood relationship with a state-diaspora dimension. It was at that point that they sought a role in the governance of that relationship.

So, between 1968 and 1971, the Jewish Agency, which had been the arm of the WZO for these relief, rehabilitation, reconstruction activities, was reconstituted (they used that term). Together, Israeli and diaspora leaders rewrote the Jewish Agency's constitution. Once that was completed, they went through a whole ceremony of recovenanting, including the signing of a new three-way covenant for the Jewish Agency, involving the state, the WZO, and the representatives of the diaspora communities in the form of their fund-raising organs.[20]

The new constitution provided for a reconstituted Jewish Agency in which the WZO and the fundraising representatives of the communities were equal partners. In fact, what was created was a nexus institution that could serve as a mediating institution between a state whose responsibilities were defined by international law and the voluntary diaspora communities.

The Jewish Agency's original constitutional configuration made it particularly appropriate for this role. Originally, it was established as a result of the League of Nations Mandate for Palestine which was given to the British in 1921. Under the terms of the Mandate, a "Jewish agency" was to be established under international law as the arm of the Jewish people for building the Jewish national home. From the first, it was to be a unique international organization, just as the Jewish people is unique. Consequently, it has a special status in international law; there is no other organization with that status, which survives to this day.[21] So the Jewish Agency exists not only by virtue of its status in Israeli law, or its recognition in the laws of the various countries in which it functions (in most cases, where there are Jewish diasporas, it also has acquired appropriate legal status), but by virtue of its status in international law which gives it a special position.

From a federalist perspective, the Jewish Agency is worthy of investigation as a model for other such arrangements since it links a group of voluntary organizations, organized on three planes—worldwide, countrywide, and local—and a politically independent state on a permanent basis in a set of common tasks.

The Jewish Agency network now comprises some seven major organizations that are linked to it as the nexus for those common tasks. They include: (1) the United Jewish Appeal, which is the principal fund-raising body of American Jewry for Israel, and its two constituting bodies, (2) the United Israel Appeal, whose task it is to transfer, oversee, and evaluate the use of the UJA funds, and (3) the Joint Distribution Committee, which offers relief, rescue, and rehabilitation services to Jews wherever they are in need; (4) the WZO and its two subsidiaries, (5) Keren Hayesod, the principal Israel fund-raising body for the rest of the diaspora, and (6) the Jewish National Fund, the entity responsible for land purchase and reclamation in the Land of Israel; and (7) the Council of Jewish Federations, the principal framing institution of American Jewry, the largest diaspora community. Each has functions of its own in Israel and in the diaspora so that all maintain their own integrities and exist in a confederal relationship with one another through the Jewish Agency and, as a result, with the State of Israel.

In addition, there is a group of organizations peripheral to the Jewish Agency that have developed to deal with problems that cannot be appropriately dealt with by those organizations clearly identified with this nexus. One of these is the World Jewish Congress, founded in 1936 at the initiative of the WZO as a vehicle for fighting anti-Semitism worldwide. At one time, the World Jewish Congress sought to be the parliament of world Jewry. It is not, but what it became over the years was a vehicle through which to represent Jewish interests in the USSR and Eastern Europe, and in those African and Asian countries that did not want direct relations with Israel. This was possible because it maintained an independent posture toward the nexus while at the same time being tied to it fiscally and organizationally. The WZO remains represented in the WJC at all levels, in recent years with less influence than previously.

There are other such functional authorities that handle a variety of tasks that serve the common needs of the Jewish people. ORT, for example, is a worldwide service for vocational training that does much to help non-Jews as well as Jews acquire the skills with which to earn a living. The Memorial Foundation for Jewish Culture, founded as a result of the joint and successful effort of world Jewry to exact reparations from the German Federal Republic for the Holocaust victims, is a worldwide body that funds Jewish cultural and scholarly enterprises. It is composed of representatives of most of the relevant institutions mentioned here. The reparations themselves were obtained through a temporary authority, the Conference on Jewish Material Claims Against Germany. All of Israel's universities are in this category. In Hebrew, these are called "national institutions," an old term designed to reflect the difference between them, the state, and the individual diaspora communities.

Federalism Out of Necessity and Culture

What is characteristic of this network is that it is confederal in both its structure and its processes. Because it is a network of interlocking institutions whose decision-making is based upon consensus and consultation, it cannot be otherwise. There is no real way to exert coercive power in such a network, though the partners can bring to bear considerable pressure on certain issues. If the State of Israel really needs something that is perceived by all to be in its interest, it is very unlikely that the diaspora communities will not respond in some way. If changes in state law regarding who is a Jew are deemed by the diaspora communities as threatening the status of a major share of their Jewish populations, they will campaign against the proposed policy changes and generally will succeed in blocking them. If there is an attack on Israel by the Arab states, obviously there is going to be a response without going through a large round of consultations, because there is a consensus as to what the issue is and what needs to be done. But on most other issues, even the state must consult with diaspora leadership if it wants to gain their support.

This is highly congruent with Jewish political culture, which is federalist in orientation, yet it has developed out of necessity.[22] There is very strong evidence that the founders of the Jewish state saw statehood as being monolithic. Their views grew out of the continental European tradition of reified statehood, in its Eastern and Central European formulations of centralized, monolithic rule. They not only expected a major ingathering of Jews, but assumed that the state would unilaterally speak for all of Jewry.[23] They and their successors changed their views very reluctantly and only out of necessity, and have never given up the theory. The history of the change is in itself worthy of exploration.

All told, there is as yet no real theory for the phenomena described here. There are principles that are becoming increasingly accepted, but there is no theory. There is an emerging set of rules as to what can and cannot be done. These rules are still in the process of being formulated, crystallized, and generally accepted.

None of this will lead to the establishment of any kind of "parliament of the Jewish people" in the near future. The period from the 1880s to the 1950s was a period in which there were a number of attempts to establish such a parliament, first through the World Zionist Organization and second through the World Jewish Congress. This idea was rejected for two reasons: the State of Israel as part of the family of independent, politically sovereign states in the world cannot subject itself to such a parliament, and the diaspora communities, as voluntary bodies composed of individual citizens of their respective countries who owe their first political loyalty to those countries, cannot identify themselves with such an extraterritorial body. Such a parliament would break the rules that bind each of the parties to other games. Since a parliament would jeopardize both sides, there is a consensus on both sides as to why not to have such a thing, albeit for different reasons.

What has developed instead is a network of functional authorities. Some multi-purpose, some single purpose, which do the business of world Jewry and, as such, have begun to provide a model of at least one form of state-diaspora organization in the postmodern epoch.

The Palestinian Arabs are now trying to develop similar mechanisms. They are learning from the Jews in that regard, quite appropriately since the Arabs are appropriately structured as a people to do so, having come out of the same general West Asian culture area as the Jews. In general, diasporas are particularly an Asian phenomenon. Other nations are building other kinds of links to their diasporas. The Chinese use trade associations as their means of connection. The Irish and other ethnic groups use fraternal associations. In no case have they become more than what are essentially private groups that may acquire some public purpose. They have not created public bodies as have the Jews. Hence, the Jewish model is one that still has no analogue. Religious institutions might have filled that void, but in the modern epoch they were reduced in scope so drastically that they could not continue to have much influence beyond what was narrowly defined by moderns as the sphere of organized religion. This may be changing, especially in Asia.

Whatever emerges it is clear that in a world grown smaller, where international migration no longer means the permanent severing of ties with the old home—a world that is, in any case, in the midst of an ethnic revival—diasporas are likely to become an even more common phenomenon. Even the most modern states, such as the United States of America, will have their own diaspora communities scattered throughout the world. Each will have to make its own institutional and legal accommodation to them. That accommodation is not likely to be in every case federal since not in every case will diasporas be organized into communities, but at least in those cases where there is a tradition of separate ethnic or religious organization, federal arrangements are likely to be important in the connection. In many cases those relationships will require new forms of federalism adapted to the asymmetries of the state-diaspora relationship.

Notes

1. The Jerusalem Center for Public Affairs has been especially active in studying state-diaspora relations, principally because of our interest in the relations between Israel and the Jewish people. This chapter draws upon some of the Center's findings to offer an introduction to this phenomenon. For a full list of JCPA publications in this field, see the JCPA Catalog, issued biennially.

2. Salo Wittmayer Baron, *The Jewish Community*, 3 vols. (Philadelphia: Jewish Publication Society of America, 1938-1944).

3. Gabi Sheffer, ed., *Modern Diaspora in International Relations* (London: Cromhelm Publishing Co., 1986); Ivo Duchacek, "Consociations of Fatherlands: The Revival of Confederal Principles and Practices," *Publius,* vol. 12, no. 4 (Fall 1982).

4. On the Chinese diaspora, see: Harley Farnsworth MacNair, *The Chinese Abroad, Their Position and Protection; A Study in International Law and Relations* (Taipei: Ch'eng Wen Publishing Co., 1971); Robert Elegant, *The Dragon's Seed: Peking and the Overseas Chinese* (New York: St. Martin's Press, 1959).

5. On Somalia and the Somalis, see Catherine Hoskyns, ed. and comp., *The Ethiopia-Somalia-Kenya Dispute, 1960-1967* (Dar es Salaam, Tanzania: Oxford University Press, 1969).

6. On the French system, see: Alain Lancelot, *L'Absentionissme Electoral en France* (Paris: A. Colin, 1968); Segun Osoba and Obaro Ikime, eds., *France in Africa* (London: Longmans, Green, 1969).

7. On American accommodations, see *The Uniformed and Overseas Citizens Absentee Voting Act* (42 U.S.C. 1973 ff(b)). (Tel Aviv: U.S. Information Service, 1988).

8. On the Arab nation, see Philip Hitti, "The Changing Scene: Impact of the West," *History of the Arabs,* 10th ed. (London: MacMillan and Co. Ltd., 1970).

9. On the Berkeley referendum, see Earl Raab and Edwin Epstein, "The Foreign Policy of Berkeley, California," *Moment,* September 1984.

10. On the Armenians and Soviet Armenia, see Aghavnie Yeghia Yeghenian, *The Red Flag at Ararat* (New York: Women's Press, 1932); Emanuel Sarkisyanz, *A Modern History of Transcaucasian Armenia: Social, Cultural and Political* (Nagpur: Udyama Commercial Press, 1975).

11. On such arrangements in the Hellenistic world, cf. Baron, *The Jewish Community*, vol. 1; Michael Grant, *The Jews in the Roman World* (London: Weidenfeld and Nicolson, 1973).

12. Cf. Howard Sachar, *The Course of Modern Jewish History* (New York, 1958); Walter Lacquer, *A History of Zionism* (London: Weidenfeld and Nicolson, 1972).

13. For an examination of this process in the context of Jewish constitutional history, see Daniel J. Elazar and Stuart A. Cohen, *The Jewish Polity*

(Bloomington, Ind.: Indiana University Press, 1984), especially Epochs 13 and 14.

14. On the Jewish Agency and its network, see Daniel J. Elazar and Andrea S. Arbel, eds., *Understanding the Jewish Agency*, 3rd ed. (Jerusalem and Philadelphia: Jerusalem Center for Public Affairs, 1993); and Zelig Chinitz, *A Common Agenda* (Jerusalem and Philadelphia: Jerusalem Center for Public Affairs, 1985).

15. On the governance of Israel with a particular eye to its place in the Jewish polity, see Daniel J. Elazar, *Israel: Building a New Society* (Bloomington, Ind.: Indiana University Press, 1986).

16. On the governance of American Jewry, see Daniel J. Elazar, *Community and Polity, The Organizational Dynamics of American Jewry* (Philadelphia: Jewish Publication Society, 1976).

17. On the governance of the Jews of France, see Ilan Greilsammer, *The Governance of the Jews of France* (Jerusalem: Jerusalem Center for Public Affairs, forthcoming); on Britain, see Ernest Krausz, *Trend Report on Jewish Social Research in Britain* (Jerusalem: Center for Jewish Community Studies, 1971); on Canada, see Harold Waller and Daniel J. Elazar, *Maintaining Consensus: The Canadian Jewish Polity in the Postwar World* (Lanham, Md.: Jerusalem Center for Public Affairs and University Press of America, 1990); and on Argentina, see Daniel J. Elazar and Peter Medding, *Jewish Communities in Frontier Societies* (New York: Holmes and Meier, 1983).

18. On the governance of the Jewish community of Brazil, see Daniel J. Elazar, *People and Polity, The Organizational Dynamics of World Jewry* (Detroit: Wayne State University Press, 1989; on South Africa and Australia, see Elazar and Medding, *Jewish Communities in Frontier Societies*; on Hungary, see Elizabeth Eppler, "Hungary: Organized Decline," *European Judaism* (Summer 1968), pp. 15-18.

19. For a comprehensive analysis of the entire structure and each community within it, see Elazar, *People and Polity*.

20. The best history of the process is to be found in Ernest Stock, *Partners and Pursestrings* (Lanham, Md.: Jerusalem Center for Public Affairs and University Press of America, 1987); Chinitz, *A Common Agenda*; and Elazar and Arbel, *Understanding the Jewish Agency*. For a study of the period from 1948 to 1968, see Charles S. Liebman, *Pressure Without Sanctions* (Rutherford, N.J.: Fairleigh Dickenson University Press, 1977).

21. See Eli Likhovski, "Memorandum on Reconstitution Agreement" in Elazar and Arbel, eds., *Understanding the Jewish Agency*, pp. 171-173.

22. See Elazar, *People and Polity*, Part I.

23. See Elazar, *Israel*, Ch. 10.

Chapter 9

WHAT SHOULD WE LEARN FROM ALL OF THIS?

What can we learn from all of this after reviewing the still rather slim body of literature on modern and postmodern confederation and supplementing it with the research for this book? We begin with some of the fundamental truths about federalism and federal solutions of any kind.

1. Statism sees the state as reified—the most comprehensive and authoritative association, which lives over and above its people. The institutions of the state have a life of their own, separate from that of the rest of civil society. As the single most comprehensive association, the state is the repository of all political sovereignty. Effective government must be centralized in the hands of the sovereign, although the composition of the sovereign may have been popularized as a result of the changes of modernity.

Federalism, on the other hand, does not concentrate on questions of sovereignty, but on questions of powers (or competences) and jurisdiction. Sovereignty is quickly disposed of by being vested in the hands of the people, who distribute governmental powers to various authorities as they deem appropriate, by constitutional means, to make certain that there will be no centralization or concentration of power in a few hands. Civil society is a matrix of associations, organized politically into various governmental arenas, most empowered directly by the people. The state is no more than a political association like all others. Federalism does not recognize any reified state or state apparatus separate from civil society. The institutions of government are simply among the institutions civil society empowered by the people and the constitution to undertake their tasks. The different arenas of government are not higher or lower than one another, but are more or less comprehensive in their scope.

Federalism rejects the power pyramid and center-periphery models in which the periphery is ruled by the elites that occupy the top or the center. By removing sovereignty from any single institution and investing it in the people in their various organized forms, federalism stands in opposition to the idea of the reified state. This is true for the entire genus of federalism, but its expressions differ in each species. It is most true for federations and least for confederations. Confederations do have a place for states with a more statist sense among their constituent units. Indeed, the state model may serve to preserve the respective integrities of the units in the confederation. In many cases, it is even necessary to make confederation itself possible; since the publics of the various state civil societies have as a foremost desire the preservation of their respective integrities, they will need to feel appropriately safeguarded through constitutional arrangements that recognize and protect that need.

2. All federalism involves some combination of self-rule and shared rule. In confederation, a premium is placed somewhat more on the self-rule of the constituent units and shared rule is more circumscribed, but they both must still be present and effective. Federalism in general emphasizes relationships, especially constitutional ones, of which the self-rule/shared rule relationship is the most important. Constitutionalized noncentralization is a means to effectuate self-rule/shared rule relationships, more so in confederations where noncentralization—the matrix model with clearly defined arenas—is a sine qua non.

3. Ethnonationalist statism is the most difficult form of statism to accommodate in any kind of federal relationship. Ethnonationalism is highly egocentric in most, if not all, cases. Consequently, there must be even more of a will to establish federal links and arrangements where ethnonationalism is involved. Confederal arrangements require a different level and kind of commitment than federal ones in this case. Confederation requires a different kind of linkage than federation. Still, the will to confederate also must exist. That is necessary for a successful confederation, if not sufficient. There is a necessity even in the case of limited confederal arrangements for all parties to be wiling to live together, to establish relationships of mutual respect, and for all parties to exercise self-control in those relationships.

4. From this general beginning, we must determine what we have learned about the special problems of confederation and confederal arrangements. Probably the most important problem is to find incentives for the confederal constituents to enter and stay in the confederation. The completeness of the constituent states and the degree of autonomy they retain, often under conditions through which their interest in or need for autonomy is already extraordinarily great, may substantially reduce the incentives for even confederal linkages. This is not necessarily so. For example, in the European Union, despite the statist nationalism of so many of the members and their ethnic uniqueness, all have had an incentive to gain economic benefits from membership in the community. Those incentives have already served well. A major issue in any confederal arrangement is to provide sufficient incentives for the members to remain in it under circumstances where secession will remain an option, either de facto or de jure.

It is clear that confederal arrangements to long survive need a commitment to permanent union. This, indeed, was one of the special points of emphasis of modern confederation. The American Articles of Confederation established a perpetual union and so did subsequent efforts at modern confederation, although, as Duchacek correctly points out, confederations are often closer to leagues than to federal unions. The term "union" is not only a paper necessity, it has to be sufficiently enforceable. We say "sufficiently" because it is clear that to be as enforceable as it would be in a federation probably would be more than the confederal partners would accept. Some element of sufficiency, that is to say, some great disincentive to secede and great incentive to remain is required. For the European Union the huge economic penalty of secession is a sufficient disincentive to have made secession an essential impossibility. So, too, is it to looser league-like international bodies like the WTO. We may anticipate that the necessity elsewhere and in general will be economic.

5. Confederations are also faced with the problem of providing a proper understanding of federal liberty. Does this have to be a special confederal understanding? Not necessarily. Our examination of the American experience suggests that there is limited conceptual difference between federal liberty in federations or confederations, though there are likely to be some differences in terms of the pact that establishes the political terms of federal liberty for the body politic in each species. In its most basic moral sense, federal liberty is the same for all people no matter what kind of regime serves them. Regarding the specifically political dimensions of federal liberty, these will,

indeed, vary from regime to regime and, as such, could also vary among confederations as between confederations and federations. Certainly, the degree to which bonds of community are called for across the federal linkages will be less in confederal arrangements than in federations, while the bonds of community in the constituent units are likely to be all that much greater. The bonds of comity, however, must be proportionate to agreements made in both.

Modern democratic republics follow one of two forms: commonwealth, in which there is a fundamental commitment to a moral and cultural homogeneity that goes beyond merely supporting the shared rules of the game; and civil society, in which far greater moral and cultural differences are acceptable and in which the emphasis is placed upon universal support for the shared rules of the game. Whatever the arguments in theory, the historical record shows that empirically, federations are more likely to be civil societies than commonwealths but may require commitment to extensive rules of the game. Duchacek identified three reasons why the Americans went beyond confederation in the new United States to invent federation. They are: awareness of common colonial experience, common sacrifice and victory in the Revolutionary War, and common language and cultural heritage.[1] In confederations, on the other hand, the constituent units are likely to be commonwealths precisely because the confederation as a whole requires adherence or commitment to fewer and less extensive rules of the game and even less in the way of cultural homogeneity. That, indeed, is why confederal arrangements have again become appropriate. They enable commonwealths to enter into federal arrangements without losing their character as commonwealths. That is why confederations and confederal arrangements are more easily appropriate for the resolution of ethnic conflicts if they can be made to work.

Vis-à-vis natural liberty, the emphasis on federal liberty certainly applies equally to both, but then it does to all civil societies, polities, and communities whose goal is to enable people to live together on more than a Hobbesian basis. Negotiating the terms of federal liberty must be appropriate to the different character of constitutionalism in federations and confederations, with constitutions, charters, and other pacts serving as the most open and honest way to reach agreements as to what constitutes the federal liberty of bodies politic on necessarily collective matters. This may be so widely recognized that it hardly need be stated. It is clearly visible in the various charters of the European Union and in the struggles over their drafting and application. It is equally visible in the covenants and charters of the United Nations where member state ratification and enforcement is far more discretionary.

6. What of the U.S. experience in all this? It may be surprising to many to recall that the United States invented modern confederation as well as modern federation. While both the Swiss confederation and the United Provinces of the Netherlands were in existence in 1776 when the United States declared its independence and began to design its Articles of Confederation, both had their origins in premodern times, Switzerland in the thirteenth century and the United Provinces in the sixteenth. Both were primarily premodern in concept and contained many premodern elements.

The American experiment, as we know, was short lived. Adopted by Congress in 1777, ratified by the states by 1781, and replaced by the Constitution of 1787 in 1789. How successful the United States was under the Articles remains a matter of dispute, with partisans of the Articles arguing that it was quite successful until replaced by the federal constitution, through sleight of hand arguments, and partisans of the Constitution of 1787 arguing quite the opposite. There is substantial literature available on both sides of the question. A good case can be made for the Articles as a modern instrumentality, perhaps flawed beyond the desirable, but still an effort to confront the problems of modernity. While the forms of confederation developed in the United States may not be useful in the postmodern epoch, the essential confrontation which those forms addressed, that between federal liberty and natural liberty remains as real as it was in the eighteenth century.

7. U.S. reliance on confederal arrangements with a federal framework can be seen to have persisted into the nineteenth century until the Civil War and even beyond, even without considering the attempted secession of the Southern states. This further demonstrates how powerful cultural expectations and sociological habit are, viewed in the face of formal constitutional arrangements alone. The ultimate triumph of formal provisions will occur, but at a much slower pace than is conventionally expected.

8. The third element of the U.S. experience from which we can learn is the postmodern emergence of regional confederal arrangements within the United States, most particularly in the South and in New England. While the future of those confederal arrangements that are other than technical in nature is not clear, they do represent a

governmental phenomenon of some importance and reflect cultural and sociological as well as constitutional and political realities.

9. They also have implications that reach beyond the United States. These have to do with two emerging phenomena on the international scene: one, the merger of the two state systems of over 180 politically sovereign states and the over 350 constituent states; and two, the development of the idea of both kinds of states as neutral service providers for all within their boundaries. Elsewhere, this writer has suggested that with the emergence of new postmodern diaspora and state-diaspora relationships, the high levels of international mobility since the end of World War II, especially those affecting Europe, and the emergence of postmodern confederal arrangements, which both encourage those migrations and limit the possibility of migrant assimilation in new lands of residence, have led to a de facto compromise that every state is required to provide essentially equal services to all of its residents regardless of citizenship. Confederal arrangements enhance the possibility of doing just that since they can distinguish between human and civil rights; the right to enjoy services and the rights of citizenship.

10. If the link between domestic and foreign affairs becomes blurred and increasingly interdependent, just as economic development, historically a domestic concern, has increasingly acquired international dimensions, as telecommunications and environmental pollution increasingly demonstrate the accuracy of the proverbial claim that they know no boundaries, federated (or constituent) states are as much involved in transborder transactions as politically independent states, while politically independent states increasingly come under the authority and the scrutiny of the "international community," not only in terms of their foreign and defense policies, but even in terms of their domestic policies' impact on their inhabitants or their neighbors. This is particularly true since the demise of the Soviet Union (in part, just because of that kind of pressure) and the emergence of the United States as the world's only superpower. The United Nations has become a more united and powerful worldwide coalition of its members, better able to act than ever before to serve the common interests of the world community and to promote certain common services. Will the linkages thus developed be those needed to develop what became in time de facto confederal arrangements?

11. All of this should explain why there is a revival of confederation. The need to establish proper partnerships while at the same time preserving communal, ethnonational, or simply national integrities

makes confederal solutions not always ideal, but often the most practical. The European Union has shown the way; certainly its member states have demonstrated a desire both to preserve their national integrities and at the same time link together for economic purposes and to maintain the security of Western Europe by harnessing the German giant to its neighbors. This volume traces, at least partially, those impulses and their consequences. The founders of the EC/EU hoped that it would start the process that would lead to a United States of Europe, but with the minimal expectation that at least it would lead to a Western European economic and defense merger to tie together the member states and thereby control a resurgent Germany. The security element foundered on a revived French nationalism in the person of Charles de Gaulle, but fortunately, NATO, established under the lead of the United States, was able to provide a very successful substitute and prevent the EC from foundering on highly divergent attitudes on the security issue at the beginning of its history.

12. If we look at the history of the EU and other new-style confederal arrangements, it quickly becomes apparent that the old reason for confederation in modern and premodern times—mutual defense—is perhaps the issue to be most avoided if postmodern efforts are to be successful. If security concerns can be accommodated by other means, particularly those linked to external powers, and great pressure is removed from parties that are, in all likelihood, somewhat reluctant or ambivalent about confederating altogether, they are able to focus on matters of mutual benefit that carry far less risk. Security matters may remain very important for federations, but for confederal arrangements they should have a very low profile.

The EC weathered some trying moments over the following decades and came very close to confronting secessionist movements in the late 1970s, but when the chips were down, it had already become clear that it was in no member's interest to pull out because of the economic integration that had already taken place. Thus, the EC overcame the problem of incentives to linkage through its economic mechanisms. Subsequently, the issue of union changed to being a question of what kind of linkage, federal union or something else, which is where the EU now stands.

Moreover, the confederal arrangements of the EU were supplemented by other European-wide and even North Atlantic-wide agreements, demonstrating once again that (quasi-) federal arrangements beget more federal arrangements. These included various kinds of agreements ranging from NATO to the Council of Europe to the

Helsinki Agreements to protect human rights centered on Europe. Although these agreements were more in the nature of the confederal agreements that Duchacek describes in "Consociations of Father-lands," i.e., augmented international treaties, since they were anchored on the EC, a true confederal arrangement, they acquired more force than ordinary international treaties. Together they have established the beginnings of a framework for permanent confederal arrangements to link all of Europe.

This trend may have suffered a setback as a result of the civil wars among the ex-Yugoslav republics, although the last word on that is not yet in. In the Yugoslav case, the EU, confronted with its own problems of linkage, did not rise to the occasion in time. Germany took the lead on its own and contributed to worsening the situation. Subsequently, the EU began to develop a concerted response, even involving the presence of troops from several EU nations as part of the United Nations peacekeeping force, but its failure was not reversible.

13. The other confederal arrangements that have emerged are, for the most part, less firm than the European Union and some are hardly more than augmented treaties. They are following the "rules" laid down by Duchacek, including the ways and means to move toward more solidly confederal arrangements when they are desired by the parties involved. Some indicate the need for dyadic arrangements, which Duchacek properly describes as the most difficult of achieving. In all, the system of developing networks of multiple authorities, some with the same jurisdiction and others with different "service-sheds," has emerged as the primary mechanism for confederal linkages. For these purposes, much can be learned from the study of intrametropolitan linkages, particularly from the studies undertaken by Holden and the Ostroms and their students in the United States.

14. The problem of ethnicity and confederal arrangements needs further study. Increasingly, the application of federal institutions and practices, especially in their confederal form, is based on the need to resolve interethnic conflicts over the same or adjacent territories. Interethnic conflicts are, thus, the greatest catalysts for confederal solutions, yet perhaps their greatest enemy. Indeed, as is indicated in this series, confederal solutions are particularly attractive when ethnic groups are involved because they seem to offer the promise of preserving ethnic group identity and political autonomy without requiring that every ethnic group be given a totally separate state. At the same time, ethnic groups in the full thrust of their ethnic separatist demands are least able to overcome ethnic egocentricity and to find a will to

confederate. Moreover, the ideology of ethnicity very often undercuts any political culture of power sharing that may exist.

With all that, nevertheless, confederal arrangements very often offer the only possible way to resolve interethnic conflict. They do not apply appropriately in every case, but there are many cases in which they will. In addition to cultural and ideological predispositions, the effective use of federal solutions is enhanced if the ethnic groups are territorially separate and weakened if they are intermixed. Perhaps the motto for all confederal arrangements should be "Good fences make good neighbors." Where it is possible to erect good fences, i.e., to maintain a certain real degree of territorial separation between ethnic groups, there is a greater chance of their cooperating with one another on a permanent basis.

If the groups are intermixed, however, and such separations are thereby physically impossible and must be secured through other means—consociational, for example—the chances for the formation and survival of confederal arrangements are much more problematic. The chances for conflict are greater because the opportunities are greater. Furthermore, the historical record with regard to consociationalism, based as it is on elite accommodation, is that consociational regimes retain their consociational character for two generations, no more, unless that character is reinforced by territorial divisions or some other independent mode of accommodation. After that time, the polity that emerges either is more integrated, as in the Netherlands and Israel, or less, as in Belgium and Lebanon. Belgium, indeed, adopted a conventional federal solution in place of its increasingly ineffective consociational structure. Lebanon collapsed into civil war, which was ended only after substantial Syrian intervention and what is, in effect, the Syrian occupation of the country.

The expanding need to build a worldwide network of arrangements for peace-keeping and economic growth is likely to further stimulate the confederal arrangements in the third arena. Attention must be paid to the problems that ethnicity poses for confederal arrangements of that kind and for the promise that confederal arrangements offer for resolving interethnic conflict on a grand scale. These ties, which inevitably will be looser, may also be less threatening, especially with positive major power involvement. They actually may assist ethnic groups toward confederal arrangements for handling more localized problems including conflicts.

Perhaps the best example to date can be found in Western Europe. The rapprochement between France and Germany, and the French and the Germans, through the European Union and the EU's contribution to it, and the rapprochement already under way for the previous forty years between the British and the French are two prime examples of this. It is questionable whether the British and the French, not to speak of the French and the Germans, are any fonder of each other than they were in the past. From the record, it seems as if they may not have to be. They may retain at least some part of their traditional prejudices toward the other as long as in areas of common concern, they are prepared to reach confederal levels of cooperation, which they have shown that they are.

It is perhaps an exaggeration to describe the divisions among islanders in the Caribbean as equivalent to ethnic tensions, but there insularity offers many of the same difficulties, even as smallness calls for certain kinds of linkage. If movement there has been slower than in the EU, there also may be less need, and the most damaging forms of insularity seem to have been contained through common confederal institutions and actions.

In a sense, almost every associated state relationship also represents an effort to resolve an ethnic conflict. The asymmetrical character of the polities involved usually has much to do with the fact that the smaller ethnic group may have little choice, while the larger may have little to fear from acting generously. Still, these represent examples of another kind of political accommodation of ethnic demands. Such demands might seemingly be more easily suppressed, while there are some kinds of arrangements that can allow a great power to be generous.

In some cases, as in interethnic conflict between more evenly balanced groups, the application of any power-sharing solution is all the more difficult. We have seen how it has erupted into full-scale, bloody, even genocidal, civil war in the territories of former Yugoslavia. Their leadership, instead of reinforcing the constitutionalization of a confederal solution already well on its way to becoming the reality in practice, disrupted the best and most peaceful era that those peoples had ever known and reintensified old conflicts that had been much reduced under the previous regime. Nevertheless, attempts to achieve a peaceful solution still have rested upon suggested confederal arrangements, such as the division of Bosnia into ten semiautonomous provinces or into Serbian, Croatian, and Muslim areas punctuated by "safe havens." There is nothing else to suggest in a democratic age. Unless the peoples on the ground and the rest of the world are willing to allow more violent and genocidal solutions such as "ethnic cleansing" with impunity, or perhaps the imposition of very severe authoritarian if not totalitarian rule, this is the only direction in which to look, where full territorial partition is not feasible. Moreover, simple partitionist solutions are becoming less and less feasible in an increasingly interdependent world. One need not see confederal arrangements as universally applicable or anything like that to understand the truth of this. Instead, more sophisticated devices that combine partition and linkage are called for.

15. One thing is clear: no confederal arrangement can be established by force. If force is used, it will not be a confederal arrangement. The experience of the ex-Communist countries with forced "federalism," all of which disintegrated with the collapse of Communism, should be an important and even salutary lesson to all. In the end, new confederal or even federal arrangements may emerge in all or parts of the territories of the former USSR, but they will be negotiated and not imposed.

16. What, then, can bring about confederal arrangements in cases of ethnic conflict? One answer is terrible fear of the alternative. The role of terror in promoting fundamental change was raised in Chapter 7. Terror in this sense is not the manufactured terror of human political revolutions that the world has come to know in the past two hundred years, but the honest terror derived from changed situations and the increasingly more widespread perception of their potential consequences if not responded to appropriately.

This, indeed, is what has led to serious efforts to resolve the great ethnic conflicts of our time—in South Africa, in the case of Israel, the Palestinians and Jordan, and in Northern Ireland. At a certain point in the conflict, fear of its consequences, at least in the minds of a major share of the leadership on the various sides, grew beyond fear of the consequences of the compromises and concessions that had to be made to achieve any resolution or movement toward peaceful resolution of the conflict. In all three cases there was sufficient latent strength in the regnant political cultures to provide a basis for developing a response to those terrors. These latent political cultural supports were not distributed equally or symmetrically among the parties to the conflict, nor were the responses symmetrical, but they were sufficient to allow moderates to begin to seize control of the relevant centers of power needed to move resolution of the conflict along. It is too soon to tell whether they were sufficient to achieve the peaceful ends sought. In that respect, South Africa has moved further down that path. In the case of Israel, the Palestinians, and Jordan, the movement has been significant, but it is too early to say whether it can continue. Unlike the situation in South Africa, where institutions and mechanisms were found that seemed to sufficiently satisfy the parties, they are still in the process of being developed in the Middle Eastern conflict. Northern Ireland is just beginning the process of negotiation that can lead to the next steps.

In contrast, where the fears of continuing along the path of conflict do not outweigh the fears of resolving it, the conflicts continue no matter what opportunities the political cultures of those engaged in those conflicts can provide in the way of movement toward resolution. In most cases, indeed, there is very little that the political cultures do provide, exacerbating the problem rather than offering a basis for its resolution, putting a greater burden on the need for fear, and even contributing to the exacerbation of the conflict. This is the case with regard to the conflicts in the former Yugoslavia, the former Soviet Union, and in black Africa.

17. In most cases those conflicts, as in the ones earlier mentioned, religion plays an important role, either manifest or latent. In none of them is religion enough to provoke the conflict; it seems that an ethnic dimension is needed as well. In this respect, they may differ from the wars of religion that contributed to the foundation of the modern state system, although it may be wise to explore the manifest or latent ethnic identities of the warring European states in the sixteenth and seventeenth centuries as well. Even among the German-speaking peoples, there were significant ethnic differences, many submerged or half-submerged by that time (Saxons, Alemannians, Teutons, Thuringians, etc.).

Religion may not cause a conflict and in no case is it the sole cause, but certain kinds of religious differences exacerbate conflicts that otherwise might occur in any case. That is the case with most modern ethnic conflicts. Conflicts caused by religion alone are more likely to be intra- than interethnic. These intraethnic conflicts may revolve around rule and power, and religion may be a means to resolve them. This has been true in the case of all three monotheistic religions at various times in their history. It is true in Islam today with regard to Muslims, even though Islam with regard to non-Muslims is one of the powerful fomenters of conflict. In the resolution of such conflicts, confederal arrangements may indeed prove to be very helpful, not so much in taking the first steps, but in taking the next steps, in providing the institutions and mechanisms to bring the resolution of the conflict to a level of sufficient stability for peace to begin to work itself out.

18. This understanding of the role of federal solutions of whatever kind is vitally necessary if federal solutions are to work. In the past, partisans of such solutions would propose them as the starting point for resolving conflicts. Not surprisingly, such solutions often failed, requiring too high a level of trust between the parties at the beginning and too compatable a political-cultural base. By considering only the structural arrangements, advocates of such solutions made no provisions for considering psychological and cultural elements.

The problem was not with the federal solutions but with the inappropriate timing used in connection with them. No doubt, there are political cultures that will never be able to sustain federal solutions. Egypt, for example, has been governed hierarchically since its emergence onto the stage of history over 6,000 years ago. Nevertheless, introduced at the proper time and in the proper manner, federal arrangements, and at times even federal principles, can be of great help in moving an interethnic conflict the next step toward resolution.

In South Africa, for example, very few whites or blacks favored any kind of federal solution to their problems. A large majority on both sides saw federalism as a means by which the other side would be able to dilute the strength and political power of their side. First, there had to be a sufficient reconciliation between the white-dominated South African government and the black-dominated African National Congress to enable them to talk with one another. They then discovered that there was enough willingness for reconciliation among their respective peoples.

When they started talking with one another, they also began listening. Both sides soon were convinced that the establishment of provincial and local governments with some governing capability was necessary in any solution. That, coupled with the unremitting federalist demands of the primarily Zulu Inkatha Freedom Party (IFP) and the federalist proposals from Joe Slovo, whose left-wing credentials were unchallengeable, led them to begin the process of designing appropriate structures and mechanisms. This, in the end, required an additional round after the interim constitution was promulgated in order to satisfy the IFP, but once the new government was in place and steps had to be taken to write a permanent constitution, it seemed that the only argument left was the extent to which full federalism would be introduced and how the provinces would be divided.

South Africa is a good example of putting federal solutions on the table at the right moment. In fact, outside experts had to raise the question of federalism and teach their colleagues responsible for the technical work of the negotiations what federalism entailed in order for the latter to be ready for the right moment.

The case of the European Union is similar in its evolving use of confederal arrangements. First, a proper measure of contact and trust had to be established, and then confederal solutions could be discussed, even if not as such, conceptualizing them in a manner that fit the dominant political culture they were to serve.

19. Are there other incentives to federalize? Thomas Hueglin has suggested with just a touch of cynicism that the European Community was founded and has survived as a network of interlocking trade-offs, each to the advantage of one of its members. There is nothing wrong with that. In general, all the members desired European peace after World War II, wanted to avoid vulnerability to Communist bloc conquests during the Cold War, and wanted to avoid the economic hegemony of the United States. For Germany and Italy and later for Spain and Portugal, the EC easily provided political respectability as they came back from their Nazi and Fascist pasts. In the small Benelux countries, the EC offered the chance for a larger voice in the new Western Europe and powers of co-determination. France gained "substantive control over the coal and steel production of its remilitarizing German arch-enemy." After World War I, it tried to gain that by detaching the Saar region from Germany—by partition—in a move that failed. German Federal Republic support for EC subsidies to support French agriculture was an additional benefit for the French.

Hueglin places himself among those who are disappointed that the results of all this were not a federal Europe but rather a confederation. Still, he points out why confederation really allows the members no effective possibilities to secede without paying huge costs. That is the other dimension of its success. In the process he describes how the institutions of the EC evolved away from federation in the direction of confederation.

20. This brings us to the larger point that postmodern confederation rests upon several principles of constitutional design that differ from the federal arrangements of modern federation as well as from premodern confederal ones. The founders of the EC saw the European Parliament as the lower house of the future European legislative assembly, and the Council of Ministers as the future upper chamber in the pattern of the German Bundesrat. The European Commission was to evolve into a supranational executive or collective government with a rotating presidency.

In fact, the Council of Ministers claimed the authority, responsibility, and power for executive decision-making. The Council remained a body for international negotiation rather than supranational policy formation, with each member state retaining veto power and its decisions requiring unanimity, at least de facto. The Commission became responsible for providing and preparing policy expertise in accordance with national prerogatives and administered the bureaucratic Community regulations which did indeed accumulate, as the major body of supranational control. The EU bureaucracy and the Commission's executive may not be fully accountable in formal democratic terms, but they have acquired immense power, while the European Parliament, even though now elected by the voters of the member states, has remained essentially an advisory body.

The direction of this slide is clearly toward confederation, but it is a tight confederation. The EU becomes a tighter confederation all the time. If asked the question how tight can a confederation be and still be a confederation, we have to conclude that we do not yet know. At the very least, the EU is breaking new ground all the time. At the same time, it teaches us much as to how a confederation can be formed and made successful. There must be multiple incentives based on trade-offs among the potential members, until leaving becomes such a disincentive for any one of them that it is rejected as a possibility.

21. It also points to the difference in the institutions of a federation and a confederation. A confederation is not built on the traditional tripartite separation of powers and three-fold set of constitutional arenas. Its separation of powers is much looser, usually based on four-fold separation of institutions and up to four or five arenas with their own constitutional standing.

It seems that postmodern confederal arrangements are best constructed out of single- and multipurpose joint authorities by those who are in the process of becoming constituent members. Thus, they weave themselves a tailor-made web, authority-by-authority, so that the authorities may or may not include all constituents uniformly. This device was used by the Swiss republics to form their Helvetic Confederation in premodern times, relying on a somewhat different set of principles. They provided full or partial exemptions from some of the linkages for some of the constituents. They also included a second set of authorities that reached beyond the original members of the confederation. In other words, the system of functional authorities allows for flexible boundaries in some cases, organized more or less on the basis of both the arenas and the populations to be served.

22. The most promising basis for confederal constitutional design in postmodern confederations is decision-making through collegial institutions with a substantial amount of equality among the constituent units built in. These three principles seem to be consistent in all of our examples. Two more may be included. In place of the traditional three-way separation of powers, a four-way separation of powers seems to be emerging in the general collective governing institutions of each confederation. The European Union is the best example, sharing power as it does between the European Council, the European Commission, the European Parliament, and the European Court, formed as a matrix. Elements of collegiality are present in all four, although the Council is the most collegial and equal. All three others have collegial components and reflect the basic equality among the members.

23. The internal federal arrangements of postmodern confederations increasingly involve more than the classic three arenas: federal or confederal, state or constituent units, and local. In the European Union, for example, there are the Union institutions, the member states, and also the constituent bodies of those member states, a number of which are federations in their own right. Germany and Belgium are federations. Spain is a federation in all but name, and Italy, which opted for regional decentralization, has increased the powers of its regions. Great Britain, while formally a Union, incorporates constitutional protections for the countries and offshore islands that together comprise the United Kingdom of Great Britain and Northern Ireland. Even historically centralized countries like France and Portugal have attempted some decentralization to their regions or provinces.

The European Union increasingly has to make arrangements for these four arenas. In addition to what already exists, there is a major EU effort to strengthen subnational regional governments in every one of its member states. This is not necessarily a matter of abstract principle. The European Commission is interested in doing so in order to strengthen the EU government vis-à-vis the national governments of the states it serves. Moreover, from the first, the local governments of the member states banded together on a Union-wide basis to strengthen their positions in the Community with some considerable success.

The same situation has yet to develop the same proportions in other examples of confederal arrangements. It does seem to exist in the West Indies where multi-island republics not only decentralize their powers to each island, but to the towns and villages on each island as well. This may be true of all island republics that have embraced federal or confederal arrangements.

24. For many of them, these arrangements are asymmetrical. As Michael Stevens has pointed out in some detail, both federacies and associated states (asymmetrical federal and confederal arrangements respectively) have become quite widespread since World War II. Since he wrote his article,[2] the United States has granted Northern Marianas Islands federacy status and federated states like the Federated States of Micronesia, the Marshall Islands, and Palau associated state status. The Netherlands, which established associated state relationships with the Netherlands Antilles shortly after World War II, has modified those arrangements somewhat, and Britain essentially sought that kind of status for China and Hong Kong when the latter returned to the Peoples Republic at the end of the decade. Most of these arrangements have proved to be remarkably stable. West Berlin, which was officially an associated state of the German Federal Republic, became a normal *land* with the unification of Germany, embracing East Berlin as well. And some years ago, India conquered Sikkim and made it a federacy rather than an associated state. There are now eleven asymmetrical confederal arrangements in the world.

This postmodern federal phenomenon is hardly recognized for what it is. Few in the way of either theoretical or empirical studies have been undertaken from that perspective. Recent analysis of confederation has relied on modern and premodern models primarily. Recent studies of specific postmodern examples have relied upon international relations or functionalist models primarily. Hence, what is needed is a considerable amount of work with both the theory and practice of postmodern confederation and confederal arrangements.

25. What remains is the question of adaptation of confederal arrangements within decentralizing federations, unions, and unitary states. It need hardly be said that this is a completely different group of confederal arrangements with its own reasons, justifications, and rules. Perhaps the most prominent example of a decentralizing federation was that of Yugoslavia. It is, at this writing, a failed example, although the last word may not have been spoken. Like most failures, there are important lessons to be learned from it.

For example, its move toward confederation was just as authoritarian and quasitotalitarian in character as its earlier move toward federation after World War II. This has had a real impact on the results. As long as the dictatorial republican oligarchies still had incentives to hold together as parts of Yugoslavia, they did. Following Tito's death, there was great economic decentralization which allowed, not only every republic, but every locality to make its own international economic policy, including rapidly building up debt for all of Yugoslavia. This reduced the incentives that had previously existed and introduced great new disincentives, as the more prosperous northern republics of Croatia and especially Slovenia found their economies being weakened by the necessity to provide assistance for the far less developed and even depressed southern republics. This led to their demands for renegotiating the Yugoslav republican arrangement and, ultimately, to their secession.

Ill-timed and misdirected outside intervention compounded the situation. When Germany, always close to those two republics, with special ties dating back to World War II if not before, insisted on recognizing the independence of Slovenia and Croatia, it awakened in the Serbs not only their traditional desire to dominate Yugoslavia, but their memories of Slovenian and Croatian collaboration with the Nazis during World War II which led to the massacre of Serbs, Jews, Gypsies, and others. Thus began the civil war. Slovenia's position and the lack of strong non-Slovenian minorities within its borders, plus German recognition, generated the conditions for its successful breakaway.

Croatia, on the other hand, with a large Serbian population within its boundaries, was invaded by the Serbian-dominated Yugoslav army, and only after considerable fighting and outside intervention was the fighting stopped in that republic, which successfully asserted claims to independence over most, but not all, of its territories, part of which are still in dispute. The scene then shifted to Bosnia, perhaps the most ethnoreligiously complex of all the republics, consisting principally of Croats and Serbs, with the Serbs divided between those who had become Muslims during the centuries of Ottoman rule, mostly the urban elites, and those who had remained Serbian Orthodox, mostly the rural peasants. The animosities of all those centuries flared up again, strengthened by the Serbian fear that the Bosnian Muslims, who had also cooperated with the Germans during World War II, were out to drive them from their lands, which were disproportionately owned by Christian Serbs.

At present, there are almost no incentives for peace and some kind of federal linkage in the ex-Yugoslav republics. Serbia, consisting of Serbia proper and the two once-autonomous provinces Kosovo and Vojvodina, and Montenegro remain as the federation of Yugoslavia.

Croatia and Slovenia are fully recognized independent states. Macedonia is recognized, but its name is not. And then there is Bosnia. Former Yugoslavia stands as a landmark of what to do wrong to sustain federal solutions of any kind. But the world cannot leave a powder keg active in the Balkans, so at the same time, the Western European powers, realizing how difficult it is to convince Balkan peoples to resolve their problems, have limited their intervention to minimal peace-keeping, including supplying civilians caught in the war. Peace-keeping intervention comes from three sources: NATO, the United Nations, and the Western European Union. They have managed to more or less contain the war, while Europe and the United States put some pressure on all the parties to reach agreement through some kind of new federal arrangement. We may yet have other lessons to learn from that situation.

Canada, on the other hand, another possible example, has exhausted itself with thirty years of constitutional struggle, principally between Quebec and the rest of Canada. The former seeks its own form of confederal arrangement which it calls sovereignty-association. A number of serious changes have been made in the Canadian political system to accommodate Quebec's demands (French Canadians have gained new recognition for their language rights throughout Canada; the Province of Quebec has gained greater authority to enact legislation which its leaders believe is necessary to maintain French as its national language; the province has gained the right to opt out of certain federal programs or to take over those programs on a provincial basis). All of these have been accomplished on a peaceful basis in a manner similar to the establishment of joint authorities in other confederations.

However, the history of Canada's federal system is one of general solutions, first through its federal constitution and subsequently, through various attempts to modify it in one direction or another. There is no place in its constitutional tradition for building the networks of authorities that have generated postmodern confederation if they do not have the same kind of legitimacy that general actions have. But general actions are only in directions that are unacceptable to one side or another. So, the Canadians go from crisis to crisis, unable to reach any final decisions and periodically exhausting themselves, thereby gaining respite until the next round.

The ex-Soviet Union, on the other hand, has moved away from general solutions to networks of authorities, often reluctantly, but making a virtue out of necessity since all of its union republics declared their sovereignty within the Soviet Union even before it was dissolved. In its place, an effort has been made to establish a Commonwealth of Independent States, based on a number of different treaties to cover different purposes or functions and at times involving different members from among the republics of the former USSR. Movement is slow. Each new treaty has to be negotiated with all parties, but there seems to be a new basis for cooperation emerging out of all of this.

While these difficulties on the way to some kind of federal or confederal relationship are continuing to be addressed slowly as opportunity permits, conflict has broken out primarily in arenas where there are clashing ethnic groups with conflicting claims—between the Armenians and the Azerbaijanis over Ngorno-Karabakh, the former Christians and the latter Muslims with bitter enmity between them, between Russians and Moldavians in Moldavia, and between Chechnya and Russia. Chechnya, which was an autonomous region in the Russian federation, was taken over by an ambitious general who was able to use the Muslim-Christian conflict to stimulate the one secessionist movement within Russia itself that has gone all the way. Others threaten to do so, but as yet have been contained.

Russia is developing internally as a federation in one way or another. The ex-Soviet Union, or most of it, at best will unite in a confederation, hopefully following a very different path than Yugoslavia. All this is barring unforeseen developments where ethnic conflicts and enmities run deep, even where all parties are of the same faith.

Meanwhile, Czechoslovakia also has separated to become two states: the Czech Republic and Slovakia. The latter sought some postmodern-style confederal ties with the former, but the Czechs were happy to be rid of the Slovaks and, with a few exceptions, have not been interested.

Senegambia failed because Senegal and Gambia tried to join together in an old-style confederation. They are now experimenting with new-style joint authorities to achieve another kind of federal arrangement.

We cannot know what the future will bring with all of this, but the world seems to be in a new dynamic, moving in a direction that is likely to produce many surprises in the near future. The revival of confederal arrangements, itself something of a surprise, seems to be one that will continue and spread as a useful and convenient means for many states and peoples to participate in the new paradigm.

In the meantime, the most powerful economic forces and agents in the world are pressing ahead with globalization. Schemes that have the effect of opening markets are also making it more difficult to maintain communities. There seems to be no practical way to control the pursuit of wealth, regardless of how it is pursued. That is to say, while procedures can prevent or at least control the most fraudulent behavior, there seem to be no procedures acceptable to the shapers of these new markets that can be used to maintain community standards. If, after the age of revolutions at the end of the eighteenth century, commerce came to replace virtue as the principal force shaping politics, in this, the postmodern age, there does not seem to be a contest between the two, or at least not one in which the competition between the two is not eliminated by the prior commitment to commerce. Thus, constitutionalism becomes even more necessary if peace and prosperity are to be maintained within a humane and truly human context.

A Last Word

Confederal arrangements can, indeed, be useful in constitutionalizing globalization, but perhaps least in the way conventionally considered until now. Conventional wisdom has had it that where conflict cannot be resolved through separation of the groups into separate states, guaranteeing the integrity and autonomy of each group in a state framework but linking them in a confederal way could be used to achieve a similar result. Evidence accumulated from the many cases in the contemporary world suggests that such confederal arrangements rarely work. Our work would suggest that there are at least two principal reasons why they are not likely to work: One, coming at a time of conflict, they must cope with groups at the moment when they are most highly inflamed and protective of their self-interest as they perceive it, clearly a poor way to begin a shared-rule arrangement. Second, linking conflicting groups forces the conflict to within too small an arena, thus exacerbating the tensions that have provoked it.

Somewhat surprisingly, perhaps, evidence is building up that confederal arrangements are useful in resolving conflicts when they are very broad-based, when the arena is widened and the sharing required within it involves many partners, not only the few engaged in the conflict. Thus, the larger regional confederal arrangements where the polities of an enlarged sphere find it useful and even necessary to share may be more effective in dampening conflict than efforts at multiethnic confederations. Then, those engaged in or reflecting ethnic conflict among them will also find it necessary and very difficult to stay out of the sharing arrangements. Thus, there is a good chance that they will dampen the consequences of conflict in the interests of self-preservation.

In a sense, this is the Madisonian principle applied to confederal arrangements, not to achieve an extended republic but a less intense form of political integration based on Madisonian principles, or, more precisely, the combination of Montesquieuian and Madisonian principles. What is missing from this equation is proper inclusion of Althusian principles, so that the further extension of the principles of civil society will not eliminate the necessities of commonwealth at the same time. We submit this as a tentative conclusion worthy of further investigation as to how those principles can be applied in concrete situations. For this, of course, there had to be the world paradigm shift from statism to federalism which opens up many new possibilities for these kinds of arrangements.

Notes

1. *Consociations of Fatherlands*, pp. 139-144.
2. R. Michael Stevens, "Asymmetrical Federalism: The Federal Principle and the Survival of the Small Republic," *Publius*, vol. 7, no. 4 (Fall 1997):177-203.

APPENDIX A: Membership of the United Nations and Its Specialized and Related Agencies[1]

Organization[2]	UN	FAO	GATT/WTO[3]	IAEA	IBRD	ICAO	IDA	IFC	ILO	IMF	IMO	ITU	UNESCO	UNIDO	UPU	WHO	WIPO
Members	185	175	128	124	180	184	159	170	174	181	154	187	185	169	189	190	158
Countries																	
Afghanistan	1946	x		x	x	x	x	x	x	x		x	x	x	x	x	x
Albania	1955	x		x	x	x	x	x	x	x	x	x	x	x	x	x	x
Algeria	1962	x	(d)	x	x	x	x	x	x	x	x	x	x	x	x	x	x
Andorra	1993											x	x				x
Angola	1976	x	w		x	x	x	x	x	x	x	x	x	x	x	x	
Antigua and Barbuda	1981																
Argentina	1945	x	w	x	x	x		x	x	x	x	x	x	x	x	x	x
Armenia	1992	x	w	x	x	x	x	x	x	x	x	x	x	x	x	x	x
Australia	1945	x	w	x	x	x	x	x	x	x		x	x	x	x	x	x
Austria	1955	x	w	x	x	x	x	x	x	x	x	x	x	x	x	x	x
Azerbaijan	1992	x			x	x	x	x	x	x	x	x	x	x	x	x	x
Bahamas	1973	x	(d)		x	x		x	x	x	x	x	x	x	x	x	x
Bahrain	1971	x	w		x	x	x	x	x	x	x	x	x	x	x	x	x
Bangladesh	1974	x	w	x	x	x	x	x	x	x	x	x	x	x	x	x	x
Barbados	1966	x	w		x	x		x	x	x	x	x	x	x	x	x	x
Belarus	1945		w	x	x	x			x	x		x	x	x	x	x	x
Belgium	1945	x		x	x	x	x	x	x	x	x	x	x	x	x	x	x
Belize	1981	x	w		x	x	x	x	x	x	x	x	x	x	x	x	x

Organization / Countries	UN	FAO	GATT/ WTO	IAEA	IBRD	ICAO	IDA	IFC	ILO	IMF	IMO	ITU	UNESCO	UNIDO	UPU	WHO	WIPO
Benin	1960	x			x	x	x	x	x	x	x	x	x	x	x	x	x
Bhutan	1971	x	w		x	x	x			x		x	x	x	x	x	x
Bolivia	1945	x	w	x	x	x	x	x	x	x	x	x	x	x	x	x	x
Bosnia and Herzegovina	1992	x			x	x	x	x	x	x	x	x	x	x	x	x	x
Botswana	1966	x	w		x	x	x	x	x	x		x	x	x	x	x	
Brazil	1945	x	w	x	x	x	x	x	x	x	x	x	x	x	x	x	
Brunei	1984		w		x	x		x		x		x			x	x	
Bulgaria	1955	x	w	x	x	x		x	x	x	x	x			x	x	x
Burkina Faso	1960	x	w		x	x	x	x	x	x		x	x	x	x	x	x
Burundi	1962	x	(d)		x	x	x		x	x		x	x	x	x	x	x
Cambodia	1955	x	w		x	x	x	x	x	x	x	x	x	x	x	x	x
Cameroon	1960	x	w	x	x	x	x	x	x	x	x	x	x	x	x	x	x
Canada	1945	x	(d)	x	x	x	x	x	x	x	x	x	x	x	x	x	x
Cape Verde	1975	x			x	x	x		x	x		x	x	x	x	x	x
Central African Republic	1960	x	w		x	x	x	x	x	x		x	x	x	x	x	x
Chad	1960	x	w		x	x	x		x	x		x	x	x	x	x	x
Chile	1945	x	w	x	x	x	x	x	x	x	x	x	x	x	x	x	x
China	1945	x		x	x	x	x	x	x	x	x	x	x	x	x	x	x
Columbia	1945	x	w	x	x	x	x	x	x	x	x	x	x	x	x	x	x
Comoro Islands	1975	x	(d)		x	x	x	x	x	x		x	x	x	x	x	
Congo	1960	x	g		x	x	x	x	x	x	x	x	x	x	x	x	x

Organization / Countries	UN	FAO	GATT/ WTO	IAEA	IBRD	ICAO	IDA	IFC	ILO	IMF	IMO	ITU	UNESCO	UNIDO	UPU	WHO	WIPO
Costa Rica	1945	x	w	x	x	x	x	x	x	x	x	x	x	x	x	x	x
Cote d'Ivoire	1960	x	w	x	x	x	x	x	x	x	x	x	x	x	x	x	x
Croatia	1992	x		x	x	x	x	x	x	x	x	x	x	x	x	x	x
Cuba	1945	x	w	x		x			x		x	x	x	x	x	x	x
Cyprus	1960	x	w	x	x	x	x	x	x	x	x	x	x	x	x	x	x
Czech Republic	1993	x	w	x	x	x	x	x	x	x	x	x	x	x	x	x	x
Denmark	1945	x	w	x	x	x	x	x	x	x	x	x	x	x	x	x	x
Djibouti	1977	x	w		x	x	x	x	x	x	x	x	x	x	x	x	
Dominica	1978	x	w		x		x	x	x	x	x	x	x	x	x	x	
Dominican Republic	1945	x	w	x	x	x	x	x	x	x	x	x	x	x	x	x	x
Ecuador	1945	x	w	x	x	x	x	x	x	x	x	x	x	x	x	x	x
Egypt	1945	x	w	x	x	x	x	x	x	x	x	x	x	x	x	x	x
El Salvador	1945	x	w	x	x	x	x	x	x	x	x	x	x	x	x	x	
Equatorial Guinea	1968	x	(d)		x	x	x	x	x	x	x	x	x	x	x	x	x
Eritrea	1993	x			x	x	x	x	x	x	x	x	x	x	x	x	
Estonia	1991	x		x	x	x		x	x	x	x	x	x		x	x	x
Ethiopia	1945	x		x	x	x	x	x	x	x	x	x	x	x	x	x	x
Fifi	1970	x	w		x	x	x	x	x	x	x	x	x	x	x	x	x
Finland	1955	x	w	x	x	x	x	x	x	x	x	x	x	x	x	x	x
France	1945	x	w	x	x	x	x	x	x	x	x	x	x	x	x	x	x
Gabon	1960	x	w	x	x	x	x	x	x	x	x	x	x	x	x	x	x
Gambia	1965	x	w		x	x	x	x	x	x	x	x	x	x	x	x	

Organization / Countries	UN	FAO	GATT/ WTO	IAEA	IBRD	ICAO	IDA	IFC	ILO	IMF	IMO	ITU	UNESCO	UNIDO	UPU	WHO	WIPO
Georgia	1992	×		×	×	×	×	×	×	×	×	×	×	×	×	×	×
Germany	1973	×	w	×	×	×	×	×	×	×	×	×	×	×	×	×	×
Ghana	1957	×	w	×	×	×	×	×	×	×	×	×	×	×	×	×	×
Greece	1945	×	w	×	×	×	×	×	×	×	×	×	×	×	×	×	×
Grenada	1974	×	w		×	×	×	×	×	×		×	×	×	×	×	
Guatemala	1945	×	w	×	×	×	×	×	×	×	×	×	×	×	×	×	×
Guinea	1958	×			×	×	×	×	×	×	×	×	×	×	×	×	×
Guinea-Bissau	1974	×			×	×	×	×	×	×	×	×	×	×	×	×	×
Guyana	1966	×	w		×	×	×	×	×	×	×	×	×	×	×	×	×
Haiti	1945	×	w	×	×	×	×	×	×	×	×	×	×	×	×	×	×
Honduras	1945	×	w	×	×	×	×	×	×	×	×	×	×	×	×	×	×
Hungary	1955	×	w	×	×	×	×	×	×	×	×	×	×	×	×	×	×
Iceland	1946	×	w	×	×	×	×	×	×	×	×	×	×		×	×	×
India	1945	×	w	×	×	×	×	×	×	×	×	×	×		×	×	×
Indonesia	1950	×	w	×	×	×	×	×	×	×	×	×	×	×	×	×	×
Iran	1945	×		×	×	×	×	×	×	×	×	×	×	×	×	×	
Iraq	1945	×		×	×	×	×	×	×	×	×	×	×	×	×	×	×
Ireland	1955	×	w	×	×	×	×	×	×	×	×	×	×	×	×	×	×
Israel	1949	×	w	×	×	×	×	×	×	×	×	×	×	×	×	×	×
Italy	1955	×	w	×	×	×	×	×	×	×	×	×	×	×	×	×	×
Jamaica	1962	×	w	×	×	×		×	×	×	×	×	×	×	×	×	×
Japan	1956	×		×	×	×	×	×	×	×	×	×	×	×	×	×	×
Jordan	1955	×		×	×	×	×	×	×	×	×	×	×	×	×	×	×
Kazakhstan	1992	×		×	×	×	×	×	×	×	×	×	×	×	×	×	×

Countries	UN	FAO	WTO/GATT	IAEA	IBRD	ICAO	IDA	IFC	ILO	IMF	IMO	ITU	UNESCO	UNIDO	UPU	WHO	WIPO
Kenya	1963	×	w	×	×	×	×	×	×	×	×	×	×	×	×	×	×
DPR Korea	1991	×				×					×	×	×	×	×	×	×
Korea, Republic of	1991	×	w	×	×	×	×	×	×	×	×	×	×	×	×	×	×
Kuwait	1963	×	w	×	×	×	×	×	×	×	×	×	×	×	×	×	×
Kyrgyzstan	1992	×			×	×	×	×	×	×		×	×	×	×	×	×
Laos	1955	×			×	×	×	×	×	×		×	×	×	×	×	×
Latvia	1991	×			×	×	×	×	×	×	×	×	×	×	×	×	×
Lebanon	1945	×		×	×	×	×	×	×	×	×	×	×	×	×	×	×
Lesotho	1966	×	w	×	×	×	×	×	×	×		×	×	×	×	×	×
Liberia	1945	×		×	×	×	×	×	×	×	×	×	×	×	×	×	×
Libya	1955	×		×	×	×	×	×	×	×	×	×	×	×	×	×	×
Liechtenstein	1990		w									×			×		×
Lithuania	1991	×	w	×	×	×	×	×	×	×	×	×	×	×	×	×	×
Luxembourg	1945	×	w		×	×	×	×	×	×	×	×	×	×	×	×	×
Macedonia	1993	×		×	×	×	×	×	×	×	×	×	×	×	×	×	×
Madagascar	1960	×			×	×	×	×	×	×	×	×	×	×	×	×	×
Malawi	1964	×	w		×	×	×	×	×	×	×	×	×	×	×	×	×
Malaysia	1957	×	w	×	×	×	×	×	×	×	×	×	×	×	×	×	×
Maldives	1965	×	w		×	×	×	×		×		×	×	×	×	×	×
Mali	1960	×	w		×	×	×	×	×	×		×	×	×	×	×	×
Malta	1964	×	w	×		×			×			×			×		×
Marshall Islands	1991				×	×	×	×		×		×	×			×	
Mauritania	1961	×	w	×	×	×	×	×	×	×	×	×	×	×	×	×	×

Organization / Countries	UN	FAO	GATT/WTO	IAEA	IBRD	ICAO	IDA	IFC	ILO	IMF	IMO	ITU	UNESCO	UNIDO	UPU	WHO	WIPO
Mauritius	1968	×	w	×	×	×	×	×	×	×	×	×	×	×	×	×	×
Mexico	1945	×	w	×	×	×	×	×	×	×	×	×	×	×	×	×	×
Micronesia	1991				×	×	×	×		×		×				×	
Moldova	1992	×		×	×	×	×	×	×	×		×	×	×	×	×	
Monaco	1993			×								×	×		×	×	×
Mongolia	1961	×		×	×	×	×	×	×	×		×	×	×	×	×	×
Morocco	1956	×	w	×	×	×	×	×	×	×	×	×	×	×	×	×	×
Mozambique	1975	×			×	×	×	×	×	×	×	×	×	×	×	×	×
Myanmar	1948	×	w	×	×	×	×	×	×	×	×	×	×	×	×	×	×
Namibia	1990	×	w	×	×	×	×	×	×	×	×	×	×	×	×	×	
Nepal	1955	×			×	×	×	×	×	×		×	×	×	×	×	×
Netherlands	1945	×	w	×	×	×	×	×	×	×	×	×	×	×	×	×	×
New Zealand	1945	×	w	×	×	×	×	×	×	×	×	×	×	×	×	×	×
Nicaragua	1945	×	w	×	×	×	×	×	×	×	×	×	×	×	×	×	×
Niger	1960	×	w	×	×	×	×	×	×	×		×	×	×	×	×	×
Nigeria	1960	×	w	×	×	×	×	×	×	×	×	×	×	×	×	×	×
Norway	1945	×	w	×	×	×	×	×	×	×	×	×	×	×	×	×	×
Oman	1971	×			×	×	×	×	×	×	×	×	×	×	×	×	
Pakistan	1947	×	w	×	×	×	×	×	×	×	×	×	×	×	×	×	×
Palau	1994																
Panama	1945	×		×	×	×	×	×	×	×	×	×	×	×	×	×	×
Papua New Guinea	1975	×	w		×	×	×	×	×	×	×	×	×	×	×	×	
Paraguay	1945	×	w	×	×	×	×	×	×	×		×	×	×	×	×	×
Peru	1945	×	w	×	×	×	×	×	×	×	×	×	×	×	×	×	×

Organization / Countries	UN	FAO	GATT/ WTO	IAEA	IBRD	ICAO	IDA	IFC	ILO	IMF	IMO	ITU	UNESCO	UNIDO	UPU	WHO	WIPO
Philippines	1945	x	w	x	x	x	x	x	x	x	x	x	x	x	x	x	x
Poland	1945	x	w	x	x	x	x	x	x	x	x	x	x	x	x	x	x
Portugal	1955	x	w	x	x	x	x	x	x	x	x	x	x	x	x	x	x
Qatar	1971	x	w	x	x	x			x	x	x	x	x	x	x	x	x
Romania	1955	x	w	x	x	x		x	x	x	x	x	x	x	x	x	x
Russia	1945			x	x	x	x	x	x	x	x	x	x	x	x	x	x
Rwanda	1962	x	w		x	x	x	x	x	x		x	x	x	x	x	x
St. Kitts and Nevis	1983	x			x		x	x	x	x			x	x	x	x	x
St. Lucia	1979	x	w		x	x	x	x	x	x			x	x	x	x	x
St. Vincent	1980	x	w		x	x	x		x	x	x	x	x	x	x	x	x
San Marino	1992		w			x			x	x	x	x	x		x	x	x
Sao Tome and Principe	1975		(d)		x	x	x		x	x	x	x	x	x	x	x	
Saudi Arabia	1945	x		x	x	x	x		x	x	x	x	x	x	x	x	x
Senegal	1960	x	w	x	x	x	x	x	x	x	x	x	x	x	x	x	x
Seychelles	1976	x	(d)		x	x		x	x	x	x		x	x	x	x	
Sierra Leone	1961	x	w	x	x	x	x	x	x	x	x	x	x	x	x	x	x
Singapore	1965	x	w	x	x	x		x	x	x	x	x			x	x	x
Slovakia	1993		w	x	x	x	x	x	x	x	x	x	x	x	x	x	x
Slovenia	1992	x	w	x	x	x	x	x	x	x	x	x	x	x	x	x	x
Solomon Islands	1978	x			x	x	x	x	x	x	x	x	x		x	x	
Somalia	1960	x	w		x	x	x	x	x	x	x	x	x	x	x	x	x
South Africa	1945	x	w	x	x	x	x	x	x	x	x	x	x		x	x	x

Organization / Countries	UN	FAO	GATT/WTO	IAEA	IBRD	ICAO	IDA	IFC	ILO	IMF	IMO	ITU	UNESCO	UNIDO	UPU	WHO	WIPO
Spain	1955	X	W	X	X	X	X	X	X	X	X	X	X	X	X	X	X
Sri Lanka	1955	X	W	X	X	X	X	X	X	X	X	X	X	X	X	X	X
Sudan	1956	X		X	X	X	X	X	X	X	X	X	X	X	X	X	X
Suriname	1975	X	W		X	X			X	X	X	X	X	X	X	X	X
Swaziland	1968	X	W		X	X			X	X		X	X	X	X	X	X
Sweden	1946	X	W	X	X	X	X	X	X	X	X	X	X	X	X	X	X
Syria	1945	X		X	X	X	X	X	X	X	X	X	X	X	X	X	X
Tajikistan	1992				X	X	X	X	X	X		X	X	X	X	X	
Tanzania	1961	X	W	X	X	X	X	X	X	X	X	X	X	X	X	X	X
Thailand	1946	X	W	X	X	X	X	X	X	X	X	X	X	X	X	X	X
Togo	1960	X	W		X	X	X	X	X	X	X	X	X	X	X	X	X
Trinidad and Tobago	1962	X	W		X	X	X	X	X	X	X	X	X	X	X	X	X
Tunisia	1956	X	W	X	X	X	X	X	X	X	X	X	X	X	X	X	X
Turkey	1945	X	W	X	X	X	X	X	X	X	X	X	X	X	X	X	X
Turkmenistan	1992				X	X			X	X	X	X	X		X	X	X
Uganda	1962	X	W	X	X	X	X	X	X	X		X	X	X	X	X	X
Ukraine	1945	X		X	X	X		X	X	X	X	X	X	X	X	X	X
United Arab Emirates	1971	X	W	X	X	X	X	X	X	X	X	X	X	X	X	X	X
United Kingdom	1945	X	W	X	X	X	X	X	X	X	X	X		X	X	X	X
United States	1945	X	W	X	X	X	X	X	X	X	X	X		X	X	X	X
Uruguay	1945	X	W	X	X	X		X	X	X	X	X	X	X	X	X	X
Uzbekistan	1992			X	X	X	X	X	X	X		X	X	X	X	X	X

Organization / Countries	UN	FAO	GATT/WTO	IAEA	IBRD	ICAO	IDA	IFC	ILO	IMF	IMO	ITU	UNESCO	UNIDO	UPU	WHO	WIPO
Vanuatu	1981	x				x	x	x	x		x	x	x	x	x	x	x	x
Venezuela	1945	x	w	x	x	x		x	x	x	x	x	x	x	x	x	x
Vietnam	1977	x		x	x	x	x	x	x	x	x	x	x	x		x	x	
Wstrn Somoa	1976	x			x		x	x		x	x	x	x		x	x	
Yemen	1990	x	(d)	x	x	x	x	x		x		x	x	x	x	x	x
Yugoslavia	1945	x	g	x					x	x		x	x	x	x	x	x
Zaire	1960	x	g	x	x	x	x	x	x	x		x	x	x	x	x	x
Zambia	1964	x	w	x	x	x	x	x	x	x		x	x	x	x	x	x
Zimbabwe	1980	x	w	x	x	x	x	x	x	x		x	x	x	x	x	x

1 This table reprinted by permission of CSA Publications, which retains its copyright. Originally printed in The Political Handbook of the World, 1997. Arthur S. Banks, Alan J. Day and Thomas C. Muller, editors. Binghamton, NY: CSA Publications, Binghamton University, The State University of New York, 1997. For technical reasons, membership in the International Fund for Agricultural Development and the World Meterological Organization have been omitted.

2 The following abbreviations have been used: UN- United Nations; FAO- Food Agriculture Organization; GATT/WTO- General Agreement on Tariffs and Trade/World Trade Organization; IAEA- International Atomic Energy Agency; IBRD- International Bank for Reconstruction and Development; ICAO- International Civil Aviation Organization; IDA- International Development Association; IFC- International Finance Corporation; ILO- International Labour Organisation; IMF- International Monetary Fund; IMO- International Maritime Organization; ITU- International Telecommunication Union; UNESCO- United Nations Educational, Scientific and Cultural Organization; UNIDO- United National Industrial Development Organization; UPU-Universal Postal Union; WHO- World Health Organization; WIPO- World Intellectual Property Organization. Dates are those of each members admission to the United Nations.

3 The 128 members of the WTO are marked by W. The 3 countries marked by G belonged to GATT but are not yet members of the WTO. The 9 states marked (d) in the table are territories to which GATT applied before independence and which as independent states maintained de facto application of the Agreement pending final decisions as to their commericial policies. (Although GATT ceased to exist on December 31, 1995, some of its provisions were carried forward under a "GATT 1994: agreement, administered by the WTO).

BIBLIOGRAPHY

Buchheit, Lee C. *Secession: The Legitimacy of Self-Determination*. New Haven, CT: Yale University Press, 1977.

Cavazza, Fabio Luca, and Carlo Pelanda. "Maastricht, Before, During and After," in *Daedalus*, Spring 1994, pp. 53-80.

Constantinesco, Vlad. "Who's Afraid of Subsidiarity?" in *Yearbook of International Law*, 1991, 1, pp. 33-55.

Davis, S. Rufus. *The Federal Principle: A Journey Through Time in Quest of a Meaning*. Berkeley and Los Angeles: University of California Press, 1978.

Deutsch, Karl, et al. *Political Community and the North Atlantic Area: International Organization in the Light of Historical Experience*. Princeton, NJ: Princeton University Press, 1957.

Diehl, Paul F., ed. *The Politics of Global Governance: International Organizations in an Interdependent World*. Boulder, CO: Lynne Rienner, 1997.

Duchacek, Ivo. "Antagonistic Co-operation: Territorial and Ethnic Communities," in *Publius*, vol. 7, no. 4, 1977, pp. 3-31.

_____. *Comparative Federalism: The Territorial Dimension of Politics*. New York: Holt, Rinehart and Winston, 1970.

_____ "Consociations of Fatherlands: The Revival of Confederal Principles and Practices," in *Publius*, Fall 1982, vol. 12, no. 4, pp. 129-177.

_____. "Dyadic Federations and Confederations," in *Publius*, vol. 18, no. 2, 1988, pp. 5-31.

Elazar, Daniel J. *Exploring Federalism*. Tuscaloosa, AL: University of Alabama Press, 1987.

_____. *Federal Systems of the World: A Handbook of Federal, Confederal and Autonomy Arrangements*. Harlow, Essex, UK: Longman Current Affairs, 1991.

231

Forsyth, Murray. *Unions of States*. Leicester: Leicester University Press, 1981.

Franck, Thomas M., ed. *Why Federations Fail: An Inquiry Into the Requisites for Successful Federalism*. New York: New York University Press, 1968.

Friedrich, Carl J. *Trends of Federalism in Theory and Practice*. New York: Praeger, 1968.

Haas, Ernst B., and Philippe C. Schmitter. "Economics and Differential Patterns of Political Integration: Projection About Unity in Latin America," in *International Organization*, vol. 18, 1964, pp. 705-737.

Hamilton, Alexander, John Jay, and James Madison. *The Federalist*. New York: The Modern Library, Random House, 1937.

Hoffmann, Stanley, "Europe's Identity Crisis Revisited," in *Daedalus*, vol. 123, no. 4, Spring 1994, pp. 1-23.

Hughes, Christopher. *Confederacies*. Leicester: Leicester University Press, 1963.

Independent Working Group on the Future of the United Nations. *The United Nations in the Second Half-Century, Report*. New Haven: Yale University Printing Service, 1995.

Jennings, Robert Y. "The United Nations at Fifty: The International Court of Justice after Fifty Years," in *American Journal of International Law*, vol. 89, no. 3, July 1995, pp. 493-505.

Jensen, Merrill. *The Articles of Confederation*. Madison: The University of Wisconsin Press, 1948.

Jillson, Calvin C. "Political Culture and the Pattern of Congressional Politics Under the Articles of Confederation," in *Publius*, vol. 18, no. 1, 1988, pp. 1-26.

Keohane, Robert O., and Joseph S. Nye, Jr. "International Interdependence and Integration," in *Handbook of Political Science*, edited by Fred L. Greenstein and Nelson W. Polsby. Andover, MA: Addison Wesley, vol. 8, 1975, pp. 363-414.

Kirgis, Frederic L., Jr. "The Security Council's First Fifty Years," in *American Journal of International Law*, vol. 89, no. 3, July 1995, pp. 506-539.

Koopmans, T. "The Future of the Court of Justice of the European Communities," in *Yearbook of European Law*, vol. 11, 1991, pp. 15-32.

Larsen, J.A.O. *Greek Federal States, Their Institutions and History*. Oxford: Clarendon Press, 1968.

Lemco, Jonathan. *Political Stability in Federal Governments*. New York: Praeger, 1991.

Lister, Frederick. *Decision-Making Strategies for International Organizations: The IMF Model.* Denver, CO: University of Denver, 1984.

_____. *The European Union, the United Nations and the Revival of Confederal Governance.* Westport, CT: Greenwood Press, 1996.

Noel, Emile. *Working Together: The Institutions of the European Community.* Luxembourg: Office for Official Publications of the European Communities, 1994.

Nye, Joseph S., Jr. *Peace in Parts: Integration and Conflict in Regional Organization.* Boston: Little Brown, 1971.

Schachter, Oscar. "United Nations Law," in *American Journal of International Law*, vol. 88, no. 1, January 1994, pp. 1-23.

Schmitt, Carl. *Verfassungslehre.* 1928. Reprint, Berlin: Duncker & Humblot, 1970.

Sheehan, James J. *German History, 1770-1866.* Oxford: Clarendon Press, 1989.

Stevens, R. Michael. "Asymmetrical Federalism: The Federal Principle and the Survival of the Small Republic," *Publius*, vol. 7, no. 4 (Fall 1977):177-203.

Temple, Sir William. *Observations Upon the United Provinces of the Netherlands*, edited by Sir George Clark. Oxford: Clarendon Press, 1972.

Treaty on European Union, Treaty Establishing the European Community. Luxembourg: Office for Official Publications of the European Communities, 1993.

United Nations Charter. United Nations Office of Public Information, undated and including amendments of 1965.

Urwin, Derek M. *The Community of Europe: A History of European Integration Since 1945.* London: Longman, 1991.

Wallace, William. "Europe as a Confederation: The Community and the Nation-State," in *Journal of Common Market Studies*, vol. 21, nos. 1-2, Sept.-Dec. 1982, pp. 57-68.

Weiler, J.H.H. "Journey to an Unknown Destination: A Retrospective and Prospective of the European Court of Justice in the Arena of Political Integrations," in *Journal of Common Market Studies*, vol. 31, no. 4, December 1993, pp. 417-446.

INDEX

Aaland Islands, 96, 99-100
Adat Bnai Yisrael, 44
Adenauer, Konrad, 94
Afghanistan, 128
Africa, 90, 210
African, 193
African National Council, 211
AFTA (ASEAN Free Trade Area), 135
Alabama, 29
Alaska, 125
Albania, 121
Alberta, 29
Algeria, 188
Allemanians, 110, 210
Allies, 27-28; United Nations, 15
Alsace, 30
Althusian principles, 220
America, 87, 109
American(s), 5, 30, 50, 69, 71-73, 77-79, 81, 83-84, 91, 105, 111, 150, 171-173, 182-183, 187, 201-203; Bill of Rights, 82; Civil War, 64, 203; confederal experience, 5, 69-70; confederation, 40, 79; diasporas, 182; federal government, 145; federal government, and the UN, 13; federation, 22; foreign economic policy, 29; Founding Fathers, 110; hegemony, 14; history, 69; Jewry, 190, 192; pluralism, 72; Revolution, 24; revolutionary constitutional period, 187; society, 72; states, 30; *see also* United States
Amphictyonic League (Greek), 44
Amphictyonies, 44-45
Anarchism, 25
Anarchy, 60, 72
Andorra, 147

Antarctica, 61
Anti-federalist(s), 40, 82, 114, 117
Anti-liberalism, 48
Anti-Semitism, 170, 193
Antigua, 134
ANZACS, 141
ANZCER, 141
Apartheid, 143
Arab(s), 146, 183, 195; diaspora, 183; states, 194
Arab League, 34
Arabic, 165
Argentina, 33, 142, 189
Armenia, 127, 184
Armenians, 184, 218
ASAS (Association of Southern African States), 144
ASEAN (Association of Southeast Asian Nations), 8, 17, 34, 135-136, 142, 144, 173-174; Secretary General, 135
Asia, Asian, 90, 145, 193, 195; Muslim, 104; republics, 128
Asia-Pacific, 174; trading and security leagues, 136
Associated state(s), 32-34, 47, 53-54, 62, 208, 215
Association(s), 2, 6, 10; as cooperatives, 6; intergovernmental cooperative, 2; intersovereign, 2
Asymmetrical confederal arrangements, 215; relationships, 54
Australia, 87, 105, 110, 136, 141, 189
Australian-New Zealand economic union, 141
Austria, 50, 103, 119
Austrian-Hungarian empire, 102-103
"Automatic society," 24
Autonomy, 185, 201, 206, 219

235

ABOUT THE AUTHOR

Professor Daniel J. Elazar, the dean of students of federalism in the world today, turns his attention here to transnational relations. His other related books include *Federalism and the Way to Peace* (1994), *Exploring Federalism* (1987), and *Federal Systems of the World* (1994). In *Covenant and Civil Society: The Constitutional Matrix of Modern Democracy* (1998) he places federalism and globalization in context.

Professor Elazar is Professor of Political Science and Director of the Center for the Study of Federalism at Temple University in Philadlephia, founder and editor-in-chief of *Publius: The Journal of Federalism,* and founder and past president of the International Association of Centers for Federal Studies. He is also Senator N.M. Paterson Professor of Intergovernmental Relations at Bar-Ilan University, Ramat Gan, Israel, and President of the Jerusalem Center for Public Affairs.